7/00

OTHER BOOKS BY JOHN STEELE GORDON

OVERLANDING

THE SCARLET WOMAN OF WALL STREET

HAMILTON'S BLESSING

THE GREAT GAME

*The Emergence of Wall Street
as a World Power 1653–2000*

JOHN STEELE GORDON

SCRIBNER

SCRIBNER
1230 Avenue of the Americas
New York, NY 10020

Copyright © 1999 by John Steele Gordon

SCRIBNER and design are trademarks of Macmillan Library Reference USA, Inc.,
used under license by Simon & Schuster, the publisher of this work.

DESIGNED BY ERICH HOBBING

Set in Fairfield

Manufactured in the United States of America

1   3   5   7   9   10   8   6   4   2

Library of Congress Cataloging-in-Publication Data is available.

ISBN 0-684-83287-9

For
Dolores Simon and Margaret Cheney
with love

ACKNOWLEDGMENTS

My first thanks must go to Scott Moyers, now at Random House, who first had the idea for this book and convinced me to write it. My present editor at Scribner, Gillian Blake, has done a wonderful job of editing, making a vast number of cogent suggestions while rescuing me from infelicities beyond number and getting me off my duff when needed, which was frequently. Steve Boldt did a wonderful job of copyediting and Andy Goldwasser, the proof-reader, did an equally good job. They each made me look better than I am on nearly every page.

David Osterlund took charge of gathering the pictures for this book and saw the potential for a television show in it. More to the point, he made a deal with CNBC to produce one. Needless to say, I am very grateful for that as well as many other kindnesses over the years.

I would also like to thank Andrew Tobias, for rooting around in his files so I didn't have to spend an afternoon with my head stuck in a microfilm machine; Wally Olson for innumerable courtesies; and Tom Dyer for lending me a very useful book for a very long time.

CONTENTS

Prologue   15

1. "A Cloacina of All the Depravities of Human Nature"   21

2. "A Line of Separation between Honest Men & Knaves"   35

3. "That Tongue That Is Licking Up the Cream of Commerce"   53

4. "What Can Be the End of All This but Another General Collapse?"   71

5. "Vanity Fair Was No Longer a Dream"   91

6. "Who . . . Could Blame Them for Doing What They Pleased?"   109

7. "The Bulls, Triumphant, Faced Their Foes"   127

8. "All You Have to Do Is Buy Cheap and Sell Dear"   147

9. "Have You Anything to Suggest?"   163

10. "Why Don't You Tell Them What to Do, Mr. Morgan?"   181

11. "Does This Happen Often?"   197

12. "The Stock Exchange Can Do Anything"   213

13. "Not Dick Whitney!"   231

14. "Wall Street Is . . . Main Street"   249

15. "It's Time We Put In a Good Word for Greed"   267

Epilogue   285

Notes   297

Bibliography   305

Index   309

Nowhere does history indulge in repetitions so often or so uniformly as in Wall Street. When you read contemporary accounts of booms or panics, the one thing that strikes you most forcibly is how little either stock speculation or stock speculators today differ from yesterday. The game does not change and neither does human nature.

—EDWIN LEFÈVRE,
Reminiscences of a Stock Operator (1923)

To what purpose is all the toil and bustle of the world? What is the end of avarice and ambition, of the pursuit of wealth, of power, and preeminence?

—ADAM SMITH,
The Theory of Moral Sentiments (1759)

THE GREAT GAME

PROLOGUE

This book covers more than three hundred and fifty years of history. It runs from an economy powered by peasants at their plows to one powered by office workers at their computers; from Galileo's handmade two-inch telescope that could not clearly make out the rings of Saturn, to the Keck Observatory's paired ten-meter instruments that can see twelve billion light-years into space; from a world where news moved at the speed of a horse to one where it moves at the speed of light. Thus this book is history on the grand scale. And history on such a scale is, of necessity, largely the history of great men, great themes, and great powers.

The classic political-science definition of a great power is "any country whose interests must be taken into account by every other country." That is why Russia, for all its economic distress, is still a great power. No one would fail to take into account the interests of a country with thousands of nuclear weapons in its arsenal. But, when it comes down to it, does a great power have to be a country at all? The answer is clearly no. Certainly in the Middle Ages the papacy was a great power, although it had sovereign control over only a relatively small territory and population. Rather, its empire was theological in nature, but no less potent for that. And as early as 1818, when France needed bank loans to pay off war debts, the Duc de Richelieu, prime minister under Louis XVIII, lamented only half facetiously, "There are six great powers in Europe: England, France, Prussia, Austria, Russia, and Baring Brothers."

Today, the power wielded by money is far greater than it was in the early nineteenth century, and the power of governments to control the world economy—and thus money—is far less. So make no mistake, "Wall Street" has become a great power. To be sure, as a piece of geography, it doesn't amount to much, just six narrow blocks of thoroughfare, running "between a graveyard and a river." As a metonym, however, it is in a class by itself. The phrase *Wall Street* has long stood for the New York financial market, but as the second millennium closes, that market has become the beating heart of world capitalism, and today sovereign governments, other markets, and mere individuals alike must all pay heed to "Wall Street" or suffer the consequences.

But how did this unimpressive little byway become so mighty a symbol? How did New York, which except for a couple of years in the late eighteenth century has never been a national or even state capital, become to global finance what the sun is to the solar system? Answering those questions is the purpose of this book.

New York began with many advantages, especially its magnificent harbor, by far the finest on the North Atlantic, and its philosophical inheritance from the money-loving, worldly Dutch. But its financial supremacy certainly wasn't inevitable. History abounds with close calls—the Duke of Wellington called the Battle of Waterloo "the nearest run thing you ever saw in your life"—and the history of Wall Street is no exception. In 1812, had Vice President George Clinton, breaking a tie, voted in the Senate for President Madison's proposal to renew the charter of the Bank of the United States instead of against it, television anchors today might very well start off the nightly financial news by saying, "On Chestnut Street today . . ." Had his nephew Governor De Witt Clinton not succeeded in pushing his proposal to build the Erie Canal through a reluctant legislature, New York might have become only one of the major cities of the eastern seaboard, not the greatest city in the Western Hemisphere.

It was also lucky that the United States was born the very same year that Adam Smith's *The Wealth of Nations,* the seminal work of systematic economics, was published. Because the United States was brand-new, it lacked an encrustation of ancient grants of privilege that are never easy to eliminate. It is estimated that in pre-Revolutionary France, someone transporting a load of goods overland from Rouen to Marseille (not that anyone would ever have done so in actuality) would have been subject to no less than fifty-odd imposts, the rights to which had been granted, one at a time, to various nobles and towns by the crown. But the American Constitutional Convention of 1787 could, and did, make the United States a vast common market by forbidding the imposition of tariffs or other restrictions on goods crossing state lines.

Further, Adam Smith's mighty work provided a philosophical basis for having governments leave economies unfettered, just as the industrial revolution was beginning to overturn the whole economic basis of Western civilization. Thus the American economy and its principal capital market could develop with minimal interference from politicians, who are quite as self-interested as capitalists.

But there was more than just luck involved in Wall Street's great game becoming, in effect, the only game in town.

In a mathematical sense, a free market is exactly that, a game. As with every game, from slapjack to world war, there are players, strategies, and a means of keeping score. Unlike slapjack, however, the game of the free market is not a zero sum one. There are winners in a poker game only because, and to the extent that, there are losers. But if the game of the free market could be played by perfectly rational players with perfect information, then it would be possible for there to be only winners. Of course, perfectly rational human beings don't exist, and perfect information is asymptotic in nature—it can be approached but never reached. That, of course, is fortunate for those who write and read history; a perfect world would also be an excruciatingly dull and predictable one. But it means there will always be losers in a free market, too.

Still, in a free market over time, the sum of the winnings will exceed the losses manyfold. That is nowhere more true than in a capital market. Capital—much denigrated in Marxist theory—is one of the indispensable ingredients of any national economy, along with labor, resources, and skills. After all, while it is impossible to build, say, automobiles without workers and without materials, it is equally impossible to build them without a factory, and that requires capital, as do inventories, payrolls, and countless other aspects of a successful business.

But notice the phrase *over time* in the first sentence of the previous paragraph. Time, all too often, is exactly what free markets lack.

Left entirely to their own devices, they tend to self-destruct. The reason is simple enough: markets are made up of self-interested human beings. Indeed, Adam Smith recognized the problem clearly. "People of the same trade seldom meet together," he wrote in *The Wealth of Nations,* "even for merriment and diversion, but the conversation ends in a conspiracy against the public, or in some contrivance to raise prices." In other words, a free market needs rules, and referees to enforce them, or the players themselves will destroy it. As has been widely noted, "If the trouble with socialism is socialism, the trouble with capitalism is capital*ists.*"

But at a crucial time in the history of Wall Street, rules and referees are just what it didn't have. In its early days, Wall Street was so small that fair play could be maintained just as it is in a neighborhood poker game, by social pressure. But the Civil War suddenly made Wall Street the second-largest securities market on earth, with billions in play. The old, informal system broke down quickly, but there was nothing to replace it. The federal government was not thought to have a role in regulating markets at this time, and New York State and City governments were so mired in corruption that most public officials were, quite simply, for sale.

For a few years, the speculators—who cared only about the next big killing—could do as they pleased. Being human beings, that, of course, is exactly what they did. But then the brokers—whose interests were with long-term stability—found a way to take control and enforce rules that curbed the power of the speculators and allowed Wall Street to function in the long term as a capital market.

In the results, one could hardly find a better example of Adam Smith's invisible hand at work. The Wall Street brokers were pursuing only their own self-interests in a stable, honest securities market. But in so doing, they provided a reliable mechanism for financing the industrialization of the American economy, and quickly that economy became the largest and most powerful on earth. That greatly increased the prosperity of Wall Street, but it increased even more the prosperity of the country as a whole. It made the American century possible.

In that American century, further reforms to meet new conditions were needed, as the interests of brokers and the interests of investors (not to be confused with speculators) increasingly clashed. The brokers resisted reform, just as the speculators had seventy-five years earlier, and this time it was largely government pressure that brought about reform. But at nearly the same time it was Wall Street, as always in pursuit of profit, that brought investing in securities to the middle class and, again, transformed and enriched the American economy and the American public.

Hardly had Wall Street come to Main Street, however, when a new technology, the computer, promised an economic revolution at least as profound as that wrought by the steam engine in Wall Street's earliest days. Among the first results of this technology was to allow Wall Street's free market to extend its power around the globe as socialism collapsed nearly everywhere.

So the story I propose to tell here is the rise of a new great power. Like Rome twenty-five hundred years earlier, Wall Street started small and inconsequential, utterly unnoticed by the mighty of the earth. But circumstances, politics, technology, sheer dumb luck—always an indispensable attribute of greatness—caused it to grow, to conquer its neighbors, to deal successfully, if often painfully, with its internal conflicts, and finally, to emerge upon the world stage as a power that other power centers could ignore only at great peril to themselves.

And like the story of Rome, Wall Street's story is a tale worth the telling. For like the Romans, the players of the great game were (and are) great, petty, noble, loathsome, smart, brainless, selfish, generous, and always, always human.

CHAPTER ONE

"A Cloacina of All the Depravities of Human Nature"

Among its innumerable other distinctions, New York is the only major city in the United States ever to have been walled.

By the 1650s, less than thirty years after its founding, Nieuw Amsterdam was becoming so prosperous that the English colonies in New England were beginning to covet the Dutch trading post in the middle of one of the world's largest and most splendid natural harbors. Even more threatening to Nieuw Amsterdam's future, the First Anglo-Dutch War had broken out in 1652.

The Dutch governor of the colony, Peter Stuyvesant, had been a soldier and thought like one. Fearing a land attack from New England, he decided to build a defensive wall on the town's northern edge. He borrowed six thousand guilders from local merchants and ordered every able-bodied man to assist in its construction. Made of sixteen-foot logs sunk four feet into the ground and sharpened at the top, the wall stretched from Pearl Street (which was then at the shoreline) on the east, 2,340 feet to what is today the western edge of Trinity Churchyard. There the land fell off sharply to the Hudson River, forming a natural defensive barrier. Gates were built at the East River, where most ships off-loaded, and at Broadway, the main land route north.

When Stuyvesant presented the bill for the wall to the brand-new city council (established only on February 2, 1653) for payment, however, the members balked. The newly appointed, self-important council members said the bill for the wall was the problem of the Dutch West India Company, which owned the colony, and refused to pay it. Not until Stuyvesant agreed to turn over the revenues from the tax on liquor in compensation did the council agree to pay for the governor's wall.

But like many a soldier before and since, Stuyvesant had failed to take sea power into account. When the English finally attacked the city, in 1664, they did not do so by land from the north, as Stuyvesant had feared and prepared for. Instead, an English fleet sailed up the harbor from the south and put the town under its guns, which far outnumbered those of Fort Amsterdam at the island's tip.

Stuyvesant, undaunted if outflanked, was prepared to defend the town no matter what the cost. But the local merchants—including his own son—were not. They signed a petition to the governor calling on him to surrender the city rather than have it—and their fortunes—destroyed. With great reluctance, Stuyvesant agreed. The next day, his beloved Nieuw Amsterdam became New York, so named because it was given as a birthday present to James, Duke of York, the younger brother and heir of King Charles II.

Stuyvesant remained in New York, living on the farm he had established far north of the city until his death in 1672. That farm, which ran from what is now Fifth Street to Seventeenth Street, Park Avenue to the East River, would make his descendants a wealthy family in the nineteenth century.

The wall, now completely useless, soon fell into disrepair and was torn down in 1698, the year the first Trinity Church was built at its western end. Had that been all there was to it, the wall would have been no more than a minor footnote in history. But on the ground immediately behind the wall, a space of one hundred feet had been reserved for troop movements, with no building allowed. As crosstown traffic was already a problem in Manhattan, just as it still is, this space was quickly and inevitably utilized as a cross street and, just as inevitably, came to be named Wall Street. That little street, thanks to another Dutch legacy to New York, would go on to become one of the most famous thoroughfares in the world.

That second legacy was the town's fundamental character. The Dutch invented modern capitalism in the early seventeenth century. Although many of the basic concepts had first appeared in Italy during the Renaissance, the Dutch, especially the citizens of the city of Amsterdam, were the real innovators. They transformed banking, stock exchanges, credit, insurance, and limited-liability corporations into a coherent financial and commercial system. The resulting explosion of wealth in turn transformed the tiny Netherlands, briefly making it one of the great powers of Europe.

It was in the Netherlands that the early techniques of stock-market manipulation were developed, such as short selling (selling stock one doesn't own, in hopes of a fall in price), bear raids (where insiders conspire to sell a stock short until the outsiders panic and sell out their holdings, allowing the insiders to close their shorts profitably), syndicates (where a group manipulates a stock price by buying and selling among themselves), and corners (where a person or syndicate secretly acquires the entire floating supply of a commodity, forcing all who need to buy the commodity to do so at their price).

And it was in the Netherlands that the eruption of "tulipomania" caused the first recorded financial bubble. Soon after the tulip was introduced into western Europe in the middle of the sixteenth century from Turkey, a craze had developed for the flower. By the early seventeenth century the prices of the more prized varieties had risen to remarkable heights, as the rich competed to display the latest and rarest varieties in their gardens. By the early 1630s, the fad had created a classic speculative madness. Tulip bulbs were being bought not for their inherent value or even their beauty, but in expectation of a continuing increase in price. (The idea that there will always be someone willing to buy an asset at a higher price than was paid for it has long been known as the Greater Fool Theory of investing.)

In 1635 a variety known as Childer was selling for 1,615 florins. To get some idea of what that sum meant in the economy of early-seventeenth-century Holland, consider that a team of four oxen, the equivalent of a tractor, could be had for 480 florins. A thousand pounds of cheese cost 120 florins. Nevertheless, the prices of tulips only continued to rise, and the following year, a single bulb of a particularly rare variety (only two bulbs were in all of the Netherlands at the time) sold for 4,600 florins plus a new carriage, two gray horses, and a complete set of harness.

But since all financial bubbles are as flimsy as their real-world namesakes, the tulip bubble burst when someone realized that, because speculation does not create wealth but only transfers it, a day of reckoning was inevitable. When that nameless person sold out (or, more courageously, sold short), others followed, and soon the frenzy to sell equaled the earlier frenzy to buy. Prices crashed and thousands were ruined in the ensuing debacle.

It was the sort of people who could precipitate such an event in Europe that founded the little colony at the mouth of the Hudson in North America. From the very first it differed from most of the other colonies that were planted on North America's eastern seaboard in that century. The Puritans of New England, the Quakers of Pennsylvania, the Catholics of Maryland, all came to the New World to worship God as they chose. In each case, the colonists' first task, as they saw it, was to build a shining city on a hill, a community to be emulated for its piety and morality.

But when the Dutch set up shop—quite literally—in their new colony, their purpose was only to make a buck. So busy were they pursuing wealth that they didn't even get around to building a proper church for seventeen years. (When they finally did, they named it for St. Nicholas, and Santa Claus has been the occasionally inattentive patron saint of New York ever since.)

New York's distinct origins and character produced a tension between it and other colonies quite early on. Even when New York extended no farther up Manhattan Island than St. Paul's Chapel at the foot of City Hall Park, Thomas Jefferson called the city "a cloacina of all the depravities of human nature."[1] This tension is noticeable even today. To the rest of the country, New York is often regarded as the epitome of all that is wicked and dangerous. To New Yorkers, the rest of the country is morally smug and, above all, boring.

The Dutch were very successful at first. Many of the new colonies were established by joint-stock companies—the forerunners of the modern corporation—that had been especially created to found a colony. All these companies soon went broke, and the colonies they founded were taken over by the crown. But the Dutch West India Company was already well established and rich from sugar and slave trading. And while the company spent twenty thousand guilders formally establishing the colony, the first shipload of furs sent back from Nieuw Amsterdam was valued at forty-five thousand guilders, a return on investment of 125 percent.

The company profits did not last long, however, thanks mostly to frequently incompetent government—another, less fortunate inheritance New York would get from its Dutch forebears. But the individual citizens of the colony fared far better. A purely commercial enterprise founded by the live-and-let-live Dutch, Nieuw Amsterdam soon possessed a cosmopolitan character. When Peter Stuyvesant, a pious member of the Dutch Reform Church, tried to expel the Jews and the Quakers who had settled in Nieuw Amsterdam, the company told him in no uncertain terms to mind his own business, so that the Jews and the Quakers could tend to theirs. A French priest visiting in the 1640s, when the town's population was still well under a thousand, counted no fewer than eighteen languages being spoken by people on its streets. They were all there to make money. Besides furs, commodities such as flour, slaves, lumber, and myriad others were also being traded in Manhattan before long. Its merchants, already firmly linked to the markets of northern Europe, soon sought to buy cheap and sell dear in the Mediterranean, the West Indies, and even the Indian Ocean.

Thus, when the town was taken over by the English, its citizens remained just as interested in money as they had ever been. They adjusted quickly and easily to English rule and English laws, and today it might seem that the Dutch left only a few place names, such as Spuyten Duyvil and Brooklyn; a few words, such as *cookie*; and a few personal names, such as Roosevelt, to mark their forty years on the Hudson. But that is not true, for they left their commercial spirit as well.

Today, somewhere deep within New York's mighty metropolis—like the child within the adult—there lives on still that little, hustly-bustly, let's-make-a-deal place that was Nieuw Amsterdam. And the making of money—for good and ill—is still the city's dearest love.

That spirit was evident as early as 1666, only two years after the English seized control, when Frederick Philipse orchestrated the first financial coup in North America by cornering the wampum market.

Philipse was born in Holland in 1626 and moved with his father to Nieuw Amsterdam in 1647. Trained as a carpenter, he actually helped to construct the wall a few years later. But Philipse did not remain a carpenter for long. Instead, he took one of the royal roads to wealth and married a rich widow. Armed with his wife's money, he began to trade in various commodities with the local Indians, with the West Indies, and with the mother country. He soon demonstrated a keen understanding of the marketplace.

The Indians provided the furs that were the mainstay of the colony's economy at that time. But they did not want to be paid for them in gold or silver. These metals, dear as they were to the hearts of Europeans, were unknown to them and therefore worthless. Instead, they demanded payment in what they regarded as "real money": wampum. Wampum were tubular beads, usually strung together in intricate patterns, that were made from the shells of the freshwater clams that abounded in the rivers and lakes of eastern North America.

In 1650, six white beads or three black beads were worth one Dutch stuiver. (Equal to one-twentieth of a guilder, a stuiver was, in effect, the Dutch equivalent of a nickel.) Unfortunately for the Dutch traders, inflation set in, and by 1659 it took sixteen white beads to equal a stuiver. This played havoc with the local economy, not only because the cost of furs skyrocketed, but because the settlers as well as the Indians used wampum in day-to-day transactions. Governor Stuyvesant tried to fix the problem with the usual government remedy, price controls. And he achieved the usual results—the price controls were ignored. Then Frederick Philipse began buying up wampum and taking it out of circulation. In fact, he buried it in hogsheads. In a matter of weeks he controlled the market in wampum and succeeded in raising its price dramatically. By 1666 it took only three white beads to equal a stuiver.

The very concept of a central bank would not develop until the end of the seventeenth century (the Bank of England was founded in 1694). But Frederick Philipse was, in effect, acting as one more than three decades earlier by regulating the money supply and, doubtless, making a tidy profit in the process. He would go on to become New York's richest citizen (marrying a second rich widow along the way), with trading interests as far afield as the East Indies and Madagascar.

As for wampum, it continued to be commonly used in New York

as a currency until shortly before the American Revolution. Then a machine was invented that cheaply manufactured counterfeit wampum, destroying the value of the real article.

New York's commercial-mindedness and live-and-let-live attitude did not make it an easy place to govern, then or now, and its citizens were soon known for their tendency to riot. It remains to this day the only American colony or state to have hanged a governor, Jacob Leisler. The Navigation Acts, first passed in 1651, were meant to ensure that the American colonies operated for the benefit of the mother country. They forbade most manufacturing and required foreign goods to first pass through British ports (paying British tariffs). But they were spottily enforced at first and, when they were, were often evaded with a timely bribe or a clandestine unloading in New York Harbor's infinity of coves and brooks. The colony flourished.

By the time the wall was torn down, Manhattan had a population of 4,937 (according to the first census ever taken in North America). Most lived at the southern tip of the island, and Wall Street was distinctly uptown. But with the construction of Trinity Church and then, in 1700, the second City Hall, on Wall Street at the head of Broad Street, the western end became a fashionable place of residence.

Only at its eastern end, at the Pearl Street waterfront, was Wall Street commercial. The first commodity regularly traded there in quantity was slaves. New York was the only northern colony to have a large slave population (14 percent of Manhattan's population in 1698), but the city also acted as an entrepôt, shipping slaves south to Virginia and the Carolinas.

Along with furs and slaves, grain also became important to the New York economy after settlers discovered that wheat thrived in the Hudson Valley. Much of this grain, in the form of flour and biscuit, was exported to the West Indies in exchange for molasses and rum. So important did flour become to the New York economy, in fact, that there is a flour barrel along with a beaver on the city's coat of arms. New York also sent such commodities as whale oil and tobacco to England in exchange for manufactured products that could not be obtained locally.

It is hardly surprising that New York was a bustling port. Its harbor was beyond compare, with miles of shoreline, deep water, and instant access to the open sea through the Narrows. Further, the Raritan and Hackensack Rivers in New Jersey, the Hudson River in New York, and Long Island Sound funneled traffic into New York. In 1699, the governor, Lord Bellomont, called New York "the growingest town in America." That was, however, a slight exaggeration. Oceangoing ships in the seventeenth and eighteenth centuries were still small enough to use the many other harbors in the New York area, such as Oyster Bay and Southampton on Long Island, and the towns on the Hudson River, such as Peekskill, that today are not thought of as ports at all.

Moreover, not long after it was founded in 1680, Philadelphia had a larger population and was the only port serving the rich Pennsylvania farmland. Meanwhile Boston served the populous New England countryside, and Charleston had an unusually rich export economy in rice and indigo. Thus toward the end of the colonial era, New York, however commercially ambitious its population, ranked only fourth among colonial ports. In 1770, Philadelphia imported 47,000 tons of cargo, Boston 38,000, and Charleston 27,000. New York imported just 25,000 tons that year.

And while New York was an active port with a thriving commerce, it was not yet a financial market. The American colonial economy grew by leaps and bounds in the eighteenth century. (That, of course, is precisely why the British government wanted so much to start taxing it, setting off a train of events that led to the American Revolution.) It exported one-seventh of the world's pig iron and possessed a merchant marine that was second in size only to that of the United Kingdom itself. But it was in many ways a primitive economy. There were no banks in the American colonies because the British forbade their establishment. Nor was there, in any real sense, a money supply, other than the wampum that served as currency in some areas.

Bank of England banknotes were not found in the colonies, nor were, to any great extent, British coins. Instead the money supply consisted of a hodgepodge of foreign coinage, paper money issued by colonial governments, and such expedients as tobacco warehouse receipts, which circulated widely in the southern colonies. The most common coin was the Spanish real. Reales, made of silver, were often called pieces of eight because they were frequently cut into halves, quarters, and eighths to supply small change. That is why a quarter is still known as two bits, and why the New York Stock Exchange until recently quoted prices in eighths, not tenths, of a dollar.

New York's position as a major port and commercial center was devastated by the American Revolution. New York was the only American city occupied during the war for an extended period, over seven years. (Indeed, no other city in modern times has been occupied by enemy forces for so long.) Those merchants who were patriots had little choice but to leave the city, and their businesses, behind. The loyalist merchants who stayed and did business with the British were forced to leave in turn, when the Americans finally reoccupied the city on November 25, 1783, a date that would be New York's major local holiday for the next century.

The physical destruction rivaled the devastation of New York's commercial strength. During the British occupation, two fires swept the city. The first, on September 21, 1776, began at the foot of Broad Street and roared unchecked up the island's west side, burning down about one-third of the developed area before it died out. Numerous commercial structures were destroyed, as were 493 houses and the first Trinity Church, which remained a blackened ruin for fifteen years afterward. The second fire, on August 3, 1778, destroyed sixty-four more buildings in Cruger's Wharf, a busy commercial area on the East River.

In all, during the turmoil of the Revolution, New York's population fell by more than half and its GDP (not that such a statistic then existed) fell by at least as much. But once the war was over and the British departed, the city recovered with astonishing speed. Its population was back to prewar levels in only four years as old residents returned and new ones were attracted to its tolerant, money-minded ways. The twenty-one-year-old John Jacob Astor, a native of Waldorf in Germany's Rhineland, came in 1784. And a steady stream of New Englanders, leaving the region's small towns, began moving to outward-looking New York in these years, rather than to stuffy, self-satisfied Boston. In 1790, the country's first national census revealed that New York had surpassed Philadelphia in population.

These newcomers continued New York's tradition of being a city of immigrants, as, indeed, it still is. The most famous of New York's eighteenth-century immigrants came earlier, however, in 1772. This was Alexander Hamilton and he would have the most influence on New York's future as a commercial center and financial market.

Hamilton was in many ways unique among the founding fathers. He was the only one not born in what is now the United States. Instead he was born on the island of Nevis, in the British West Indies. And except for the by-then venerable and world-respected Benjamin Franklin, he was the only one not born rich. In fact, in John Adams's memorable if not altogether accurate phrase, Hamilton was born "the bastard brat of a Scotch pedlar."

Hamilton was indeed a bastard, but his father was not a peddler, just an incompetent businessman. As a younger son of the laird of Cambuskeith, Hamilton's father sprang from a family far more ancient and more distinguished than Adams's own. But he soon deserted his mistress and her two sons, and Hamilton's mother opened a small store in St. Croix, then part of the Danish Virgin Islands, to feed herself and her family.

Hamilton went to work, at the age of nine, for a New York merchant named Nicholas Cruger, who operated a trading post in St. Croix. Cruger was mightily impressed with the highly intelligent and ambitious youth. When Cruger returned to New York because of his health, he left Hamilton, aged only thirteen, in charge. Two years later, he paid for Hamilton's passage to New York. It would be his home for the rest of his life.

Hamilton studied at King's College (now Columbia University), trained in the law, and served as an aide-de-camp to George Washington during the Revolution. When Washington became president, he asked Hamilton to be his secretary of the treasury, the post that would have to deal with the most pressing problem facing the new republic: its chaotic finances. This Hamilton did, and in an astonishingly short time.

While the Continental Congress had been able to borrow from France and the Netherlands to buy arms in those countries, it had not been able to sell nearly enough bonds domestically to finance the war. Instead it had no choice but to resort to forced loans, requisitioning supplies and paying for them with IOUs, and to issue fiat money, the so-called continentals. This paper money was money only because the government said it was. And as fiat money always does, the continentals induced a great inflation. Within a few years, Congress had to revalue earlier issues at only 2.5 percent of their face value. For a hundred years and more, the phrase "not worth a continental" would be part of the American vocabulary.

There had been speculation in the bonds, IOUs, and continentals in New York and elsewhere even while the war (and the British occupation of New York) continued. Speculators held auctions in these securities at coffeehouses (where so many financial institutions had been born, including the London Stock Exchange and Lloyd's of London), but they were sporadic and informal and attracted little attention. But when Hamilton began to construct the financial underpinnings of the country under the new Constitution, speculation in these securities became one of the country's first great political issues.

Hamilton wanted to do three things. First, he sought to establish a federal tax system to provide a dependable revenue stream. (Under the old Articles of Confederation, the federal government lacked the power to tax and was obliged to ask the states for money.) Second, he wanted to refund the national debt, both foreign and domestic, and the debts incurred by the several states during the war, on generous terms by issuing new bonds on the full faith and credit of the United States. Finally, he envisioned a central bank, modeled on the Bank of England, to act as the government's fiscal agent and as a regulator of the country's money supply.

The group of politicians who would soon be known as Jeffersonians, after their most distinguished leader, bitterly opposed Hamilton. They felt that the speculators, who had bought the old bonds and other paper at low prices, should not be allowed to profit by having them redeemed at higher prices. Only the original bondholders, the Jeffersonians argued, should benefit. This was hopelessly impractical, as it would have been, at the least, time-consuming, and quite often impossible, to determine who the original holders were.

The refunding act passed Congress, but not without a good deal of horse-trading. For instance, to get the Jeffersonians to accept the refunding of the state debts, Hamilton had to sacrifice the chance of making New York the new federal capital. (While it is, of course, impossible to know how history would have developed had New York become the country's political capital as well as its commercial, cultural, and financial one, there is no doubt that this country, and New York City as well, would have been a very different place.)

Once Hamilton's program was in operation, the effect on the economy of the new United States was extraordinary and immediate. But a bitter legacy among his opponents has lasted to this day. In fact, the whole history of American politics can largely be seen as the ongoing battle between the Hamiltonians and the Jeffersonians. Because Wall Street became the center of American finance, it became to a large extent the symbol for all that the Jeffersonians and their heirs—from Andrew Jackson to William Jennings Bryan to Ralph Nader—thought wrong with the country.

But that was in the future. In the 1790s what mattered was that Hamilton's program caused the American economy to flourish. In the 1780s the United States had been in financial chaos, not altogether dissimilar to Russia today. But by 1794 it had the highest credit rating in Europe, its bonds selling at a 10 percent premium over par. Talleyrand, soon to be the French foreign minister but then in exile in this country from the Terror, explained why. The new bonds, he said, were "safe and free from reverses. They have been funded in such a sound manner and the prosperity of this country is growing so rapidly that there can be no doubt of their solvency."

Although by the 1790s it was growing much more slowly than New York, Philadelphia remained the country's financial center. The first bank in the country, the Bank of North America, had been formed there, and the first stock exchange in the country, the Philadelphia Stock Exchange, was organized in 1790. Because Philadelphia was to be the nation's capital for ten years, while Washington was under construction, Hamilton's central bank, the Bank of the United States, was established there in 1791 as well.

But under Hamilton's program, New York's financial activity also greatly increased, and the pieces were all in place. New York's commerce was growing swiftly, as was its population. National as well as local prosperity was on the rise. Merchants had more and more need for credit, insurance, and other financial services. Alexander Hamilton himself had founded New York's first bank, the Bank of New York, in 1784. Hamilton's program provided a reputable and unified money supply and a predictable value to the currency. Speculators and brokers, familiar with finance and risk, were looking for opportunity and profit. They were ready, willing, and able to provide the liquidity all financial markets need. And the speculative techniques bequeathed New Yorkers by their Dutch ancestors were there for the taking by the bold and the artful.

A city, a street, and destiny were coming together.

CHAPTER TWO

"A Line of Separation between Honest Men & Knaves"

Wall Street first gained national fame not for financial reasons but for political ones. On April 30, 1789, George Washington took the oath of office as the first president under the new Constitution, on the second-floor balcony of what had been New York's City Hall, located on Wall Street at the head of Broad. Renamed Federal Hall when appropriated as a temporary capitol, it had been refurbished with $32,000 of New Yorkers' money. Added to the cornice and frieze were such national decorative touches as clusters of thirteen stars and thirteen arrows surrounded by olive branches. (Torn down in the 1830s to make way for the new Customs House that is still there, now a national monument and museum, all that remains of Federal Hall is a section of the wrought-iron railing before which Washington took the oath. It is on display at the New-York Historical Society.)

Federal Hall, however, was hardly the only building on Wall Street to be the scene of construction at this optimistic time. A block to the west, the second Trinity Church was nearing completion, its two-hundred-foot steeple still swathed in scaffolding. It would be consecrated less than a year later, with the president in attendance. Many of the mansions on the western end of Wall Street were spruced up at this time as well. Alexander Hamilton, slated to be the new secretary of the treasury, moved into one at the corner of Wall and William Streets.

Thanks largely to Hamilton, however, the days of these handsome, classical-style mansions were already numbered. In the rapidly expanding economy that Hamilton's financial program fostered, commerce quickly overtook the residential section of Wall Street. In 1791, the Bank of New York moved into the McEvers mansion at the corner of Wall and William Streets, directly across from Hamilton's residence. (Hamilton had helped found the bank, but sold his stock when he became secretary of the treasury to avoid any appearance of a conflict of interest.)

The eastern end of Wall Street, where it met the East River, had always been given over to commerce, although not all of it was financial in nature by any means. Because of the prevailing winds, the captains of oceangoing sailing ships preferred to dock on that side of Manhattan. The services these ships required, from warehouses to ships' chandlers, formed the hub of New York's commercial district. Many of the buildings at that end were two stories tall, with shops for hairdressers, tailors, candle makers, and such on the first floor and the proprietor's dwelling on the second. Others were given over to brokers of various types.

Broker connoted something much broader at the end of the eighteenth century than it does today. The word had entered the English language as early as the fourteenth century, coming from the French *brocour,* one who broaches a cask of wine to sell it by the glass or bottle. The word was applied to wholesalers and retailers until the seventeenth century, and after that simply referred to an intermediary, someone who does not produce a product himself. Rather a broker came to mean someone who brings together buyers and sellers and makes his profit by taking a commission on any resulting transaction.

Today, brokers are usually highly specialized, dealing only in one product or group of closely related products, such as insurance or real estate. Only relatively recently has the unmodified word *broker* come to mean a specialist in the buying and selling of securities. At the dawn of the Republic, a New York broker was a generalist, often having interests in a dozen different forms of trade. It was not unusual for one man to buy and sell securities, run a private lottery, insure cargoes, sell interests in tontines (a cross between life insurance and gambling, long since outlawed), and be a partner in a private bank.

Because there was as yet little manufacturing in the United States above the artisan level, other than shipbuilding and pig iron production, most "businessmen" were, in fact, brokers. But they constituted a small percentage of the workforce. The overwhelming majority of Americans at the end of the eighteenth century lived on farms. Those who lived in cities were more likely to be shopkeepers, domestic servants, or professionals such as lawyers and clergymen.

Hamilton's program produced a sudden flood of tradable securities, including federal bonds, new state bonds, and stock in newly chartered banks (there were only three state banks in 1790; by 1800 there were twenty-nine) and insurance companies. These new, tradable securities increased the volume of securities business for the generalist brokers, although it would be another generation before any of them specialized only in securities trading.

While the federal and state bonds were the meat and potatoes of the new securities brokerage, the "hottest" security was the stock in the Bank of the United States, which was capitalized at $10 million, a vast sum for that time and place. Its size and its monopoly position as the federal government's fiscal agent made it, in a sense, the country's first blue-chip stock (although that phrase itself would be invented only in the fateful year of 1929). The government was obligated to purchase 20 percent of the bank's shares (Hamilton raised the money by floating a bond issue in Europe through the Amsterdam firm of Hope and Company). The other 80 percent was to be sold to the public, with the limitation that no individual could own more than one thousand shares. A subscriber was required to pay 25 percent of the purchase price in gold, but the rest could be paid for in the 6 percent government bonds that had been issued as part of Hamilton's refunding program.

Trading in the stock of the BUS, as it was soon called, began in the spring of 1791 on a when-issued basis. When the subscription was held in early July of that year, it sold out within the hour and began to rise steadily. What amounted to the country's first major IPO set off the country's first bull market.

European firms began sending agents, and capital, across the Atlantic to participate in the new market. Short sales (the sale of borrowed stock, in hopes of a decline in price) and what are now called puts and calls (the right to buy or sell a security at a future time at a guaranteed price) were first employed at this time (although both had long been known in Europe), greatly adding to the speculative possibilities. As activity began to pick up, newspapers turned their attention to the new market, and of course, as the market went higher, predictions of disaster appeared. On August 31, 1791, the *New York Gazette* even offered a bit of doggerel, entitled "Speculation":

> What magic this among the people,
> That swell a may-pole to a steeple?
> Touched by the wand of speculation,
> A frenzy runs through all the nation;
> For soon or late, so truth advises,
> Things must assume their proper sizes—
> And sure as death all mortal trips,
> Thousands will rue the name of SCRIPTS.[1]

Scripts was a contraction of *subscription stock,* and these were the equivalent of what we now call *securities.* The words *stock* and *bond* were also in use, but often used interchangeably. Restricting the word *stock* to mean a security representing an ownership interest and the word *bond* to represent debt securities would come about only in the later decades of the nineteenth century. The brokers and customers, presumably, were not confused. But many writers of the period were, and a considerable majority of historians have been ever since.

As some brokers began to increase their business in financial instruments, they needed a place in which to trade. Many of the local coffeehouses, like those in Amsterdam and London a century and more earlier, welcomed brokers to meet at their facilities, making their profit on food and drink, while the brokers sought theirs in trading. Often, however, there still wasn't enough business to occupy the brokers' full attention, and they would spend the time gossiping and gambling at cards and dice. A betting slip survives from this period with two New York brokers wagering on whether a particular French politician will be guillotined on or before a certain date.

Some of the more successful brokers, such as McEvers & Barclay, Leonard Bleecker, and John Pintard, began holding regular auctions at their offices to accommodate the new business. Then, early in 1792, John Sutton, his partner Benjamin Jay, and several others decided to form a central auction at 22 Wall Street, called the Stock Exchange Office. Sellers would deposit the securities they wanted to sell, and the auctioneers would take a commission on the sale. Brokers wanting to buy for their own account or for their customers' accounts would attend the auction.

This system soon collapsed, however. Many of the outside brokers attended the auction only to learn the latest prices and would then offer the same securities at a lower commission outside. Even the insiders would often trade away from the auction to ensure their own profits. To correct the problems, the most important of the brokers met at Corre's Hotel on March 21, 1792, to try to hammer out an agreement that would stop these abuses. They agreed to form a new auction, beginning on April 21, and furthermore agreed that "we the Subscribers, Brokers for the Purchase and Sale of Public Stock, do hereby solemnly promise and pledge ourselves to each other, that we will not buy or sell from this day for any person whatsoever any kind of Public Stock, at a less rate than one quarter per cent Commission on the specie value, and that we will give preference to each other in our negotiations."[2]

Twenty-one individual brokers and three firms signed this agreement, known as the Buttonwood Agreement because it was supposedly signed beneath a buttonwood tree (they are now usually called sycamores) outside 68 Wall Street, where brokers often met in good weather to carry on their trading. Whether or not the agreement was actually signed beneath it, the huge buttonwood tree, already several hundred years old in 1792, became a beloved Wall Street icon until it fell in a storm on June 14, 1865.

The first meeting of the new exchange was held at the Merchant's Coffee House. But that winter the members decided to build a meeting place of their own. They didn't build a stock exchange, however, as there simply wasn't enough business in stocks and bonds to justify it. Instead, they built another coffeehouse, named the Tontine Coffee House, at the corner of Wall and Water Streets. Its name derived from its being financed by a tontine. Two hundred and three shares were offered at $200 each, and its act of incorporation called for the corporation to hold the property developed with the money until only seven survived among the original stockholders. At that point the property was to be sold and the proceeds distributed among the survivors. Although the coffeehouse was open to all, only the members were allowed to participate in the securities auctions held there. Less substantial brokers continued to operate on the street and at their own offices.

While the New York Stock Exchange would not be formally organized for another quarter century, this agreement is traditionally regarded as its ultimate foundation. But it was also a price-fixing cartel, designed to keep the insiders in and the outsiders out of a closed club that was restricted to New York's most affluent brokers. It would remain to some extent a closed club, operated first of all for the benefit of its members, for nearly another century and three-quarters, long after the New York Stock Exchange had become the largest and most important stock exchange on earth.

One of the major operators in the bull market that had brought the nascent stock exchange into existence—indeed, one of its prime creators—was William Duer. He would prove an archetype whose successors would appear in every bull market to follow, right up until the present day.

Born in England in 1747, Duer was the son of a successful West Indian planter. Educated at Eton, he joined the British army, serving in India with Clive. He spent some time managing his father's estates in the West Indies and then settled in New York, where he secured a lucrative contract to supply masts and spars to the Royal Navy. He purchased an expansive, timbered property near Saratoga, New York, to fulfill this contract and built a large house there.

When the Revolution began, he sided with the rebels and was elected to the Continental Congress. After he left office, he made a fortune supplying the Continental Army and married Catherine Alexander, often known as Lady Kitty, the daughter of the immensely rich American general William Alexander, who claimed the extinct Scottish earldom of Stirling.

Following the Revolution, Duer and his wife lived in almost royal style in their New York mansion, with liveried servants and as many as fifteen different wines at a single dinner. He could afford this opulent existence owing to a number of financial coups during the 1780s, involving land and the Revolutionary debt. In 1785 he was appointed secretary of the Treasury Board of the national government under the Articles of Confederation, a position tailor-made for obtaining insider information. In 1789, Alexander Hamilton (whose wife was a cousin of Duer's wife) appointed him assistant secretary of the treasury.

Hamilton was personally honest and never tried to profit from his position in the government or to help his friends with insider information. When Virginia's Henry Lee asked his friend Hamilton for information on the Treasury's refunding plans, Hamilton refused to tell him anything. Duer was not so fastidious. For instance, William Bingham, a rich Philadelphian and intimate of Duer's, was so sure of the future that he borrowed £60,000—a very considerable fortune at that time—in Amsterdam to more profitably speculate in the federal debt. No evidence survives, but it is hard to imagine he would take such a tremendous risk without having shortened the odds with insider information.

Federal law forbade Treasury officials from speculating in federal securities, and Duer resigned rather than obey it. But he had always been more interested in Treasury connections, and especially a reputation for having them, than in the job itself. He became more and more involved in speculative schemes, until Hamilton felt he needed to caution his former subordinate. "I feared," he wrote in a letter as early as the autumn of 1790, "lest it might carry you further than was consistent either with your own safety or the public good. My friendship for you, and my concern for the public cause, were both alarmed."[3] Duer's answer, if any, does not survive, but Hamilton's caution did not cause Duer to alter his behavior in the least.

Operating for himself and for others, Duer continued to speculate. Among those he borrowed money from to do so was Henry Knox, the secretary of war. The principal speculative vehicle for Duer and others was the stock in the Bank of the United States, which had been issued at $100 a share. It reached as high as $185 before declining in September 1791. But it never dipped below $130 and was soon back up to around $170.

At the end of 1791, Duer entered into a partnership with Alexander Macomb, one of New York's richest and most prominent citizens. Their plan was to operate together for one year, speculating in stocks, especially the stock of the Bank of New York. The trades were to be made in Macomb's name and the stock held in that name, but Duer was the real power behind the speculation. In effect, the agreement called for combining Macomb's money with Duer's speculative talents and insider connections with the Treasury Department. At the end of the year they were to divide the profits equally.

Duer began buying Bank of New York stock when rumors were circulating that the Bank of the United States planned to buy it and convert it into its New York branch. If that was true, then the stock was certain to rise, and Duer and Macomb would make a handsome profit. But Duer, it seems, was playing a deeper game. While long in the market with Macomb, he was short Bank of New York in his own account. So were several Livingstons, members of New York's most powerful family, on his advice. Thus Duer was betting in public that the Bank of New York would be acquired and in private that it would not be. If the merger failed, Duer and Macomb would lose, while Duer, on his own, would make a fortune. But since his agreement with Macomb called for using Macomb's money, not his own, all Duer had to lose by double-crossing Macomb was honor, a sacrifice he seemed perfectly willing to make.

As the speculative fever increased, the incorporations of several more banks were announced. The Million Bank of the State of New York was to have an eponymous capital of a million dollars. Its charter had a provision allowing it to merge with the Bank of New York, presumably prior to that bank's own alleged merger with the BUS. Investors mobbed the office, and rights to buy the stock when offered were soon selling for $92. When an issue of 4,000 shares of stock of the Tammany Bank, capitalized at $200,000, was announced, the bank received subscriptions for no less than 21,740 shares.

In the heightening frenzy, Duer was the center of all attention, and, it seemed, he could do no wrong. His trades, supposedly private, quickly became public knowledge and were duplicated by other speculators. And Duer contributed to the rising market by leveraging. He borrowed from banks and from individuals, including $203,000 from Walter Livingston in early March 1792. More, he made speculative agreements with other notables, including John and Nicholas Roosevelt. He began to buy bank stocks for future delivery, betting that rising prices would enable him to pay for them when the time came.

Hamilton was appalled. "'Tis time," he wrote on March 2, 1792, "there should be a line of separation between honest Men & knaves, between respectable Stockholders and dealers in the funds, and mere unprincipled Gamblers."[4] Finding that line of separation, of course, has occupied the finest minds of Wall Street and the government ever since, with mixed results at best.

Among the people Duer had bought bank stock from were several members of the Livingston clan. Thus they had an interest in seeing that prices fell rather than continued to rise. To ensure this, they began to withdraw gold and silver from their bank deposits, contracting the local money supply, and forcing banks to call in loans. In other words, they instituted a credit squeeze. Interest rates soared to as much as 1 percent a day.

This was ruinous to Duer and others who had borrowed to speculate on rising prices. Matters only worsened for Duer when an audit uncovered shortages amounting to $238,000 at the Treasury in accounts Duer had been responsible for. Hamilton, who had been giving Duer time to straighten the mess out, now ordered the Treasury to sue for the money.

Duer desperately tried to borrow to cover his obligations, but the man who had been having money thrown at him just a few weeks earlier, now couldn't borrow a dime. Despite his troubles, he maintained a brave front, as the desperate on Wall Street usually do. On March 22 he wrote Walter Livingston, who had loaned him a fortune, that "I am now secure from my enemies, and feeling the purity of my heart I defy the world."[5]

Needless to say, he was anything but secure, and less than a day later he was in debtors' prison, where he would remain the rest of his life. With Duer's fall, panic ensued and prices plunged. The next day twenty-five failures were reported by brokers in New York's still tiny financial community. Walter Livingston, who had gone from door to door among New York's fashionable assuring anyone who would listen that he was still solvent, announced that he was not. Alexander Macomb failed in early April and was also incarcerated.

Jefferson, then secretary of state, wrote to a friend that "at length our paper bubble is burst. The failure of Duer in New York soon brought on others, and these still more, like nine pins knocking one another down."[6] Hardly able to contain his glee at the discomfiture of the speculators he hated so passionately, Jefferson calculated their total losses at $5 million. He also calculated that this sum was the total value of New York real estate at the time and equated the losses caused by the panic to the losses that would have occurred had the city been destroyed by some natural catastrophe.

In fact, the situation was not nearly that bad. Many speculators had, indeed, been ruined, but they had been playing the game with their eyes open and had no one to blame but themselves. And many of them were young and able to recover from their losses, wiser for the experience.

And Hamilton moved quickly to ensure that the panic did not bring down basically sound institutions, which would have injured innocent investors, not just speculators. He ordered the Treasury to purchase several hundred thousand dollars' worth of federal securities to support the market and urged banks not to call in loans. Further, to ease the money shortage, he allowed merchants to pay import duties—usually payable only in gold or BUS banknotes—at the customs house with notes payable in forty-five days. Praising the Treasury and the banks, Hamilton wrote that "no calamity truly *public* can happen, while these institutions remain sound."[7]

Hamilton was acting exactly as public monetary and fiscal authorities should behave in the midst of a financial panic. His sound plan prevented the contagion of fear from getting out of hand and assured that the panic would not have long-term adverse consequences to the American economy as a whole, however devastated individual speculators were.

Unfortunately, the lessons implicit in Hamilton's actions were lost on the Jeffersonians, who, unable to distinguish between investors, speculators, and gamblers, saw only a bailout of gamblers. When they rose to power, they would destroy the Hamiltonian system, exposing the country to financial disaster again and again. It would be 1987, 195 years later, before the federal government would once again step in decisively to prevent a major speculative panic from becoming a national calamity.

Among the other consequences of the Jeffersonian attitude would be that Wall Street would develop in a power vacuum. Its only leadership and regulation came from within. For years to come, the Street would set its own rules, devise its own procedures. This made its financial market freer than any other in the world. But unregulated free markets are inherently unstable, likely to break down under stress.

None of the banks, such as the Million Bank of the State of New York, whose organizations had been announced at the height of the frenzy ever opened their doors. But even if the panic had not intervened, it is questionable how many ever would have. To issue stock to the public, a company needed a corporate charter, which at the end of the eighteenth century required an act of the state legislature.

The corporation was an invention of the Renaissance that was vital to the development of the capitalist system and, indeed, the modern world. Before the corporation, a person who invested, either individually or in a partnership, was risking his entire net worth. But a corporation is, at least in legal fiction, a "person." A corporation can be sued, it can own property, it can go broke, it can even be criminally indicted (although it would be hard to jail one). And, of course, a corporation can be taxed. But the stockholders are *not* the corporation. They can be held to account for their own actions, but not for the actions of a corporation they own an interest in. Nor do stockholders risk any more money than they invest.

It was this crucial distinction—limited liability—that made the corporation indispensable, allowing capitalists to pool their resources in pursuit of profits, without risking personal bankruptcy.

But while anyone can form a partnership, only the state can create a legal person. In England, this was the prerogative of the crown. But the crown created only seven corporations based in the American colonies during the entire colonial era. After the Revolution, the crown's power to create corporations passed to its successors, the various state legislatures. And as with any piece of legislation, politics always played a far greater role in the fate of a corporate charter than all other factors, including economic.

Today it is difficult to grasp just how intimately intertwined business and politics were before the middle third of the nineteenth century. Most political offices were, effectively, part-time positions, and their holders were perfectly free to carry on their private affairs when not engaged in public ones. Further, the ethics of using one's public office for the purpose of private gain had hardly been explored or elaborated. While some, such as Hamilton and Washington, were above reproach even by the standards of today, most of their contemporaries were not. As late as the 1830s, *lawyer* Daniel Webster would send a private law client a bill for $500 because *Senator* Daniel Webster had inserted an amendment favorable to the client's interests into a piece of legislation. Neither Webster nor the client nor, presumably, anyone else saw anything wrong with this, legally or ethically.

At the same time, New York politics were quite as complicated as they are today. "Man and boy I have known New York politics for sixty years," John Adams would write, "and to me they have always been the devil's own incomprehensible." These two factors together account for why, when Aaron Burr, a New Yorker whose public and private interests were particularly tangled, wanted to open a bank, he had to start a water company to get one.

After the dust of the William Duer debacle had settled, only two banks remained in operation in New York City, the Bank of New York (which was not taken over by the BUS; it remains independent to this day) and the local branch of the Bank of the United States. Both had been founded by Alexander Hamilton, who detested the corner-cutting Burr and would eventually die at his hands. While he held stock in neither, Hamilton influenced both decisively, even after he had left office as secretary of the treasury in 1795. His position as leader of the Federalist Party in New York ensured that local Jeffersonian merchants could have a difficult time obtaining credit and other banking services.

Aaron Burr, the state's leading Democratic-Republican (as the Jeffersonians were coming to be called), was determined to beat this system. A bank controlled, or at least heavily influenced, by him would strengthen his position and that of his political allies considerably. It might even help lure wavering Federalists into the Democratic-Republican camp with the promise of financial assistance. (Also, it is reasonable to assume that the high-living Burr was thinking of ways to ease his own chronic financial distress.) The problem was how to get the Federalist-controlled state government to grant a corporate charter.

Certainly Burr knew that the merest hint that he was trying to start a bank would create deep suspicion among many of his fellow legislators in Albany. So Burr, one of the cleverest politicians in American history (much too clever for his own good, it would turn out), came up with a scheme to bury the authority for a bank deep in the fine print of a charter for a company nominally intended to supply desperately needed potable water to the residents of New York City.

Of all the world's great cities, only New York and Hong Kong are surrounded by salt water. In the early days, New York's residents drew their water from individual wells, some private, some dug by the city. But by the end of the eighteenth century, these wells were grossly contaminated by street runoff and sewage from an ever-expanding number of privies. The rich could afford to buy drinking water from vendors who brought it in from outside the city, but the rest of the population had to make do with what they could get. Epidemics of typhoid and cholera were becoming increasingly common (although the connection between these diseases and bad water was not understood until the middle of the nineteenth century).

City officials realized that water would be a significant limiting factor in future growth unless they dealt with the problem effectively. In 1796, Dr. Joseph Browne suggested that the Common Council petition the state legislature to create a private water company. Browne just happened to be Burr's brother-in-law, and he was probably acting on Burr's behalf. The Council adopted Browne's idea, but asked the legislature to empower the city, not a private company, to establish and operate a water-supply system. This was not what Burr had in mind at all, of course.

But Burr possessed formidable powers of persuasion and soon convinced five leading citizens of both parties to serve on a committee with him to convince the city of the merits of a private company. Among the members of this committee was Alexander Hamilton himself. Hamilton even wrote the committee's formal memorandum to the city on the advantages of a private company over a public one.

Hamilton certainly knew of the city's already desperate need for clean water. And he may well have been unaware of Burr's actual intentions. As usual, Hamilton did not profit personally; still, plenty of Federalists were cut in on the action, and another brother-in-law—this time Hamilton's—would become one of the first directors of the new company.

After securing the city's approval, Burr returned to Albany and presided over the committee of the Assembly that drafted the charter establishing a company, "for supplying the city of New-York with pure and wholesome water." Waiting until the last minute before adjournment to submit the bill, Burr slipped an additional clause into the proposed charter. "And be it further enacted," it read, "that it shall and may be lawful for the said company to employ all such surplus capital as may belong or accrue to the said company in the purchase of public or other stock, or in any other monied transactions or operations . . . for the sole benefit of the company."[8] Translated from the legalese, this meant that the new company, along with building a water system, could engage in virtually any business it wanted to, including, of course, operating a bank.

In the rush to adjournment, no one in the Assembly or the Senate, it seems, even noticed the clause. Only one member of the Council of Revision—which under the original state constitution held the power of executive veto—objected. The others, perhaps, had good reason to be quiet. State Chancellor Robert R. Livingston, for one, held an option on two thousand shares in the new company. Even the Federalist governor, John Jay, did not speak out against it and signed the bill into law on April 7, 1799.

Only five months later, long before it had created a water system or even laid a single length of pipe, the company opened a bank. Hamilton soon regretted his part in the company's creation, calling it "a perfect monster in its principles but a very convenient instrument of profit and influence."[9]

Certainly Burr found it very convenient. When he stepped

down as a director three years later, while serving as vice president of the United States, he owed the bank no less than $64,903.63, a fortune by the standards of the day.

Eventually the company did get around to providing a rudimentary water system, serving perhaps a thousand houses through about twenty-five miles of wooden pipes. These pipes, heavily coated in tar inside and out, still occasionally turn up during excavations. But the water was never "pure and wholesome." Of course, the company's heart was never in the water business, which it abandoned just as soon as it could, in the 1840s, when freshwater from the upstate Croton River began to flow into the city through a city-built aqueduct, giving New York its first system for reliably clean water.

The bank, however, continued as a major player in New York's financial community. In fact it's still a major player. Today known as Chase Manhattan, it is the largest bank in the United States.

The power to create corporations might have remained indefinitely with state legislatures, doubtless resulting in all sorts of adverse consequences. But the number of applications began to accumulate rapidly as the eighteenth century ended. In just the last four years of the 1790s, 335 businesses were incorporated in the United States, mostly for the purpose of internal improvements, such as canals and toll roads. After the turn of the century, the pace only accelerated. Between 1800 and 1860 the state of Pennsylvania alone incorporated over two thousand businesses.

States had no choice but to pass general incorporation laws, specifying the circumstances and rules under which a corporation could be formed without a specific act. New York was the first to do so, in 1811, and other states soon followed. But the legislatures gave up this power only reluctantly, and the corporation laws would always lag behind the new economic realities brought about by the accelerating industrial revolution.

At first, states restricted limited liability to companies with a special legislatively granted charter. The stockholders of companies with charters granted under general incorporation laws were personally liable just as partners in a partnership are. It would be the middle of the nineteenth century before this all-important attribute of a corporation was universal. And in the latter half of the century, as the economy became increasingly integrated nationally, industrial corporations were still forced to operate under charters limited by often parochial state incorporation laws. Many state incorporation laws, for instance, forbade a company from owning property in another state.

As the American economy grew, the securities markets in New York, Boston, Philadelphia, and Baltimore grew as well. Gross domestic product has only been retroactively calculated by economic historians, with increasing uncertainty, back to the 1860s. But government revenues can serve as a rough measure of the country's economic growth. In 1792, the first year for which figures are available, federal revenues were $3,670,000. By 1808 they were $17,061,000. By 1817 they were $33,099,000, a ninefold increase in only twenty-five years.

Philadelphia remained the nation's financial center because of its big banks. The Bank of the United States was killed in 1811, when Congress, now dominated by Jeffersonians, refused to renew its charter, even though President James Madison requested it. Stephen Girard, a Philadelphia shipowner and the country's richest man, had taken over its assets and opened his own bank.

Congress followed its refusal to renew the charter of the government's prime fiscal agent and borrowing mechanism by declaring war on the only military power in the world capable of seriously attacking the United States, Great Britain. The result of this folly was a near fiscal disaster, forcing the secretary of the treasury, Albert Gallatin, to go hat in hand to Stephen Girard and beg him to underwrite a bond issue so that the country could continue the war. In 1816, a chastened Congress chartered the Second Bank of the United States. Capitalized at $35 million, it was by far the largest bank in the country and the only one able to operate across state lines. It, too, was headquartered in Philadelphia.

The huge number of federal bonds issued to finance the War of 1812 (the national debt rose from $45 million in 1811 to $127 million in 1815) caused an increase in the brokerage business in the country. But much of this business went to Philadelphia because of its great banks and its well-organized stock exchange. The major New York brokers, still operating under the casual Buttonwood Agreement, decided that a more formal structure was needed. In 1817, they sent a broker named William Lamb to Philadelphia to examine how the Philadelphia Stock Exchange worked. When he returned, several leading brokers met in the office of Samuel Beebe on February 25 and drew up a constitution that was nearly identical to that of the Philadelphia Stock Exchange. Twenty-eight individuals, belonging to just seven firms, became the original members of the Board of Brokers, soon renamed the New York Stock and Exchange Board.

The constitution called for a president and a secretary, who would run the daily auction. New members had to have been in the brokerage business for at least a year to be eligible and were to be elected by a vote of the current membership. Three blackballs, however, were enough to exclude a potential member. To discourage wild speculation, the constitution required next-day delivery, unless other terms were agreed to. It also forbade "matched sales," where two or more brokers trade a stock among themselves to give the illusion of a price movement. This last provision would prove impossible to enforce, and matched sales would be a common feature of Wall Street for more than a hundred years.

The new board rented the second floor of the building at 40 Wall Street at $200 a year, heat included, and New York finally had a real stock exchange.

The city had been growing quickly since becoming the nation's largest in 1790. But Philadelphia still held its own with a population of 112,000 compared to New York's 123,700. But another development in 1817 was about to make New York not only the nation's largest city, but its only metropolis: the Erie Canal. It remains to this day the most consequential public work in American history.

CHAPTER THREE

"That Tongue That Is Licking Up the Cream of Commerce"

It would be hard to exaggerate the problem of overland transportation before the nineteenth century, and the extent to which that problem restricted economic growth. Roads were few and miserable where they existed at all, and the only way to move freight on them was by horse- and ox-drawn wagons. As a result, in the American colonies most overland freight moved by river. Unfortunately, most rivers on the eastern seaboard are navigable by sizable vessels for only short distances.

When independence was achieved, the problem became especially acute. While most citizens of the new republic lived east of the Appalachian Mountains, most of its land was to their west. With the removal of British restrictions on western settlement and the generous granting of land there to veterans of the Revolution, the population of the trans-Appalachian west expanded rapidly as soon as the Revolution was won.

The cost of transportation made it extremely costly to ship produce back over the mountains to eastern markets. Instead the farmers either had to consume the produce themselves in a subsistence economy or ship it by one of two routes. The first, via the Great Lakes, the St. Lawrence River, and Montreal, required a portage around Niagara Falls. It also wasn't available in winter and passed through British territory. The other, via the Mississippi River and New Orleans, passed through Spanish territory. In the 1790s, the transportation of western produce was one of the major concerns of the new nation's leaders. Washington himself remarked that the loyalty of the western settlers was "hanging by a thread," because their economic interests lay more with New Orleans and Montreal than with the eastern seaboard.

Jefferson's purchase of Louisiana removed the threat of a foreign power closing the Mississippi to American commerce, but did nothing to solve the transportation problem. That was solved by a New Yorker named De Witt Clinton, who in doing so not only helped to cement the union and its western territories, but also quite accidentally assured that Wall Street would become the dominant financial market in the United States.

Clinton was born in 1769 into a prominent New York political family (his uncle George Clinton would be governor of New York and vice president of the United States). Tall, commanding in appearance, and highly intelligent, Clinton graduated from Columbia College at the age of only seventeen, delivering an address in Latin at the commencement ceremonies. He soon won election to the State Senate and in 1802 was appointed to the U.S. Senate. But he resigned from that body the next year to become mayor of New York, then a one-year appointive office. Appointed over and over again, he would hold the mayoralty for most of the next twelve years. While running the city, he also devoted considerable attention to statewide matters, including transportation.

Clinton was shrewd enough to see a great opportunity in two linked geographic peculiarities of New York State. The first was the Hudson River. Technically, for most of its length the Hudson is not a river at all. Instead, as far north as Albany, which has measurable tides, it is an estuary, an arm of the sea that allowed ocean-going vessels to sail far into the heart of New York State. The second peculiarity was that the Appalachian Mountains, which run from Maine to Alabama, have a gap in them near Albany, where the Mohawk River flows into the Hudson from the west. Between Albany and Lake Erie, the land never rises above six hundred feet. Thus a canal—the only form of inland transportation then capable of hauling freight at low prices—was feasible.

Clinton became determined to build that canal, and certainly, no one could accuse him of thinking small. The Erie Canal was, by order of magnitude, the greatest engineering enterprise undertaken in the United States before the Civil War. And because the federal government refused to help in 1811, New York State had to build it alone.

From the beginning, political opposition was considerable. The settlers in the vicinity of where the canal would be built, of course, were all for it. The construction alone would be a great economic benefit to that area, whether or not the canal turned out to be economically viable in the long term. But downstate and in New York City, where the bulk of the state's population lived, many short-sightedly thought the project was nothing more than an upstate boondoggle that would have no benefit for them. They fought it tooth and nail. Regardless, Clinton, an adroit politician, was able to coax the proposal through the legislature, and in 1817, the year he was first elected governor, work began.

Clinton turned the first shovelful of dirt on July 4, 1817. Although many predicted the canal would take decades to build if it could be built at all, Clinton said—in a statement strikingly similar to President Kennedy's announcement a century and a half later that the country would put a man on the moon—that "the day will come in less than ten years when we will see Erie water flowing into the Hudson."[1] And just like the Apollo program, that was a tall order.

The canal was to be 363 miles long, descending 555 feet from Lake Erie to the Hudson through eighty-three locks. It was to be forty feet wide and four feet deep and would have to be dug entirely by hand. The state legislature authorized borrowing $7 million to fund the project, at a time when the typical yearly outlay of the federal government totaled less than $22 million.

With the goal of getting as much of the canal into operation as quickly as possible, Clinton concentrated work on the "long level," the sixty-nine miles between Syracuse and Herkimer that did not require any locks. It was completed within a year and helped cement political support for the project. By 1821, 220 miles of the canal were in operation, but construction of the hardest parts had not begun. Two aqueducts to carry the canal over the Genesee and Mohawk Rivers, 802 feet and 1,188 feet respectively, had still to be built, as had several locks.

Clinton nearly lost the governorship that year thanks to continuing opposition to the canal in areas of the state not directly served by it. But finally, in 1825, two years ahead of Clinton's self-imposed deadline, the canal was ready. On October 26, Governor Clinton set out from Buffalo in a decorated canal barge drawn by four gray horses. The barge also carried two kegs of Lake Erie water. What followed was a five-hundred-mile-and-two-week-long party as all along the canal and the Hudson River, New York State celebrated what one orator called the building of "the longest canal, in the least time, with the least experience, for the least money and to the greatest public benefit."[2]

On November 7, Clinton, amid a flotilla of boats, barges, and ships carrying thousands of celebrants, was rowed out to Sandy Hook for a ceremony dubbed the Wedding of the Waters. Clinton poured water from Lake Erie into the Atlantic, where it mingled with water that had been carried from the Rhine, the Ganges, the Nile, and twelve other great rivers of the world. Thus did the celebrants symbolize, with typical New York panache, the city's coming greatness as a center of commerce when, in the words of another orator, "the valley of the Mississippi . . . [will pour] its treasures in this great emporium through channels now formed and forming."[3]

The canal was already a success by the time it officially opened. In 1825, some 13,110 boats passed between Buffalo and Albany, paying a total of half a million dollars in tolls, more than enough to fund the debt the state had incurred to build it. Forty thousand passengers flowed by the city of Utica that year. And traffic only increased. "Having taken your position at one of the numerous bridges," an early witness wrote, "it is an impressive sight to gaze up and down the canal. In either direction, as far as the eye can see, long lines of boats can be observed. By night, their flickering head lamps give the impression of swarms of fireflies."[4]

Although many of the passengers were farm families leaving the hardscrabble hills of New England to find better land in Ohio and points west, the vast majority of those boats' cargoes had originated in, passed through, or were destined for New York City. The rapidly increasing agricultural production of the Middle West, once forced to take the long route down the Mississippi, could now speed through the far shorter one built by De Witt Clinton. Before the canal was built, a ton of flour in Buffalo, worth $40, could be transported overland to New York City in three weeks at a cost of $120, quadrupling its cost. Using the canal, however, that same ton of flour could be shipped in eight days at a cost of $6, or to put it another way, at one-twentieth the prior cost and in one-third the time. All other commodities benefited similarly.

Indeed, within a few years, the Boston poet and physician Oliver Wendell Holmes (the father of the Supreme Court justice) grumpily complained that New York had become "that tongue that is licking up the cream of commerce and finance of a continent."[5]

As a result of the Erie Canal, New York's growth exploded. In 1820 its population was 123,700, while Philadelphia's was close behind at 112,000; by 1860, the figures were 1,080,330 and 565,529. Equally impressive was New York's growth as a port. In 1800, about 9 percent of the country's foreign commerce passed through New York. By 1860 the figure had leaped to 62 percent.

New York quickly became the greatest boomtown the world has ever known. The line between the built-up city and the undeveloped land to the north raced up Manhattan Island at a rate that averaged about two blocks per year. As Manhattan Island is about two miles wide, that meant that the city was adding about ten miles of new streetfront per year. These streets were often blocked with construction materials, constricting the city's traffic, which soon acquired a reputation for snarls it has never lost.

Needless to say, this vast expansion of New York's commercial activity and population was immediately reflected in greatly increased business for the city's brokers. But they remained generalists in the 1820s, dealing in everything from securities to cotton to insurance. However, the building of the Erie Canal created a mania in canal securities, adding significantly to the volume on Wall Street and other major markets in Boston and Philadelphia. No small part of that increased volume came from orders from Europe, as capitalists there sought opportunities in the fast-growing American economy.

Indeed, many American canal companies were controlled by London bankers such as Baring Brothers, whose New York agent was the shrewd Thomas W. Ward. By the end of 1823, Baring Brothers owned no less than $240,000 worth of various canal stocks and added another $82,000 the following year. This considerable English presence, and influence, in the American markets would continue for decades. In 1833 a member of Congress joked that "the barometer of the American money market hangs up at the stock exchange in London."[6] Today, of course, the situation is exactly reversed and the rest of the world's financial barometers hang in Wall Street.

As a result of this demand for American canal shares, offerings were often oversubscribed. The Blackstone Canal in Providence, Rhode Island, received bids for more than three times the number of shares being offered. The Morris Canal in New Jersey, the subject of much later speculation on Wall Street, was also initially oversubscribed many times. Often these new ventures, if they came to fruition at all, did not turn out to be nearly as profitable as their prospectuses had so confidently predicted. Many were just badly managed. A few were outright frauds. Others incurred unanticipated costs that made them uneconomic. The Chesapeake and Ohio Canal Company, designed to be a more southerly version of the Erie Canal, turned into a bottomless pit for cash as its route ran into endless engineering difficulties. By 1827, the estimates of its eventual costs reached $22 million, more than three times what the Erie had cost. It was, in fact, never to be completed.

This phenomenon would repeat itself over and over on Wall Street as the ongoing industrial revolution provided a continuing supply of new possibilities. The rosy hopes engendered by the possibilities induce great demand for the securities in untried companies, as investors try to latch onto the future. Prices soar. Then, when the companies actually go into business, reality sets in, and the prices crash. This would happen with the railroads in the 1840s and 1850s. In the late 1920s, investors snapped up the stocks of airline companies, most of which had never operated a single airplane. So eager were they to partake in the future of air travel that they also ran up the price of the stock of Seaboard Air Lines, although that company was actually a poetically named railroad, not an airline at all. In the 1960s investors flocked to new franchising companies, trying to cash in on the market uncovered by McDonald's and Kentucky Fried Chicken. Few of these companies actually prospered after their initial offerings were sold.

With demand for new American securities—both for new companies and for state bonds—booming and with incorporation and securities laws in their infancy, both the crooked and the naive were often able to sell securities that were dubious at best. Maryland and Pennsylvania, both with securities markets as large and active as Wall Street's in the 1820s, allowed companies, and indeed the state governments as well, to pay interest and dividends out of new loans and stock issues. That New York State law forbade this Ponzi-scheme financing would be a significant factor in the establishment of Wall Street's dominance in securities trading when, in 1837, the boom came to an inevitable end.

As the bull market of the late 1820s developed, many brokers found that they could begin to abandon their other lines of brokerage, such as insurance and lotteries, and more profitably concentrate on stocks and bonds. But much of this activity was not occurring at the New York Stock and Exchange Board. In 1821 the board began meeting at 21 Broad Street in the office of Samuel Beebe, one of the most successful brokers. Only in 1827 did it move to quarters of its own at the new Merchants' Exchange, on the south side of Wall Street, between William and Hanover Streets.

But much of Wall Street's activity took place, quite literally, on the street, as brokers who were not members of the board would meet under various lampposts to trade securities. This trading often exceeded the volume on the board itself, at least in terms of the number of shares traded if not in what is now called market cap, just as Nasdaq volume today often exceeds that of the New York Stock Exchange. Many new issues were first traded at the offices of the underwriting brokerage firm before moving to the Exchange Board. Volume on the board could often fall to less than a hundred shares a day, and on March 16, 1830, a mere thirty-one shares changed hands at the New York Stock and Exchange Board, a record for low volume that has not since been approached.

During this boom another modern Wall Street–character archetype appeared. His like had not been seen before, but would not leave the Street again, right up to the present day. His name was Jacob Little. Born in Newburyport, Massachusetts, the son of a shipbuilder, Little arrived on the Street in 1817. That was a seminal year in the history of New York City. Construction of the Erie Canal began, the New York Stock and Exchange Board was formally organized, and the Black Ball Line, the first shipping firm to run passenger vessels on a regular schedule across the North Atlantic, between New York and Liverpool, was established. A revolutionary concept at the time, scheduled passenger service would soon become the standard, and New York would become the dominant American terminus for transatlantic passenger travel until well into the jet age.

Little clerked for Jacob Barker, one of the early all-purpose brokers, for a few years before setting up his own firm in 1822 in a basement office. (Because of the high cost of real estate in the Wall Street area, every square foot of space was utilized even then, and basement offices were common.) Blackballed several times, he finally gained membership in the New York Stock and Exchange Board in 1825.

Little was very different from William Duer of a generation earlier. Duer specialized in inside government information (or, perhaps more accurately, the appearance of inside government information). More, Duer had been perfectly willing to betray his partners, whose money he invested, in the interest of his own profits. By modern standards, Duer was a crook.

But Little was an independent trader, with no ties to government and no long-term partnerships. He sought his profits by outguessing the other traders as to which way the market in a particular issue would go, and using his own money to buy and sell accordingly. In other words, Jacob Little was a speculator, someone who hopes to profit by short-term market moves rather than by long-term investing in growing enterprises.

Speculation has always had a dubious reputation, at least away from Wall Street. Speculators are often seen as parasites on the capitalist process, contributing nothing toward wealth creation themselves, but profiting from it. But in fact, besides endearing themselves to brokers by generating large commissions with their frequent trades, they also add greatly to the liquidity of the market, increasing the volume of trades and the number of potential buyers and sellers, which in turn helps to ensure that the best prices are available. But because speculators have always been the designated fall guys of Wall Street, they have been blamed for every market excess and every bear market that follows such excesses.

These bear periods have inevitably provoked people who do not understand how markets work to lobby for the removal of speculators from the nation's financial system. That speculation has not only survived, but continues to flourish, despite ever-increasing regulation and discouragement (such as higher taxes on short-term capital gains), testifies to both speculation's inevitability and desirability when properly regulated. Besides, like pornography, speculation is much easier to identify than to define. As Sir Ernest Cassel, the great British financier of the turn of the twentieth century, explained, "When I was young, people called me a gambler. As the scale of my operations increased, I became known as a speculator. Now I am called a banker. But I have been doing the same thing all the time."[7]

Wall Street's first great speculator, Jacob Little usually operated on the downside of the market, preferring to bet on a fall in prices. Because of this, he was the first on Wall Street to be known by the sobriquet of the Great Bear, but by no means the last. His initial fame, however, came from a bet on the upside, in one of the hottest stocks of the early 1830s, the Morris Canal and Banking Company. In 1834 the market had been rising briskly and Morris Canal and Banking was among the main engines of this advance. But Little had learned that many of Wall Street's biggest players had sold the stock short, expecting it to fall.

Little saw opportunity in this situation. At that time, a person selling short promised future delivery of the stock in question at a specified time at a particular price. If the price fell in the interval between the sale and the delivery date, the short seller needed only to buy the stock at the lower price and deliver it to receive the higher price and make a profit.

But if the price rose, the short seller was forced to take a loss. Worse, a stock price, at least theoretically, can rise to infinity. Therefore the potential loss is also unlimited because of one of the oldest and most sacred rules of Wall Street, usually expressed in a famous bit of doggerel, often attributed—almost certainly erroneously—to Daniel Drew:

> He who sells what isn't his'n,
> Must buy it back or go to prison.

Little organized a pool of fellow speculators to quietly buy the stock of Morris Canal. When the short sellers went into the market to make good their contracts, they discovered to their horror that Little and his friends had cornered the stock and owned the entire floating supply. Little's group had bought much of it for around $10 a share. Needless to say, they were not inclined to sell it at that price, and within a month the price had rocketed to $185 a share, making a fortune for Little and his allies.

Little was suddenly the most famous operator on Wall Street and would remain the Street's best-known plunger for another twenty years, despite going bankrupt three times. Each time he managed to bounce back, a speculative phoenix rising from the ashes of insolvency. Finally he went bankrupt for a fourth time in the great panic of 1857 and did not recover. He remained on Wall Street for the next few years until he died, but he was only able to trade in penny stocks and odd lots, his glory days long past. William Worthington Fowler, whose memoirs of his days on Wall Street would become a great best-seller in the 1860s, described such men as Little became:

> "No one who has entered the precincts of the stock exchange will have failed to notice certain nondescripts who constantly frequent the market. They are men who have seen better days, but having dropped their money in the Street, come there every day as if they hoped to find it in the same place. These characters are the ghosts of the market, fixing their lack-lustre eyes upon it, and pointing their skinny fingers at it, as if they would say, 'thou hast done this!' They flit about the doorways and haunt the vestibules of the Exchange, seedy of coat, blackingless of boot, unkempt, unwashed, unshorn, wearing on their worn and haggard faces a smile more melancholy than tears."[8]

What made Little's rise to greatness possible was the first great bull market on Wall Street. In turn, the bull market arose from the financial policies of the administration of Andrew Jackson.

Jackson was the first president not to come from a privileged background. Born in poverty and orphaned as a boy during the Revolution, Jackson studied law and, in 1788, emigrated to Nashville,

Tennessee, then little more than a collection of cabins. He soon prospered as a lawyer and began acquiring large tracts of land, whose value rose quickly as settlers poured into the lush country of Middle Tennessee. But when one land deal with complicated financing went awry, Jackson found himself responsible for another man's notes. It would take Jackson more than a decade to settle this matter, and as a result, he developed a lifelong horror of speculation, debt, and paper money.

When he became president, in 1829, Jackson's financial program was simple: pay off the national debt as quickly as possible and destroy the second Bank of the United States, which he hated as a symbol of the "money power" of the East. The second bank had been chartered by Congress in 1816, after the near disaster of the War of 1812. But, like Hamilton's first Bank of the United States, the charter was issued for twenty years, after which a renewal was necessary.

The bank was incompetently managed at first. But when Philadelphia banker Nicholas Biddle took control in 1823, it quickly developed into the largest and most powerful bank in the country. Because it was nationally chartered, it was the only bank able to operate across state lines. As the federal government's fiscal agent, with a branch in every major city, its notes were accepted without question throughout the country.

Biddle was an extraordinary man, one of the greatest bankers this country has ever produced. He completed all the work necessary to earn a degree at the University of Pennsylvania by the time he was thirteen, but the university refused to grant it because of his age. So he went to Princeton, earned a B.A. there in two years, and at the age of fifteen, was class valedictorian.

By the time Jackson became president, Biddle was probably the second most powerful man in the country, and many thought Biddle would run for president himself one day. But his very success proved his undoing. Biddle's aristocratic ways (the Biddles were among Philadelphia's best-known families) turned Jackson against him and his bank. But there wasn't much Jackson could do to thwart him until the bank's charter ran out in 1836. Meanwhile Jackson concentrated on reducing the national debt. The country was running large surpluses, and the number of federal bonds to be traded in the nation's financial markets steadily diminished as a result. As the Bank of the United States handled federal bond issues, this reduced the bank's power. The capital no longer needed by the federal government was taken up by state bonds, canal companies, and the first railroads. But the smaller supply of securities in the marketplace increased demand for what was left, driving up prices.

By 1834, Jackson had virtually eliminated the national debt, the only time in the history of the country—indeed the only time in the modern history of any major nation—that the debt has been paid off. He did it by a combination of a high tariff and by ruthlessly vetoing spending bills, especially those for internal improvements, such as roads.

The country's increasing prosperity also increased the number of traders on Wall Street. In the late 1820s volume on the New York Stock and Exchange Board had often fallen below a hundred shares a day. But by the mid-1830s the auction was averaging about six thousand shares a day. On June 26, 1835, volume reached a record 7,825 shares. The auction, however, was not the continuous auction of today. Rather the members sat in chairs (the origin of the term *seat on the stock exchange*) at desks, and twice a day the president or whoever was presiding would call out the name of each security in turn. In 1836 the stocks listed on the board, although not all of them were regularly traded, consisted of thirty-eight banks, thirty-two insurance firms, four railroads, four canals, and three gas companies (the new technology of gaslight was rapidly spreading through America's cities at this time).

Much trading in listed securities still took place on the street. The board requirements for membership excluded many people who, at least in good times, made their livings as brokers. And many more were eliminated by blackballs. Still, the board set the pace and the prices, and most trading on the street took place in the afternoon, after the board's auction was concluded and prices had been determined. Nonmember brokers would often listen at the door to be the first to hear the latest prices.

On December 16, 1835, right in the middle of this heady bull market, Wall Street was hit not by a financial disaster, but by a physical one. On that day the Great Fire of New York broke out, its exact origins never determined, and raged, unchecked, for two days. Although firemen from as far away as Philadelphia came to the city's aid, they could do little. Bitter cold weather and high winds impeded firemen's efforts and fanned the flames, the glow of which lit up the night sky as far away as Philadelphia, Poughkeepsie, and New Haven. And because New York still lacked an adequate water supply, the hand-drawn fire trucks were forced to continually leave the scene to refill at the East River, where firemen had to continually chop through the ice.

When the fire was finally controlled, the heart of the business district of New York was in ruins. The fire consumed more than 700 buildings in the twenty-square-block area bounded by Wall Street, Broad Street, Coenties Slip, and the East River. Gone, too, was almost all that was left of colonial New York. Today Manhattan, the center of the oldest big city in the United States, has only a single major structure that predates the Revolution, St. Paul's Chapel, at the corner of Broadway and Fulton Street.

Because of the fire, twenty-three of the twenty-six fire insurance companies in the city declared bankruptcy, taking down with them many stockholders and policyholders alike. A functioning stock market, obviously, was crucial to sorting out the consequences of the Great Fire. But among the buildings lost was the Merchants' Exchange, where the New York Stock and Exchange Board had been holding its auctions since 1827. Fortunately, a brave employee of the stock exchange, J. R. Mount, managed to rescue the exchange's records from the burning building before it collapsed in a roar. Mount was given a hundred-dollar reward and the board was soon up and running once again in temporary quarters. And while the economy of New York City was badly injured by the fire, the national economy continued to boom, helping to get the New York brokers back on their feet quickly.

At the heart of that national prosperity was a land boom developing in the West, financed by new state-chartered banks. In 1829, only 329 banks existed in the entire country. Just eight years later there were 788. But while the number of banks more than doubled, the face value of the notes these banks had issued more than tripled, from $48.2 million to $149.2 million. And the loans outstanding almost quadrupled, from $137 million to $525.1 million. Many of the states had slapdash banking laws, and many of these new banks were badly—if not fraudulently—managed, undercapitalized, underregulated, and overly sanguine about the future.

The Bank of the United States had been able to enforce some discipline by refusing to accept the notes of banks it regarded as unsound. But as its power diminished, its ability to control the situation diminished as well. Further, as part of his campaign to destroy the Bank of the United States, Jackson withdrew government deposits from the bank and placed them instead in these state banks (quickly dubbed "pet banks" by Jackson's political opponents). With increased deposit bases, these banks were able to issue still more banknotes and make still more loans on the collateral of real estate, the most illiquid of all investments.

Thus the policies pursued by President Jackson, who hated speculation and paper money, had the entirely unintended effect of causing the country's first great speculative bubble, financed by paper money. Ironically, much of the land involved in this spiraling boom was sold by the federal government, to settlers and speculators alike. Sales by the government's General Land Office had totaled a mere $2.5 million in 1832. By 1836 sales totaled $25 million and in the summer of that year were running at the rate of nearly $5 million a *month*. The phrase *to do a land-office business* originated in this frenzy to acquire government land.

Jackson understood perfectly well what was happening. "The receipts from the public land were nothing more than credits on the bank," he wrote later. "The banks let out their notes to speculators, they were paid to the receivers, and immediately returned to the banks to be sent out again and again, being merely instruments to transfer to the speculator the most valuable public lands. Indeed, each speculation furnished means for another."[9]

Typically, Jackson resolved to stop this speculation in its tracks. He proposed to his cabinet that the Land Office accept only specie—gold and silver—in payment for land. But the cabinet, many of whose members were deeply embroiled in the speculation themselves, strongly opposed him. Congress, equally involved, would also have nothing to do with the plan. So Jackson just waited until July 11, after Congress had adjourned for the year, then issued the so-called specie circular as an executive order. It required, with a few exceptions, payment in gold or silver after August 15.

Jackson had hoped that his action would dampen speculation in land, but it did more than that, bringing it to a screeching halt. As the demand for specie soared, holders began turning in banknotes and demanding gold and silver. Banks, to raise the needed money, called in loans as fast as they could. Western banks drained gold and silver from eastern banks, but they then held on to the metal as best they could, because of yet another government program.

With the federal government running large surpluses and having no debt, money tended to pile up uselessly in the Treasury and was deposited in the pet banks. But in 1836, Congress decided to give much of this surplus money to the various state governments to use as they saw fit. It directed the Treasury to withdraw $9 million every quarter, beginning in January 1837, from its bank deposits and divvy it up among the states according to population. The banks had to be ready to absorb this considerable shrinking of their deposit bases.

The weaker ones, with small gold reserves and large note issues, began to fail. The country's businessmen, who needed bank credit to operate, were crippled. Stock prices declined. Philip Hone, the New York diarist and former mayor, had laid the cornerstone of his new mansion on Broadway in June 1836 and then gone to Europe to see his daughter. He returned to New York in October to find the financial climate completely altered. "Hard times," he wrote in his diary on November 12. He listed several stocks that had been selling at over a hundred when he had sailed for Europe and were now selling for sixty or seventy. The *New York Herald* reported on January 2, 1837, the day that the first $9 million was transferred from mostly eastern banks to the state governments, that interest rates that had been 7 percent a year had risen to 2 or even 3 percent a month.

Bankruptcies began to spread. When the Bank of England raised interest rates to prevent gold from flowing out of that country, British cotton purchases declined, further injuring the American economy. With higher interest rates at home, British capitalists were less inclined to invest in American securities, and prices on Wall Street plummeted still further.

The first great bull market in American history had been succeeded by the first great bear market. Volume stayed high. Indeed,
it reached ten thousand shares a day several times in March 1837
as Martin Van Buren replaced Jackson in the White House, just in
time to reap the economic whirlwind that Jackson had so uninten-
tionally sown. Now stocks were headed south with a vengeance.
Morris Canal had opened the month at 96. It ended it at 80 (by
1841 it would be worthless). Long Island Railroad fell from 78 to
64. Several states, trying to refinance their debts, found no takers
for their bonds.

By April, Philip Hone, himself badly burned, reported in his
diary, "The immense fortunes which we heard so much about in
the days of speculation, have melted like the snows before an April
sun. No man can calculate to escape ruin but he who owes no
money; happy is he who has a little and is free from debt."[10]

By the end of the next month every bank in the nation, at least
those that had not already failed, suspended gold payments. Government revenues, which had reached $50.8 million in 1836,
plunged to a mere $24.9 million the following year, and Andrew
Jackson's vision of a debt-free federal government vanished, never
to be seen again. By the early fall of 1837, about 90 percent of the
country's factories had closed, and the country's first (and still its
longest) great depression was under way. Given the depth and
extent of the depression of 1837, it was fortunate that the vast
majority of the American population still lived on farms and outside what economists call the cash economy. They could make do,
providing for themselves, until better times returned. Those in the
cash economy, the factory workers and owners, the merchants,
and of course the brokers on Wall Street, suffered far worse.

As panic gave way to depression, business on Wall Street dried
up. The New York Stock and Exchange Board moved several times
in these years, in search of smaller and less costly quarters. But if
Wall Street had been badly hurt, Philadelphia's financial market
had been far more grievously crippled.

New York's market had been growing faster than Philadelphia's
for a number of years as the city's population exploded. By the
mid-1830s, it was clearly the largest and most important. Further,
the political and economic events of the midthirties exerted a far

deeper impact on Philadelphia than on New York. The loss of its national charter had forced the Bank of the United States to seek a state charter, under the distinctly clunky name of the Bank of the United States of Philadelphia. But without a national franchise, it became just another state bank, with little of its old power that had fueled, in turn, the Philadelphia financial market.

The following year, when the depression hit, the state of Pennsylvania found itself unable to service its huge state debt of $20 million. It had no choice but to default on payments of both principal and interest. As the Philadelphia banks had large amounts of their reserves in state bonds, they were as devastated by the default as they were by the depression. New York, which had state debt of a mere $2 million, was able to meet its obligations. While many New York banks closed their doors, the sounder ones survived. As a result, Philadelphia, already in second place, fell far behind New York in total financial activity.

It is hardly coincidental, therefore, that it was just at this time that the phrase *Wall Street* entered the American lexicon as a metonym for the country's financial system as a whole. It would become an increasingly accurate one as time went on. It is not the least of ironies that Wall Street, the symbol, should arise out of fire, panic, and depression.

CHAPTER FOUR

"What Can Be the End of All This but Another General Collapse?"

Wall Street was a gloomy place in the years immediately following the crash of 1837. Those brokers who still maintained other lines of business than securities usually survived, but many who had begun to specialize did not. And, of course, the brokers who were well enough established to be members of the Stock and Exchange Board fared better than those who operated on the curb. At the height of the bull market of the 1830s, the curb brokers, unable to get into the Stock and Exchange Board, had formed a rival exchange known as the New Board. But by 1839 three-quarters of these brokers were in bankruptcy and the New Board itself disappeared in 1848.

Europe as well as the United States was in the midst of a deep recession, and demand for American securities in England and on the Continent was considerably reduced. Needless to say, the fact that no fewer than nine state governments had defaulted on their bonds by 1842 did not help the European market for American securities. Even some South American municipal bonds were selling in Europe at higher prices than American federal ones. The head of the Paris branch of the Rothschild bank told an American visitor, "You may tell your government that you have seen the man who is at the head of the finances of Europe, and that he has told you that they cannot borrow a dollar, not a dollar."[1]

Wall Street itself had greatly changed in appearance since the early days. The handsome brick mansions that had lined the western end of Wall Street had largely given way to four- and five-story office buildings faced with brownstone. The old City Hall that had served briefly as the federal capitol was torn down in the 1830s and replaced on its site at the head of Broad Street with the Customs House. Built in the Greek Revival style so popular in the 1830s and 1840s (but containing within it a most un-Greek rotunda and dome), it has served as the backdrop for much Wall Street history ever since. It would become the Subtreasury in 1862 and acquire its famous statue of George Washington on the front steps in 1883, the hundredth anniversary of Evacuation Day.

The Merchants' Exchange on the south side of Wall Street, a victim of the fire of 1835, was replaced with a new and larger Merchants' Exchange that opened in 1842. It, too, is still there (although with a second colonnade added above the first in 1907).

But the most notable architectural change in this period was the building of the third Trinity Church on the site of the first two, across Broadway from the western end of Wall Street. The second church, completed in 1790, had been a relatively simple structure. But as New York City had grown, so had its most important Episcopal parish. In 1705, Queen Anne had endowed the infant parish with some land north of the city known as the Queen's Farm. Amounting to about 275 acres of what is today the lower west side of Manhattan, the value of the Queen's gift had grown enormously as the city had exploded in size during the early nineteenth century. By 1840, Trinity had become what it remains today, the richest church parish on earth. Its building already in serious disrepair by this time, the vestry decided to replace it with a larger and grander edifice.

Built of brownstone, the new Trinity Church was by far the largest church in New York City at the time. Its spire, thrusting 275 feet into the sky, would be the highest point in the city until the 1870s, when the Manhattan tower of the Brooklyn Bridge finally surpassed it. (Being the Empire State Building of its day, it attracted a steady stream of tourists, and the church sextons made a tidy income charging them for the right to climb the steeple staircase and admire the view.) Consecrated in 1846, just as the Mexican War was finally bringing an end to the depression, Trinity Church—a godly enterprise that also happens to be extremely rich—has been the somewhat ironic symbol of Wall Street ever since, far more recognizable than even the New York Stock Exchange or the Morgan Bank.

*   *   *

Just as Wall Street was undergoing a physical transformation, so the American economy was changing as well, despite the depression. The linchpin of this transformation was the railroad, the seminal invention of the nineteenth century. The railroad solved the problem of overland transportation that the canals could only partially alleviate. Canals were not only extremely expensive (the Erie had cost about $20,000 per mile at a time when $1,000 a year was a middle-class income), but limited as to where they could be built. Because they needed prodigious quantities of water to operate, canals were only feasible in areas of good rainfall and, in northern areas, were useless in winter. Nor, as the stockholders of the ill-fated Chesapeake and Ohio Canal found out, were they cost-effective in mountainous terrain, because the locks that were needed to raise and lower the barges were, by far, the most expensive element of canal-building. But railroads could be built nearly anywhere and were, within reason, all-seasonal.

In the middle of the seventeenth century, miners discovered that a draft animal could pull a much heavier load if the wagon it was hitched to was seated on rails. The concept did not have much application outside of mines, however, until a motive power more potent than horses was available. But as soon as James Watt's rotary steam engine was perfected in 1784, engineers began to think of putting the steam engine together with a carriage on rails. Watt's design, which cycled only about twelve times a minute, did not generate enough power to move even its own weight, let alone a cargo of goods or people. It took the high-pressure steam engine, developed independently by Richard Trevithick in England and Oliver Evans in the United States, at the turn of the nineteenth century, to make the railroad a practical possibility. Watt's engine used steam to push the piston down, but utilized a vacuum to return it to its original position. The engines designed by Trevithick and Evans used steam to move the piston in each direction and at much higher pressures than Watt's engine. The sound of the exhausting steam gave these devices the nickname puffer engines, and this type of steam engine would power the nineteenth century by making overland transportation nearly anywhere fast and cheap. To get an inkling of the scope of the ensuing transformation, consider that in the second decade of the century, building a canal just across New York State had been at the outer limit of the possible. Only a half century later, the Union Pacific Railroad was flung across the entire continent.

Oliver Evans, one of this country's forgotten geniuses, saw the future clearly as early as 1813. "The time will come," he wrote that year, "when people will travel in stages [i.e., stagecoaches] moved by steam engines, from one city to another, almost as fast as birds fly. . . . A carriage will set out from Washington in the morning, the passengers will breakfast in Baltimore, dine at Philadelphia and sup at New York on the same day. . . . To accomplish this, two sets of rails will be laid . . . to guide the carriage, so that they may pass each other in different directions and travel by night as well as by day."[2]

Evans, who died in 1819, did not live to see his vision become a reality. The railroad was not a single invention but a technological complex, one that took decades to reach full fruition. The British engineer George Stephenson first put all the pieces of the puzzle together into a practical whole. In 1829 he opened the Manchester and Liverpool Railroad between those two cities, giving the manufacturers of fast-growing but inland Manchester an outlet to the sea.

Stephenson's railroad was an immediate commercial success and was soon and widely imitated. The Baltimore and Ohio Railroad, already under construction when the Manchester and Liverpool opened, at first depended on horsepower, for engineers thought that its tight curves made steam power impractical. But the New York engineer and industrialist Peter Cooper proved that wrong in 1830 when he built the first locomotive in this country, the Tom Thumb, out of bits and pieces. Lacking good piping, for instance, he used gun barrels to connect the boiler to the steam engine. The Tom Thumb ran on the Baltimore and Ohio at speeds up to eighteen miles per hour, a breathtaking pace in a world accustomed to the rhythms of a trotting horse.

The Baltimore and Ohio was the first of many new railroads, and by 1835 a thousand miles of track were in operation in the United States. By 1840 there were three thousand; by 1850, ten thousand. By the outbreak of the Civil War, thirty thousand miles of track knitted the country together.

The railroads dramatically transformed the pace of life. In 1829,

Andrew Jackson had needed a month to travel by coach from Nashville, Tennessee, to Washington for his inauguration. By 1860 the trip could be made in three days. The greatly increased speed made long-distance travel much more appealing. Until the Charleston and Hamburg Railroad, one of the first in the country, began operations in 1830, passenger traffic between the two South Carolina cities had been handled by a stagecoach making three trips a week. Only five years later, the railroad was handling thirty thousand passengers a year.

Even more important than passenger traffic, however, was the freight traffic. Just as the Erie Canal had reduced freight charges between the Great Lakes and New York City by a factor of twenty, so the railroads reduced charges on a similar scale between all the inland points they connected. As a result, no invention in history had so swift and decisive an effect upon the world economy as did the railroad. Indeed, it might almost be said that the railroad created the world economy out of a myriad of local ones. "Two generations ago," the economist Arthur T. Hadley wrote in 1886 in his classic *Railroad Transportation,* "the expense of cartage was such that wheat had to be consumed within two hundred miles of where it was grown. Today, the wheat of Dakota, the wheat of Russia, and the wheat of India come into direct competition. The supply at Odessa is an element in determining the price in Chicago."[3]

Not only commodities such as wheat were affected. Before the railroad, manufactured products could often be made efficiently by hand, because local markets meant that demand was small. But with the dawn of the railroad age, economies of scale became possible in manufacturing, and more and more products could be produced on an industrial scale at greatly reduced prices. And the railroads, with their ever-growing demand for rails, locomotives, carriages, and coal (although for fuel early railroads in the United States mostly exploited the country's vast abundance of cheap timber), spurred the first heavy industries employing workforces of unprecedented size and the first great industrial fortunes, such as Peter Cooper's.

Much of the rest of the economic and political history of the nineteenth century involved the country's learning to manage, regulate, and equitably distribute the profits of what the railroads made possible. But first, new methods of financing were required to build the railroads. For while the construction of railroads was much cheaper than that of canals, they were too expensive to be financed by individuals and their families as most enterprises had been before the nineteenth century. Railroads were not only capital-intensive, in the early days they represented an economic unknown.

The first railroads were usually short, local lines, intended to connect a town to the nearest existing transportation, usually a river or port. These were often financed by the towns and the local inhabitants who would be the immediate and direct beneficiaries of the improved transportation. But many of these locally sold bonds soon made their way to Wall Street and the country's other financial centers, and more and more brokers began underwriting issues of railroad securities.

Railroad securities became the meat and potatoes of Wall Street's daily business, just as state and federal bonds had been a generation earlier. In 1835 only three railroads were listed on the stock exchange; by 1840, ten were being regularly traded; and a decade later the number had swelled to thirty-eight. By the outbreak of the Civil War, railroad stocks and bonds accounted for one-third of all American securities.

Unique among the early American railroads was the Erie. Rather than originating as a local line, the Erie was conceived from the beginning as a great trunk route, and at its completion in 1851 it would be, briefly, the longest railroad in the world. But the Erie had been born of politics, not economics, and it would never fully escape its tainted birth. To gain political support for his beloved Erie Canal, De Witt Clinton had promised the counties along the Pennsylvania border, known as the Southern Tier, an "avenue" of their own, to be built with the substantial aid of the state government, from the Hudson to the Great Lakes.

A canal was out of the question across the rugged Catskill and Allegheny Mountains, and at first, a toll road was planned. But when the Manchester and Liverpool Railway proved an immediate success, the Southern Tier began pushing for a railroad as the fulfillment of Governor Clinton's promise. The counties where the Erie Canal lay, naturally, wanted no competition from a more southerly route, and only with the greatest difficulty was the New York legislature induced to grant the Erie Railway a charter at all, on April 24, 1832. But, as agreed, the terms of the charter made actually building the railroad very difficult.

The charter called for the company to raise $10 million but prohibited it from organizing formally until half the stock had been subscribed to, an enormous underwriting by the standards of the day. Further, it specified that the route of the railroad lie entirely in New York State and that it not connect to any out-of-state railroad. (By 1850, the New York legislature, realizing the folly of such a prohibition, passed a railroad act *mandating* its railroads to connect with other railroads where possible.)

And the line was required to have a gauge of six feet, to further impede its interconnection with other lines. The very first railroads had been built to whatever gauge suited the engineers in charge, but a standard gauge of four feet eight and a half inches had soon become the norm. (The exact origin of this curious measure is one of the enduring mysteries of railroad history.) But because of its charter, the Erie would not adopt the standard gauge until close to the turn of the century.

Also because of its charter, the original route of the Erie ran 483 miles between Piermont, a small town on the west side of the Hudson River north of the New Jersey line, to Dunkirk, an equally small town on the shores of Lake Erie. Only politicians could have designed the world's longest railroad to run between two towns of no importance whatsoever. And because of its rugged route, engineering difficulties abounded. Originally capitalized at $10 million, the Erie Railway would end up costing an awesome $23.5 million to construct. The company was forced again and again to turn to the state and Wall Street to raise the needed money. The result was a capital structure that is a near textbook example of how not to finance the building of a railroad, with issue after issue of debt and crushing interest payments. Some of this debt was issued as convertible bonds (meaning that the holder could convert them into stock if so desired). One issue, unique in the history of Wall Street, was even convertible at will back and forth between stock and bonds as often as the holder desired, a nearly perfect speculative vehicle. Because of its vast issuance of securities, the Erie was tailor-made for speculation, and the railroad would in future years become known as the Scarlet Woman of Wall Street, because of all the brokenhearted investors who were tempted by her.

Long before the Erie had moved a single passenger or load of freight, it had become a speculative football on the Street. The railroad's capital needs were too large a sum for Wall Street to handle in the 1830s, and much of the Erie's paper was sold in London. This supply of Erie stock and bonds in London, largely forgotten about by the New York brokers, allowed Jacob Little to engineer one of his most famous coups. In 1837, just before the market crash, the Street knew that Little had been selling Erie short for future delivery, and several brokers decided to corner the stock and squeeze Little when the time came to fulfill his contracts. They quietly bought up the floating supply of Erie stock in the New York market and waited for Little to try to close his shorts, when the price would surely skyrocket.

But Little had been buying Erie convertible bonds in London, and on the day when he had to fulfill his contracts, he simply strolled into the Erie offices, asked that his bonds be converted into stock, and used the latter to met his obligations. The rival brokers were left holding large amounts of Erie stock they could unload only at a considerable loss.

The second great transforming invention of this period was the telegraph, and like the railroad, it had a profound impact on Wall Street as well as on the rest of the country.

Long-distance communication was second only to overland transportation as a limiting factor of the pre-industrial economy. Since time immemorial, communication had largely been restricted to the speed of human travel. News could take a week to get from Boston to New York. And it was even possible to outrun the news. Philadelphia brokers learned to dread the sudden appearance of a stagecoach full of Wall Streeters because it meant that they were in exclusive possession of important news from London that might make them a small fortune.

Before the nineteenth century, the only alternatives to human travel were either one-message solutions (such as the string of bonfires Queen Elizabeth I ordered built along England's south coast to inform London of the sighting of the Armada) or too expensive for most people to afford. For instance, in the 1790s the French government constructed a string of semaphore stations between Paris and important military bases such as at Brest, at the end of the Brittany peninsula, some 330 miles away. Each station consisted of a mast and two arms with flags that were raised and lowered on pulleys by four or five men. With what amounted to a string of gigantic Boy Scouts, a message could be wigwagged between Paris and Brest in only a few hours, while a message conveyed by courier required several days. But the cost per message was astronomical, and of course, the system was useless at night or in foul weather. Further, because the message had to be repeated many times, the transmission error rate was high.

Timely information is so important to securities markets that, in the 1830s, a semaphore line sprang up between Wall Street and Philadelphia. Men were stationed on tall buildings and hills every six or eight miles, armed with flags and telescopes. The man on the top of the Merchants' Exchange on Wall Street, where the Stock Exchange was then located, would signal opening prices to a man in Jersey City across the Hudson, and the information could get to Philadelphia in about thirty minutes.

The idea that electricity might be used for sending messages at high speed over long distances dates to the 1770s. A Swiss inventor built a device in 1774 with one wire for each letter of the alphabet. Electricity sent down the appropriate wire would charge a pith ball with static electricity. This, in turn, would ring a bell, creating a sort of alphabetical carillon. This, of course, was hardly a practical device. Another seventy years passed before a failed American artist named Samuel F. B. Morse created a system that worked efficiently in the real world.

Like George Stephenson and the railroad, Morse did not so much invent the telegraph as assemble existing pieces into a working system. Morse's one wholly original contribution was his marvelously efficient code. It took Morse several years of lobbying before the government paid for a demonstration project between Washington and Baltimore, but as soon as Morse, in the Capitol, telegraphed "What hath God wrought?" to his partner, Alfred Vail, in Baltimore and Vail repeated the message, the telegraph began to spread like a spiderweb across the country. That same year, 1844, Morse and partners formed the Magnetic Telegraph Company to run a line between New York and Philadelphia. By 1846 the company was profitable and paying dividends. Within ten years, twenty-three thousand miles of telegraph wires tied together most major American cities, and by 1861, a telegraph line stretched all the way to San Francisco. Like the railroads, at first telegraph companies were strictly local affairs. But beginning in the 1850s, one company, Western Union, began buying up small, independent telegraph companies and assembling a nationwide system that would dominate American communications until the telephone and the coming of the Bell system at the end of the century.

In a classic case of economic synergy, the early telegraph lines often ran along the ready-made rights-of-way of the burgeoning railroads. In turn, the railroads soon developed a system of telegraph signals that allowed the trains to run safely on the often single-tracked lines at much higher speeds than had been possible before.

Needless to say, brokers in the country's financial centers were early and heavy users of the new communications medium. In the Street's early days, boys known as runners, had indeed run, knitting together the brokers, the exchange, the curb, and the banks into a single market. This is the reason messengers on Wall Street are still known as runners, even though today they are often elderly men who only amble along.

It is axiomatic that a market cannot be larger than the area in which communication is, effectively, instant. For that reason, although New York was the largest securities market by the middle of the 1830s, the others in Boston, Philadelphia, and elsewhere remained important and independent. They were affected by the New York prices, as the primitive semaphore line between the country's two biggest cities indicated, but could not be bound by them, as by the time the prices reached the other cities, they were already stale.

But the telegraph allowed New York prices to reach Philadelphia and elsewhere in seconds, all day long, regardless of the weather. As a result, those cities' days as major financial centers were soon over. The reason was understood even at the time. "Money," wrote

James K. Medbery in 1870, "always has a tendency to concentrate itself, and stocks, bonds, gold rapidly accumulate at those points where the most considerable financial activity prevails. The greater the volume of floating wealth, the more conspicuous this peculiarity. It resulted from this law that New York City became to the United States what London is to the world. Eminent before [the telegraph], this chief metropolis of the seaboard now assumed an absolute financial supremacy. Its alterations of buoyancy and depression produced corresponding perturbations in every state, city, and village in the land."[4]

Thus in a very real sense, the development of the telegraph in the 1840s assured that New York would become the financial center of the country. Had Morse perfected the telegraph in the 1820s, which would have been technologically possible, Philadelphia would probably have been able to exploit it and sweep up the liquid wealth of the nation.

Even before the telegraph, however, express services—companies that transported freight and mail by the fastest means possible, just as FedEx does today—delivered securities and money between New York and other cities. Alvin Adams, a Bostonian, began making regular trips between Boston and New York for this purpose in 1840. Once the telegraph was established, these express services became vital for maintaining New York's dominance. Curiously, many of the early express companies, set up merely to transport money and securities, evolved into banks and brokerage houses themselves. American Express and Wells-Fargo both began in this way, and so did the financial career of one of the most colorful characters in the history of the Street, Daniel Drew.

Daniel Drew was born in 1797 on a poor, hillside farm in what was then southern Dutchess County, about sixty miles from New York City, then a long day's journey. Raised in a poor family, Drew's schooling was minimal, little more than reading, writing, and basic arithmetic. His mother was religious and she taught her son a fundamentalist, fire-and-brimstone form of Christianity. But while he would be deeply and genuinely religious all his life—he would found a seminary and build several churches—Daniel Drew was always to separate his religious instincts from his business behavior.

E. C. Stedman, a Wall Street broker and author (he coined the word *Victorian,* in 1875, to designate the age in which he lived), knew Drew well and was bemused by Drew's seemingly effortless moral dichotomy. "Ethical teachers," he wrote, "are frequently known to impress upon those committed to their care the necessity of taking their religion into the routine of daily life. Among the characteristics of 'Uncle Daniel' Drew was the capacity to carry religion whithersoever he went without any laudable effect upon either his religion or his life. He seemed actually to draw aid and inspiration from his faith for the execution of the schemes in which he appeared at his worst."[5]

As a child Drew earned money working around the circuses that wintered in the area, and possibly this is when he learned the skills of a circus barker that he would put to such good use on Wall Street. In 1812, when he was fourteen, his father died and Drew joined the militia to get the hundred-dollar bonus being offered enlistees after the outbreak of the War of 1812. The British did not choose to attack well-defended New York City, however, so Drew never saw action. But his hundred-dollar bonus would prove the foundation of a fortune that at one time reached as high—at least by Drew's reckoning—as $16 million. Had there been a *Forbes* Four Hundred list at that time, Drew would have ranked among the top twenty richest individuals in the country.

Striking out on his own, Drew became a drover, buying cattle from local farmers and driving them into New York City where they were sold and butchered. At the end of one of these drives, according to a Wall Street legend so ancient and so universally accepted that it might as well be true—although it almost certainly is not—Drew had a moneymaking idea. The night before the end of the drive, Drew allowed his herd all the salt they would eat, but denied them water, until they reached a stream that then flowed through the meadows of rural upper Manhattan and now runs somewhere under Seventy-seventh Street. The cattle, half-mad with thirst, rushed into the stream and sucked up gallons of water. With the cattle now considerably, if only temporarily, heavier, Drew then drove them quickly into New York, where he sold them, on the hoof and by the pound, to the city's butchers.

Since cattle have been a staple of commerce for thousands of years, Drew was likely not the first to think of this particular scam, and he would probably not have jeopardized his future dealings with the city's butchers for a onetime profit. But he has the credit for it, if that is the term, and the story is the undisputed origin of the term *watered stock,* a notion that has bedeviled many writers of the history of Wall Street ever since. They think it was solely a nefarious practice of the mid–nineteenth century. In fact, watered stock means nothing more than issuing stock in amounts above the paid-in capital, which *could* be done with nefarious intent, as we shall see, until rules were developed to prevent misuse. But every stock dividend and stock split is also watered stock, and few investors object to them. The term has disappeared from today's Wall Street not because the practice has disappeared but because the practice has become universal.

Drew steadily expanded his cattle business, and by the end of the 1820s, he was bringing herds as large as two thousand head to New York, making a profit of as much as $12 on each animal. In 1829, Drew used his accumulating capital to buy the Bull's Head Inn, located at what is today the corner of Third Avenue and Twenty-sixth Street. Then still considerably north of the city proper, it had become the center of the city's cattle market.

Drew began making regular trips to Wall Street for business, often delivering papers and money for others as well, acting as an express service between what was then the suburbs of New York and downtown. The Street held an immediate attraction for him. Like Jacob Little, Drew loved the great game for its own sake, the thrill that came from outsmarting his fellow players. And while Drew affected a country-bumpkin style of dress and talk and had a laugh that sounded "like a hen thrown suddenly off from her propriety,"[6] soon no one doubted his brains or his capacity to concoct remarkably original schemes. "We have said his intellect was subtle," William Worthington Fowler, a fellow speculator, wrote. "The word *subtle* does not altogether express it. It should be *vulpine.* . . . The hounds of the Street for twenty years have been following his track, now in silence and now baying in deep-mouthed chorus when they run him to earth, but his twistings and doublings and countless devices have foiled them."[7]

Drew executed a typical ploy one day when he walked into the Union Club, the city's most prestigious men's club. He seemed quite agitated, as though looking for someone, and pulled a large handkerchief from his pocket several times to mop his brow, causing a piece of paper to fall out of his pocket, which he seemed not to notice. When he left the club, the other brokers present immediately retrieved the paper. It read, "Buy all the Oshkosh stock you can get at any price you can get it below par."

Oshkosh, according to Henry Clews, who told this story in his memoirs, was a railroad company, regarded at the time as overpriced and headed for a tumble. But the brokers reasoned Drew must have known something they didn't and formed a syndicate to buy thirty thousand shares. They were careful to buy the stock from a broker that Drew had never used before but, alas for them, was using then, and the stock fell "at the rate of twelve points a day."[8]

In 1836, Drew formed the brokerage firm of Drew and Robinson and three years later sold the Bull's Head Inn. He was in the great game for good and by the 1850s was one of the Street's major players. And by then, as well, the American economy had awakened from the doldrums induced by the panic of 1837.

The depression, as defined by economic contraction, ended in 1843, but the economy recovered only slowly. Not until the Mexican War of 1846–48 did the economy move into high gear as a result of the new territories the country gained. And it was the California gold strike of 1848 that really transformed both the country and its economy.

On January 24, 1848, James Marshall was inspecting a millrace that he had just constructed on the American River, not far from Sacramento. A millrace carries water from a stream to the top of a waterwheel, and he had turned the water into his new apparatus the night before to clear the debris. Now something "about half the size and shape of a pea" glinted in the water. "It made my heart thump," he remembered later, "for I was certain it was gold." "Boys," he said to his workmen, "by God, I believe I have found a gold mine."[9]

He had indeed.

It is an oddity of the American past that one of the most significant events in the nation's history—the California gold strike—

should have taken place in a foreign country. But negotiations to end the Mexican War did not conclude until February 2, 1848, with the signing of the Treaty of Guadalupe Hidalgo. Only on May 30, four months after Marshall's discovery, did the Stars and Stripes rise over the Southwest in exchange for $15 million and the assumption of Mexican debts to Americans.

In the middle of the nineteenth century gold reigned supreme in the world financial system. The Bank of England had gone on the gold standard in 1821, declaring itself ready to buy or sell unlimited amounts of pounds sterling for gold at the rate of one ounce of gold for £3/17/10½ (a ratio set more than a century earlier by Sir Isaac Newton, of all people, enjoying the perks of a largely no-show job as Master of the King's Mint). As the United Kingdom dominated the world's economy in the nineteenth century, the Bank of England quickly became the world's de facto central bank, and pounds sterling became the currency of international trade. Major nations had little choice but to peg their own currencies to gold, at least for trade purposes.

The good thing about a gold standard is that it makes inflation impossible. If a country begins to create too much paper money, gold will begin to flow out of its treasury, as people exchange the money for gold. But that means that under a gold standard, the money supply is limited by the amount of gold available to back the currency. In England, only the Bank of England issued banknotes, and their supply could easily be controlled.

But the United States government, lacking a central bank of its own, did not issue banknotes. The federal government's contribution to the money supply was limited to coins, including gold coins at the ratio of $20.66 to the ounce of gold. The nation's paper money was provided by thousands of state-chartered banks that ranged from unquestionably sound to totally fraudulent. These banknotes tended to be worth less the farther from the issuing bank they traded, and publishers issued "banknote detectors" that told people which notes were sound and which dubious.

The United States was not a major gold producer in the early nineteenth century. In 1847, a typical pre–gold rush year, the United States produced only 43,000 ounces, mostly as a byproduct of base-metal mining. The following year, however, the country turned out 484,000 ounces, thanks to California. In 1849 the output was 1,935,000 ounces. By 1853 output was no less than 3,144,000 ounces, worth almost $65 million.

The result of this sudden influx of gold into the American economy was great prosperity and economic growth. (And because a myriad of local banks funded loans by issuing banknotes, inflation.) Government revenues, a rough measure of economic activity, had been only $29 million in 1844. By 1854 they were over $73 million.

James Marshall and his employer had tried to keep the news of the gold strike a secret. Needless to say, they failed dismally. San Francisco was soon nearly deserted as men rushed to the hills in hopes of instant wealth. Because of California's remoteness—the telegraph wouldn't reach California until 1861—the news took months to reach the East Coast. But on December 8, 1848, President James K. Polk sent Congress a message declaring that rumors of the gold strike were authentic. He sent along a guaranteed-to-get-your-attention piece of proof, a twenty-pound gold nugget. About the size of a man's fist, it was worth about $5,000, then enough for a large family to live on in comfort for two years or more.

The result was mass hysteria. Ninety thousand people set off for California in 1849 and as many again in 1850, sharply moving the country's center of gravity westward. (In 1851, John B. L. Soule wrote in the *Terre Haute Express*, "Go west, young man"—a phrase quickly picked up by, and forever after attributed to, Horace Greeley.)

The influx of gold spurred a major economic boom as it expanded the money supply and greatly increased the backing of the dollar. Foreign investors, who had shunned American securities in the 1840s, now flocked back into American railroad and government bonds. In 1847, the country's foreign indebtedness amounted to $193.7 million. Within a decade it had almost doubled to $383.3 million.

Railroad mileage increased by nearly 150 percent as the railroads rushed westward to the Mississippi, the jumping-off point for wagon trains to California. Pig iron production in turn soared from only 63,000 tons in 1850 to 883,000 tons in 1856. Coal production more than doubled as well.

As settlers and gold diggers flocked west, New York remained the hub of the nation's financial and mercantile system. "Every beat of this great financial organ," wrote the *Louisville Courier* in 1857, "is felt from Maine to Florida, and from the Atlantic to the Pacific."[10] State banks thought it necessary to keep deposits in New York institutions to assure that their customers would be able to do business there. Only around $8 million in 1840, by 1857 these interbank deposits were estimated as high as $50 million. Nearly all foreign investments in American securities now came through New York, and New York commodities brokers handled the foreign sales of southern cotton planters and western wheat farmers. Indeed, the cotton trade between the South and Europe was so profitable to New York bankers and commodities brokers that when the Civil War erupted, New York's mayor, Fernando Wood—"of whom no man need fear he holds too low an opinion"—suggested that the city secede as well.

This swelling economic activity was, of course, reflected on Wall Street. Mining shares, many of them of highly dubious value, traded briskly on the curb, and a Mining Exchange was soon established to handle the business in a more formal manner. But while volume increased significantly, especially on the curb, prices did not climb as quickly as the economy as a whole. The main reason for this was that the pool of American securities available became much larger. Nearly as many companies were incorporated in the United States in the 1850s as in the first half of the century. Twenty-seven new banks were founded in New York City alone in the years 1851–53, with $16 million in capital, much of it raised on Wall Street.

By 1856, 360 railroad stocks were being traded, 985 bank stocks, 75 insurance stocks, as well as hundreds of corporate, municipal, state, and federal bonds. Most of these were not traded on the New York Stock and Exchange Board, however, as the board refused to admit new and untested issues. As always in times of change and economic optimism, the new issues attracted the most speculative attention. So while volume on the board remained steady at around six thousand shares a day, volume on the curb often soared above seventy thousand shares.

By 1857 the mood on the Street was exuberant. The dark days of the late thirties and early forties were forgotten or unknown by new traders, who now flocked to Wall Street to make their fortunes. And as in other Wall Street booms before and since, many fortunes were made, and lost, nearly overnight. That year George Francis Train expressed the mood on Wall Street in a bit of doggerel:

> *Monday,* I started my land operations;
> *Tuesday,* owed millions by all calculations;
> *Wednesday,* my brownstone palace began;
> *Thursday,* I drove out a spanking new span;
> *Friday,* I gave a magnificent ball;
> *Saturday,* smashed—with just nothing at all.[11]

While newcomers to the Street and to New York were especially susceptible to this easy-come-easy-go atmosphere, even the well established could be affected by it. Robert Schuyler, grandson of General Philip Schuyler and Alexander Hamilton's nephew, was president of both the Harlem and New Haven Railroads. An examination of the New Haven's books during the summer of 1854 uncovered a few irregularities, but Schuyler assured stockholders and journalists that they could be explained, and few doubted his word. Further examination, however, revealed that among numerous other frauds, Schuyler had clandestinely printed twenty thousand shares of New Haven stock and sold it—this is what is really meant by *watered stock*—pocketing $2 million, a vast fortune in those days. By the time the news of this enormous theft became public, Schuyler was, of course, well on his way to Canada with the money. He was never brought to justice. Schuyler was perhaps the most prominent of the crooks who operated on Wall Street at this time, but he was by no means the only one.

By mid-1857 the boom gave signs of eroding. "What can be the end of all this but another general collapse like that of 1837, only upon a much grander scale?" wrote James Gordon Bennett, founder and publisher of the *New York Herald,* the country's largest and most influential newspaper, on June 27. ". . . Government spoilation, public defaulters, paper bubbles of all descriptions, a general scramble for western lands and town and city sites, millions of dollars, made or borrowed, expended in fine houses and gaudy furniture; hundreds of thousands in silly rivalries of fashionable parvenus, in silks, laces, diamonds and every variety of costly frippery are only a few among the many crying evils of the day."[12]

But the supposed evils of greed were one thing, the reality of the economic data was quite another. California gold production had leveled off, and the Crimean War and poor harvests in Europe, which had stimulated American exports, were over. In June the *Herald* noted, "Our wharves are crowded with ships, most of them without employment; and those that have found something to do have accepted it at rates ruinously low."[13] A Boston paper revealed at the same time that the New England textile industry was suffering—six thousand cotton looms were idle for lack of demand.

Making matters worse, money tended to flow out of New York banks in the summer and early fall, as western farmers drew down their local deposits to pay for the harvest and pay down their loans. Thus August was in any event a month when money was tight in New York, and by the middle of the month the *Herald* noted, "The supply of weak, sickly stock securities pressing for sale is very great, and there are no buyers, no demand from any source."[14]

Then, on August 19, Edwin C. Litchfield, president of the Michigan Central Railroad, resigned "in order," he wrote, "to spend more time on personal matters."[15] Even in 1857, such an excuse was recognized as code for "the company is in big trouble." Michigan Central led the list of major railroad stocks plummeting in value. On August 7, Michigan Central had been at 85; by August 29 it stood at only 67. The Erie tumbled from 34 to 21; New York Central from 83 to 74. The Michigan Central was soon in receivership.

On August 24, the New York branch of the Ohio Life Insurance and Trust Company, a bank despite its name, suspended operations, admitting insolvency. Massive fraud was soon revealed, and the home office in Cincinnati followed it into suspension. Its stock fell 85 percent in four days, and its depositors lined up outside the bank, hoping against hope to retrieve some portion of their money. A local newspaper, expropriating a phrase from the recently published *David Copperfield,* wrote that all they could do was "wait for something to turn up."[16]

The more vulnerable Wall Street brokers and speculators began to fail. On August 27, Jacob Little, unable to meet his obligations, suspended—for the fourth and, it turned out, last time in his long career. By September the weaker banks were going under, and on September 12 the market suffered another blow when the steamer *Central America* sank in a hurricane off Cape Hatteras. Lost with it were more than four hundred passengers and, of more immediate concern on the Street, $1.6 million in California gold.

Although the Atlantic telegraph cable would not be finished until the following year (and even then it failed in only two weeks), London and Paris markets soon learned of Wall Street's troubles, and the first truly international financial panic ensued. European interest rates shot up as the Banks of England and France moved to protect their currencies. As a result European investors pulled out of American securities and into safer ones at home.

By mid-October most banks in the country, and all the major ones in New York, had suspended payments in gold. In effect, the banks had declared a bank holiday, and the sound ones used the opportunity to build their species reserves and call in loans in an orderly manner. The worst was over on Wall Street, and the banks were able to resume specie payment in December.

But the effect of the crisis on the New York financial market had been brutal. About half the New York brokers had gone bankrupt, as had 985 New York merchants, who left liabilities of about $120 million, a titanic sum for that time. The short-lived Mining Exchange vanished as quickly as it had appeared, and the curb became a near ghost town. Even many of the old established brokers, who had survived the panic of 1837, were broken by this one. One reason, of course, was that in the earlier panic, most of them still had other businesses besides securities brokerage. By 1857, they did not.

Because so many of the older brokers left the business, the New York Stock and Exchange Board, virtually a closed club for years, now had seats available, and younger, more aggressive brokers joined. Not bound to the old ways by ties of family or long association, such men as Henry Clews, Leonard Jerome, Cornelius Vanderbilt, Daniel Drew, and August Schell would revolutionize business practices on Wall Street. The Civil War would give them unprecedented opportunities, and the result would be the greatest example of capitalism "red in tooth and claw" and its consequences the world has yet seen.

CHAPTER FIVE

"VANITY FAIR
WAS NO LONGER A DREAM"

Wars, according to an ancient Chinese saying, are fought with silver bullets. While individual battles are decided by tactics, firepower, courage, and of course luck, victory in the long haul has almost always gone to the side better able to turn the national wealth to military purposes.

The American Civil War was the first great conflict of the industrial age. Indeed it was the greatest military event of the hundred years that came between the fall of Napoleon and World War I, fought on a scale previously unimaginable and foreshadowing the desperate global struggles of the early twentieth century. As a result, both sides confronted wholly new and completely unforeseen fiscal demands and were forced to invent new ways to address them without wrecking their domestic economies. That the North succeeded in rising to these economic challenges and the South did not played a major part in the eventual outcome.

From the first, both sides faced desperate financial problems. Because of the depression that had begun in 1857, the government in Washington had been operating in the red for four years, borrowing mostly short term to make up the deficit. The national debt, only $28.7 million in 1857, had more than doubled to $64.8 million in 1861. In December 1860, as the states in the Deep South began to secede one by one, there was not even enough money in the Treasury to pay congressional salaries.

The expenses of the federal government averaged only about $172,000 a day that month. But by early summer, 1861, after the war had begun, expenses were running at $1 million a day. By the end of the year they were up to $1.5 million. In December 1861, most northern banks stopped paying their debts in gold, and the federal government was forced to follow suit a few days later. The country had gone off the gold standard, and Wall Street panicked. "The bottom is out of the tub," Lincoln said. "What shall I do?"[1]

There are basically only three ways to finance a great war. First, the government can raise taxes. By the end of the war the federal government was taxing nearly everything that could possibly be taxed, including, for the first time, incomes. Roughly 21 percent of the cost of the war was raised by taxation. The Bureau of Internal Revenue, the ancestor of the IRS, is by no means the least of the legacies of the Civil War.

The second way is by issuing printing-press money, the principal means by which the Revolution had been financed. During the war the federal government issued $450 million in so-called greenbacks, financing about 13 percent of war costs and triggering the wartime inflation that drove prices to about 180 percent of their prewar levels. The South, with far fewer financing options, was forced to use printing-press money to pay for more than half of its wartime expenses. This caused the Southern economy to spin out of control, with a virulent inflation that reached 9,000 percent by war's end.

The issuing of greenbacks had a curiously unanticipated effect on Wall Street. With both greenbacks and gold coins in circulation, the most ancient of economic laws—Gresham's law, which says, "Bad money drives out good"—began to operate. Given a choice of using gold or greenbacks, which the law required be accepted at par with gold, spenders, naturally, chose to spend the greenbacks and keep the gold. The precious metal, then, tended to disappear into mattresses. But gold was necessary for certain purposes, such as customs duties. (The federal government, which required everyone else to accept greenbacks, excepted itself from that requirement.) Thus trading, and speculating, in gold began immediately on Wall Street. At first the New York Stock and Exchange Board permitted trading in gold, but because the price of gold tended to fall after Union victories and rise with Confederate ones, the board decided gold trading was unpatriotic and banned it in 1862. But to meet the continuing demand, curb brokers quickly organized

Gilpin's News Room, presumably named for one of the organizers, and beginning in 1863, anyone willing to pay the annual $25 fee was welcome.

As at the Regular Board, prices at Gilpin's tended to vary according to the fortunes of the Union Army, reaching a low just before the Battle of Gettysburg, when it took 287 greenback dollars to buy 100 dollars in gold. Needless to say, along with the people who legitimately required gold for business and tax purposes, hundreds of speculators were hoping to make a profit by guessing right on the vicissitudes of war. Because news from the front could be worth a fortune if possessed even a few minutes before it became generally known, brokers often employed agents attached to the armies, both Union and Confederate, and were routinely better informed of what was going on than was the government in Washington. Indeed, Wall Street knew the outcome of the Battle of Gettysburg before President Lincoln did.

These traders often endured heavy criticism for their unpatriotic willingness to bet against the Union cause. The press often referred to them as "General Lee's left wing in Wall Street," and Abraham Lincoln publicly wished that "every one of them had his devilish head shot off."[2] But the gold traders were hardly affected by the opprobrium. For the lucky or the skillful, there was just too much money to be made.

Transferring gold from seller to buyer could be a hazardous business, and several major robberies took place before the Bank of New York began to act as a gold depository, allowing the transfers to take place within the safety of the bank. Even then, risk existed. In 1865, E. B. Ketchum of Ketchum, Son & Company, a previously distinguished firm with a seat on the Regular Board, forged several million dollars' worth of drafts on gold deposited at the Bank of New York and managed to get clean away.

On June 17, 1864, Congress made it illegal to trade in gold at any place other than a broker's office. The primary result of the law—besides closing Gilpin's and forcing trading out onto the street—was to increase the spread between gold and greenbacks. So obvious was the effect that the law was repealed a mere two weeks later, and Gilpin's reopened, as wild and speculative a place as ever. Realizing that gold trading was inevitable, members of the

Regular Board and others of the Wall Street establishment, including J. P. Morgan, Levi P. Morton (later vice president of the United States), and Horace Clark, Commodore Vanderbilt's son-in-law, were instrumental in establishing the New York Gold Exchange, soon known as the Gold Room, in October of that year.

At one end of the room that, according to a contemporary, looked "like a cavern, full of dank and noisome vapors"[3] was a large, clocklike dial, with a single hand that showed the current price of gold. Even the smallest movement could signal the making or breaking of traders. Although the Gold Room was a far cry from the rowdy, raucous early days at Gilpin's (which shut down after the Gold Room opened), it was still no place for the faint of heart or the overscrupulous.

The third method for financing a war is to borrow. This the federal government did, and on a scale no sovereign government had ever before contemplated. The national debt, $64.8 million in 1861, had by 1865 reached $2.755 billion, an increase by a factor of over forty-two. Total annual government expenses before the war had never exceeded $74 million. By 1865 interest expense alone was well over twice that.

A few days after the disastrous battle of Bull Run, Treasury Secretary Salmon P. Chase personally went to Wall Street to float a bond issue for $50 million at an interest rate of 7.30 percent. (He apparently chose that rate because it would yield two cents a day in interest for each hundred dollars of face value.) Although he was able to raise the money, Chase realized that while it was a considerable sum for the Wall Street banks to handle at that time, it was only a drop in the bucket of the government's long-term needs.

Clearly the old ways of government borrowing would no longer suffice. Fortunately for Chase (and the country), accompanying the treasury secretary to New York was a young banker named Jay Cooke. Cooke, the son of a lawyer and congressman, was raised in Ohio but settled in Philadelphia, where, just as the war began, he opened a private bank named Jay Cooke and Company. The federal government hired Cooke (whose father was an old associate of Chase's) as the agent to sell a new series of bonds, called five-twenties, because they could be redeemed in not less than five years or more than twenty, meanwhile paying six percent interest in gold.

Instead of trying to place them quietly with banks and brokers, who would hold them in their reserves, Cooke advertised the bonds widely in newspapers and handbills and convinced the Treasury to issue them in denominations as small as fifty dollars. He planted stories in the newspapers, trying to convince the average workingman that buying them was not only a patriotic duty, but a good investment as well. He succeeded beyond his wildest hopes.

Before the war, far fewer than 1 percent of all Americans owned securities of any kind. For all but the rich, the mattress was the place for any surplus cash. But Cooke sold bonds to about 5 percent of the population of the North. By the end of the war, Cooke was selling bonds even faster than the War Department could spend the money.

This vast influx of bonds, and bondholders, into the country's financial markets transformed Wall Street almost overnight. Although the stock market had plunged at the outbreak of war—as stock markets almost always do—investors began to realize that the war would be protracted and not only would there be a vast increase in the amount of securities to be traded, but that much of the money that the government was spending would go to such firms as railroads, iron mills, textile manufacturers, and munitions companies whose profits would be invested in, and capital needs met by, Wall Street.

By far the biggest boom the Street had yet known was soon under way.

Almost overnight the Wall Street securities market swelled to become the second largest market in the world, surpassed only by London's. In the midst of this frenzy, the New York Stock and Exchange Board still held its two regular, sit-down auctions at 10:30 A.M. and 1 P.M., but they were not nearly adequate to handle the volume. Other exchanges began to form to take up the slack, as they often did in boom times on the Street during the early and mid–nineteenth century. One such exchange first held meetings in a basement room, known with no great affection as the Coal Hole. Before long its volume was exceeding that on the Regular Board, which in 1863 changed its name to the one it has borne ever since, the New York Stock Exchange.

This new exchange, reorganized in 1864 as the Open Board of Brokers, would have a profound effect upon the history of Wall Street, although it was in existence for only five years. For one thing, it abandoned the old, gentlemanly sit-down auctions that the Regular Board still clung to. Instead it instituted what is known as the continuous auction, in which trading in various securities took place simultaneously at designated places on the trading floor. These places are still called posts, because they were modeled on the trading action at the curb market, where individual lampposts marked the spots where brokers gathered to trade particular stocks.

This new system allowed a much more precise knowledge of current prices and also a much higher volume of trading. By 1865, the Open Board was doing ten times the volume of the Regular Board. For the first time the New York Stock Exchange had a truly serious rival for its spot as the most important institution on the Street. Its leaders began to realize that the old days on Wall Street were gone and that they would have to institute change if the exchange was to survive.

Trading volume on Wall Street by 1865 was estimated to have reached an unprecedented $6 billion a year. "Many brokers earned from eight hundred to ten thousand dollars a day in commissions," wrote James K. Medbery in 1870. (At that time $1,500 a year was a comfortable, middle-class income.) "The entire population of the country entered the field. Offices were besieged by crowds of customers. . . . New York never exhibited such wide-spread evidences of prosperity. Broadway was lined with carriages. The fashionable milliners, dress-makers, and jewelers reaped golden harvests. The pageant of Fifth Avenue on Sunday, and of Central Park during the week-days was *bizarre,* gorgeous, wonderful! Never were there such dinners, such receptions, such balls. Anonyma startled the city with the splendor of her robes and the luxury of her equipages. Vanity Fair was no longer a dream."[4] Of course, on real battlefields, real men were dying by the thousands in a war that cost more American lives than all the others combined.

The Mining Exchange, which had been among the casualties of the crash of 1857, was reorganized that year and was soon doing a brisk business in such stocks as the Woolah Woolah Gulch Gold Mining and Stamping Company. Some of these companies were legitimate, some plain frauds, and some a mixture of both. One Wall Streeter of the time reported that something called the Garner Hill Company issued a million shares at a price that "would have made the mine worth $1,600,000, giving the promoters, who had paid only thirty thousand dollars in cash, the net profit of a million and a half, with seventy thousand thrown in as contingent expenses!"[5]

Another exchange, the Petroleum Board, was formed in 1865 to handle trading in the exploding number of new companies formed to exploit the Pennsylvania oil field, where Edwin Drake first drilled for oil in 1859. Petroleum was so new that its uses were still highly speculative. Some thought that its chief use would be medicinal or cosmetic, such as hair oil. The absence of certainty, of course, only added to the speculative fever on the Petroleum Board.

But many brokers operated without any formal organization. Some even had no offices and (if the market turned against them) often simply vanished, leaving their creditors holding the bag. The word *guttersnipe*, coined in 1857, became a common term for these curbstone brokers. But by 1863 they may well have been trading as much as a million shares a day on the street.

In the frenzy of trading, brokers didn't have time to go home for lunch as they regularly had before the war. To meet the demand for eating on the run, the lunch counter—a fixture of every American business district since—made its first appearance. The American love affair with fast food was under way, thanks to Wall Street. And, a hundred years later, Wall Street would be instrumental in changing fast food from a mom-and-pop industry to a national one with the franchising boom of the 1960s.

When the Wall Street markets closed at the end of the business day and darkness halted trading on the street, brokers migrated to informal uptown exchanges, principally the one at the Fifth Avenue Hotel—New York's most fashionable hotel, located on Madison Square—which met the demand for evening trading. For a while it was possible to trade twenty-four hours a day in New York City, a circumstance that would not recur for well over a century.

But because of this multiplicity of exchanges and the ever-expanding number of brokers and customers, oversight of the market was nonexistent. Before the war, when Wall Street was still a small place where everyone knew each other, regulation could be as informal as the rules in a backyard touch-football game. Now the situation had completely changed. It was every man for himself and caveat emptor was the only rule of the new game.

At this time Wall Street began to attract others, new personalities whose names remain familiar to this day because of the fortunes they created or the influence they had. John Tobin, Leonard Jerome (the grandfather of Winston Churchill) and his brother Addison, Frank Worth (the great-great-great-grandfather of the late Diana, Princess of Wales), Henry Clews, J. P. Morgan, Jay Gould, and Jim Fisk all came to the Street at this time. One, however, stood out, even in this crowd of giants. Cornelius Vanderbilt was not a broker or banker, never speculated, seldom even set foot on Wall Street. Nonetheless, for the last fifteen years of his life, he was the most important player in the great game.

Vanderbilt was born in 1794 on Staten Island, where his father owned a farm overlooking New York Bay. Although providing for his large family, the father was unambitious, and Vanderbilt's mother was the major influence on his early life. From the first he was strong and active. When he was only six, he nearly drowned his horse in a race with a neighboring slave boy two years older than he. (Vanderbilt, who was never in the least a snob, let alone a racist in an age when racism was taken for granted, encountered his childhood playmate again at the end of his life. By then the richest man in America, Vanderbilt invited his friend, who had become a Methodist minister, to his home and entertained him there.)

Although highly intelligent, Vanderbilt was bored by abstractions and found the knuckle-rapping, rote-learning education that was the norm at the turn of the nineteenth century nearly unendurable. Although he stayed in school for about six years, far longer than many of his contemporaries, he would never master the intricacies of English grammar and spelling. More, he would be famous for both the quantity and quality of his profanity.

By the time he was sixteen, he was anxious to set out on his own. He saw opportunity in a periauger for sale at Port Richmond. Periaugers were the everyday workhorses of New York Harbor in the age before steam, brought there by the Dutch. Flat-bottomed and two-masted, they were up to sixty feet long and twenty-three feet wide, with ample room for cargo. Shallow-drafted, they could sail nearly anywhere in New York's endless waterfront.

Vanderbilt asked his mother to lend him the hundred dollars he needed to buy the vessel. That was no small sum in 1810, and his mother drove a hard bargain. She told him that if he could clear, plow, harrow, and plant a previously untilled eight-acre field before his birthday—about four weeks away—he could have the money. Vanderbilt enlisted some neighborhood boys and got the task done.

"I didn't feel as much real satisfaction," Vanderbilt recalled in his old age, "when I made two million dollars in that Harlem corner as I did on that bright May morning sixty years before when I stepped into my own periauger, hoisted my own sail, and put my hand to my own tiller."[6] Vanderbilt began his career by ferrying passengers back and forth from Staten Island to Manhattan and soon had a reputation for being the most reliable captain in the port. At the end of the first season he was able to pay his mother back the hundred dollars and give her another thousand besides.

The War of 1812 assured Vanderbilt's success. The army needed someone completely reliable to supply the forts that guarded New York Harbor and gave Vanderbilt the contract, even though he had not submitted the lowest bid. But most of the time the boat business in New York did not operate by contract. Rather it was a matter of getting to the job first and keeping it. Vanderbilt soon proved himself to be as tough as they come. At six feet one he was well above average height for his generation, with broad shoulders and immense physical strength that stayed with him long into middle age. In 1844, when he was fifty, he was leading a parade of Henry Clay supporters up Broadway when "Yankee" Sullivan, a Tammany tough and the best New York boxer of his day, grabbed his horse's reins. The enraged Vanderbilt leaped off his horse and beat Sullivan senseless.

By the end of 1817, Vanderbilt figured he was worth about $9,000 as well as being the owner of a respectable fleet of sailing ships. But Vanderbilt was always alert to change and the opportunities it presented, and he soon saw the future in steam. He sold his sailing vessels and went to work for Thomas Gibbons as captain of Gibbons's steamboat *Stoudinger*. The vessel, popularly known as the *Mouse* because of its small size, operated on the run between New York and New Brunswick, New Jersey.

At the time, Gibbons had a big problem. New York State had granted the well-connected Robert Livingston (who had funded Robert Fulton's *Clermont,* the first commercially successful steamboat) a monopoly of steamboat navigation in New York waters. The legislature arrogantly defined these waters as running to the high-tide mark on the New Jersey shore. The monopoly, needless to say, was highly unpopular with the people at large. A gifted naval architect, Vanderbilt persuaded Gibbons to build a larger vessel of his own design. He named it the *Bellona* after the Roman goddess of war, and New Yorkers, much more classically attuned in those days, quickly got the implication.

While Vanderbilt, with endless ingenuity, evaded the day-to-day efforts of the Livingston monopoly to seize the *Bellona,* Gibbons pursued his rights in court. The monopoly attempted to bribe Vanderbilt, offering him the colossal salary of $5,000 a year to switch sides, but he refused. "I shall stick to Mr. Gibbons till he is through his troubles," he said.[7] While often ruthless when crossed (and especially when double-crossed), Vanderbilt was always a man of honor. "His word is his bond when it is freely given," wrote a contemporary, "he is equally exact in fulfilling his threats."[8]

In 1824, Gibbons won a total victory when Chief Justice John Marshall, writing for a unanimous Supreme Court, declared the Livingston monopoly unconstitutional because the federal government alone had jurisdiction over interstate commerce. The case, *Gibbons v. Ogden,* is easily one of the half dozen most important decisions ever handed down by the Court, for it ensured that the economy of the United States would develop as a true common market. Thus, when the concept of "Wall Street" hardly existed, Cornelius Vanderbilt, pursuing private gain, had unwittingly played a major part in advancing the Street's (and the country's) future interests. There could hardly be a better example of Adam Smith's "invisible hand" at work.

Vanderbilt stayed with Gibbons until 1829, when he struck out on his own as a steamboat owner. His first vessel, the *Caroline* (named for his sister), would have the singular distinction of ending her days by going over Niagara Falls. But that was long after he had sold her. Vanderbilt, in an age when steamboats did "a whole-sale business in human slaughter," would never lose a vessel to fire or shipwreck. By the 1840s, Vanderbilt was the greatest shipowner in the country, and the *Journal of Commerce* had bestowed upon him the title he has been known by—to his contemporaries and to history—ever since: commodore.

As always, Vanderbilt was a tough competitor. Convinced that he could run any venture better and cheaper and faster than the next man, Vanderbilt loved to attack the cozy cartels that then often dominated the steamboat business. The cartels often decided that it was much cheaper to pay Vanderbilt *not* to com-pete. This was fine with Vanderbilt, who would simply take his vessels and compete somewhere else. By the 1850s he was oper-ating as far afield as Central America (where he personally pio-neered a route across Nicaragua) and Europe, where he found that even he could not compete against the heavily subsidized British Cunard Line. By the time the Civil War began, Vanderbilt was worth perhaps as much as $20 million.

But again, Vanderbilt had been observing the changes taking place around him. And in the late 1850s he saw the future in rail-roads. The Commodore had had a long and understandable antipathy to the new technology. At the dawn of the railroad era, in 1833, he had been involved, and very nearly killed, in the first major railroad accident in the United States. The car ahead of his had broken an axle while the train was traveling at the then high rate of speed of twenty-five miles per hour. Everyone else in Van-derbilt's car had been killed, while he was thrown out and dragged along before being flung down an embankment. With several bro-ken ribs and a punctured lung, he was months recovering.

But as early as 1854 he was looking closely at the New York and Harlem Railroad, which ran from New York to a point across the Hudson River from Albany. Packing a lunch, he would ride from one end of the line to the other and back. "After I made my collec-tion," a conductor remembered, "the Commodore would ply me with questions about the Harlem road. How many gallons of milk did we haul a day? How many engines had we? Were they good? Did the farmers patronize the road?"[9]

Well into his sixties and already one of the half dozen richest men in the country, Vanderbilt decided to abandon his beloved steamboats and move into railroads. To do that he knew he had to go to Wall Street, for the stock of the Hudson and Harlem lines had been among the staples of the Street for years.

Vanderbilt was surely the greatest nineteenth-century railroad man never to build a railroad. Instead he bought them, ran them with matchless efficiency, expanded them, and exploited their possibilities to the fullest. The Harlem, for instance, was generally thought a railroad of little importance or promise. Completed in 1852, it ran mostly through declining farming country. Its annual passenger revenues only once exceeded half a million dollars before the Civil War, and its freight revenues reached that level only in 1859. Even by the standards of the mid–nineteenth century, that was small potatoes. As late as March 1863, the *New York Herald* reported that "of all the railroad shares dealt in, the Harlem probably possesses the least intrinsic value."[10]

But the Commodore noticed something others seem to have overlooked. The New York and Harlem Railroad and its competitor running a few miles to the west, the Hudson River Railroad, were the only two railroads with direct access to Manhattan Island, their tracks running right into the heart of the city. The Harlem's tracks ran down Fourth Avenue (now Park), originally as far as Twenty-sixth Street. But the city council soon ordered the dirty and dangerous locomotives to stay north of Forty-second Street, which is why Grand Central Terminal is located where it is. Railroads approaching the city from the east, such as the New York and New Haven, had to pay for the right to use the Harlem's right-of-way. The railroads coming from the west were blocked by the Hudson River, then unbridged south of Troy.

Thanks to his close personal inspection, the Commodore further realized that the Harlem was a poorly managed operation. Demonstrating the same confidence with which he had approached steamboating, Vanderbilt was convinced that he could run it far more efficiently and thus profitably. And he saw one more opportunity for profit. The state legislature, in granting a charter to the Harlem, had empowered the city council to grant the Harlem such streetcar franchises as it saw fit. Vanderbilt began to accumulate Harlem stock.

Obtaining a streetcar franchise from the city council, just as from the legislature, required bribing the members. But at least the city council was a much smaller, and thus less expensive, body. The Harlem, undoubtedly feathering council members' nests left and right, obtained the best possible streetcar franchise, the one that ran the length of Broadway, the city's greatest and busiest street. One writer of the time estimated that up to 200 million people a year passed up or down Broadway. Besides whatever the Harlem paid the council members personally (the members also, of course, used the inside information to buy Harlem stock for their personal accounts), the railroad also agreed to pay the city 10 percent of its total revenues from the franchise.

Vanderbilt was not part of the Harlem's management, but he had steadily been buying the stock, even though many on the Street thought it a good short sale. "The Commodore moved about through the turbid waters of the Street," William Worthington Fowler reported, "making no secret of his doings and quietly absorbing into his vast financial maw the huge slices of Harlem fed out to him by the frolicsome and infatuated bears."[11]

The bears were looking for a tumble in the price of Harlem, and they seemed to have information to back up their hunch. The council had passed the Broadway franchise bill on April 23, 1863, when the price of Harlem was in the low 50s. By May 19, the price had soared to 116⅝, but that day a wave of short selling hit the stock. The prime mover behind the short sales, apparently, was the Commodore's old friend Daniel Drew, a member of the board of directors of the Harlem.

The price fell to the 80s, but Vanderbilt kept buying it, particularly if "the sellers wished to *go short of it*. A great hand was always extended to receive the stock and pass it away out of sight, in a deep, broad iron chest."[12]

The reason for the short sales became apparent on June 25 when, late in the afternoon, the council suddenly rescinded the Broadway franchise they had granted only two months before. The stock fell "like a shot partridge" to 72,[13] and the bears on the Street were keenly anticipating the Commodore's embarrassment the next day.

But the next day the stock did not fall. Instead it shot up to 97, and the following day hit 106. The *New York Times* explained that morning, "The chief owners of the Harlem property are Mr. Cornelius Vanderbilt and his immediate friends, and that portion of the capital stock which they have not already paid for and transferred to their names they have the cash means in bank to pay for, whenever the short sellers—who have contracted for more than the entire capital—are ready to make their deliveries."

Investors who had shorted the stock, of course, would have to buy it from Vanderbilt to make their deliveries. The Commodore, who had never been involved in Wall Street before, had bested the most sophisticated speculators in the country in the biggest corner the Street had yet seen. On Monday, June 29, as the *Herald* was gleefully reporting that the shorts might need as many as fifty thousand shares to make good their contracts, the city council—many of whose members were short of Harlem—hastily reversed course and gave the Harlem back its franchise. Vanderbilt then allowed the price of Harlem to fall to 94, so that the city council members—who might prove useful in the future—could get off the hook.

The *Times* was delighted. "The public sympathies," it wrote, "are wholly with Mr. Vanderbilt in this transaction, and there are the most hearty congratulations exchanged in the Street today that the shameless trick and fraud of the City Council and their stock-jobbing co-conspirators have been paid off with compound interest."

But while Vanderbilt let the potentially useful city council members off easy, he had no intention of being so charitable with the speculators on the Street. He steadily ratcheted up the price of Harlem through the summer "amid the execration of the whole ursine tribe,"[14] until the last of the bears made peace at a price of 180. Vanderbilt had not only bought control of the New York and Harlem Railroad, he had made a fortune, to add to the one he already had.

The Commodore had also been steadily buying the stock of the Hudson River Railroad, which ran along the east side of the Hudson River as far as East Albany, where, via a ferry, it connected to the New York Central, which ran parallel to the Erie Canal to Buffalo. By 1863 he was on the board and one of the principal stockholders.

Apparently a group of speculators who were not involved in the

Harlem corner thought that that corner would give them an opportunity to play with the stock of the Hudson River Railroad. Just as the Harlem corner was reaching a climax, they launched a bear raid on the Hudson. They sold the stock short, hoping to force enough margin calls and panic among the stockholders to lower the price to where they could close their shorts at a profit.

Vanderbilt reacted immediately and told his brokers to buy all the seller's options that were offered. At that time, stock was often sold for future delivery within a specified time, usually ten, twenty, or thirty days, with the precise time of delivery up to either the buyer—in which case it was called a buyer's option—or the seller. Most short sales were effected not by borrowing the stock as is done today, but by using seller's options. These options differed from modern options—puts and calls—in that the puts and calls convey only a right, not an obligation, to complete the contract.

By buying up all the seller's options offered, Vanderbilt and his allies were in effect announcing their intention to corner the stock. But the Commodore had something more elegant in mind than a mere corner. As the financier Russell Sage described it, Vanderbilt was about to prove that "he was to finance what Shakespeare was to poetry and Michelangelo to art."[15]

Given the Harlem corner, many speculators assumed that Vanderbilt must be short of cash. And the Commodore did nothing to dispel those rumors. Indeed he acted as though they were true, by having his brokers approach other brokers and ask them to "turn" the stock. Turning was a means whereby, with a maximum of luck, a corner could be achieved with a minimum of cash. To turn a stock, a purchaser would immediately sell it, buying back from the buyer a "buyer's option" on the stock at a slight increase in price, thus preserving his cash. But the buyer had no obligation to keep the stock. If he thought the corner would fail, as the vast majority did, he could increase his profit by selling it and buying it back cheaper when he had to fulfill his buyer's option.

Many of the brokers who sold the Commodore buyer's options took advantage of this and, confident that Vanderbilt was at the end of his financial rope, sold the stock in the Hudson railroad at once. But they were wrong. Vanderbilt had plenty of money. They didn't know it, of course, but they were selling to intermediaries for the Commodore, for cash, stock they had already contracted to sell him later.

In the first ten days of July 1863, Cornelius Vanderbilt closed the trap. When the seller's options came due, the sellers went into the market to buy Hudson River stock. There was none to be had, for the Commodore owned it all. As the price shot from 112 to 180 virtually overnight, he called for the stock he had bought on buyer's options, and these unfortunates as well discovered that Vanderbilt was the only seller. The Commodore, magnanimity personified, did not insist that the bears who had been caught in their own trap fulfill their contracts immediately. He was willing to lend them the necessary stock, but at an interest rate of 5 percent per day.

Thus, as Grant took Vicksburg, as the greatest battle ever fought in the Western Hemisphere settled the nation's destiny at Gettysburg, as a thousand bodies piled up in the streets of New York City itself in the greatest riot in the country's history, Cornelius Vanderbilt played Hannibal at Wall Street's Battle of Cannae. His double envelopment of the bears netted him and his allies $3 million and was recognized immediately as a masterpiece of financial manipulation. "Wall Street has never known so successful a corner," the *Herald* declared on July 13.

The following year a court ruled that the city council lacked the legal authority to grant any more streetcar franchises beyond what it had authorized thirty years earlier. Vanderbilt therefore had to go to Albany to get legal sanction for the Broadway line, which was already under construction. Undoubtedly he paid good money for the pledge he received both from the legislative leaders and the governor that they would pass the needed legislation. Daniel Drew and others also went to Albany to testify in favor of the bill. But Drew, as was his wont, was playing a double game. He told the legislators privately that if they were to short Harlem stock and then defeat the bill, they could make a bundle.

Drew's scheme was, of course, a near carbon copy of what had cost the members of the city council so dearly the previous spring. One is at a loss to explain how they could have been tempted. "The statesmen at Albany," E. C. Stedman, a veteran of Wall Street in the 1860s, wrote at the turn of the century, "in the spring of 1864, were well aware of the misfortune into which the statesmen at

New York had plunged themselves, less than a year before, by their bear campaign against this stock. Yet they rushed fatuously into a similar attempt, as if Vanderbilt had proved an easy victim. Perhaps the public treasury, the customary object of their conspiracies, had lately been too well guarded. Perhaps the opportunities for fleecing corporations were more restricted than they are today. Or perhaps they had achieved such success, in raids of one sort or another, as to become intoxicated by good fortune and reduced to the mental condition of a beast of prey which has tasted blood."[16]

To be sure, the Commodore was, while formidably rich, not as liquid as he might have liked. He was holding huge blocks of Hudson and Harlem stock and would have been loath to use them as collateral for loans. Certainly Drew had been right about Harlem rising swiftly. At the beginning of 1864 it had been selling for about 90. By March 26, it was at 140. That day the committee that had been hearing testimony regarding the bill reported it unfavorably—usually the prelude to its being shelved or defeated—and Harlem dropped immediately to 101. The legislators could have covered their shorts at that point and made a lot of money. But, apparently, they had not learned or did not heed one of the Street's oldest truisms: bears make money and bulls make money, but pigs don't make money. They held on, hoping to see it drop to 50.

Vanderbilt quietly called on his allies, notably John M. Tobin and Leonard Jerome. Together they pooled no less than $5 million—a huge sum at that time—and set about buying all the Harlem stock that was offered. On March 29, Harlem opened at the first auction at the New York Stock Exchange at 109. By the afternoon auction, however, it was at 125. By the end of April, it was at 224, and Vanderbilt and his allies were informed that they now owned 137,000 shares, while only 110,000 shares had been issued. The rest had been sold by the shorts to the men who now owned all the stock there was.

"Five hundred strong men," Fowler wrote, "hard of head and deep of coffer," were in the Commodore's grasp.[17] Asked what to do, he bellowed, "Put it to a thousand!"[18]

Fortunately, Leonard Jerome counseled Vanderbilt to temper justice with some self-interested mercy. He pointed out that with Harlem at a thousand, half the houses on the Street would fail and a panic would result so awesome that no one could predict the outcome. "The Commodore," the powerful broker Henry Clews cackled gleefully in his memoirs, "yielded to that touch of nature that makes all the world akin, and under the magnetism of Jerome's prudent entreaty, like Pharaoh with the Israelites, agreed to let the Legislature go—at 285 for Harlem."[19]

The second Harlem corner was over and there would not be another. Indeed, for a full generation on Wall Street, the phrase "short of Harlem" meant much the same thing as "up the creek."

And Vanderbilt would, until his death in 1877, enjoy a reputation and a stature such as no other man has had on Wall Street before or since. In 1869, England's *Fraser's Magazine* reported that among the denizens of Wall Street, Vanderbilt "assumes the royal dignity and moral tone of a Gaetulian lion among the hyenas and jackals of the desert."

But for all his power and reputation on Wall Street, Vanderbilt was never of the Street. He was out to build an empire in railroads, not buy and sell stock. In 1867 he was asked to become president of the New York Central, and he soon merged it with his Hudson River Railroad. This put him in direct competition with the Erie, which likewise ran from New York to Buffalo, although on a far less geographically favorable route. Had the Erie been competently run, Vanderbilt would undoubtedly have ignored it and allowed his competitive advantages to win the lion's share of the traffic.

But the Erie soon fell under the sway of Daniel Drew and two younger men, Jay Gould and Jim Fisk. To the triumvirate, Drew brought a total lack of scrupulosity, Gould financial genius, and Fisk a talent for showmanship so primal it is still remembered on the Street. Together they gave the Commodore no end of grief. And when he decided he had no choice but to go into the Street and buy control of Erie, all hell broke loose.

CHAPTER SIX

"WHO . . . COULD BLAME THEM FOR DOING WHAT THEY PLEASED?"

There has never been another speculative football on Wall Street to equal the Erie, with its debt-heavy, crazy-quilt capital structure; its politically determined route; and lack of rules and public accountability that are now taken for granted. The sheer speculative genius of the major players in the Erie game enabled them to take advantage of these qualities and repeatedly lure the unsuspecting into Erie securities.

"The mania seemed to possess everybody," *Fraser's Magazine* told its readers in 1869. "Old-fashioned merchants abandoned the principles of a lifetime and *'took a flyer,'* or in other words, bought a few hundred shares of Erie. Professional men, tired of their slow gains; clerks sick of starvation salaries; clergymen, dissatisfied with a niggardly stipend, followed fast in the same course. Even the fair sex, practically asserting women's rights under the cover of a broker, dabbled in Erie shares."[1]

Coincidentally, the mania in Erie and an important new technology, the stock ticker, came along at the same time. The telegraph had made possible the rapid dissemination of prices across the entire country. But a telegraph line requires skilled operators at each end to function. In 1867, however, Edward A. Calahan produced the first stock ticker, a mechanical device that could print out, on a paper tape, stock prices sent to it by telegraph from the floor of the exchange. Now, instead of getting just periodic reports on the action on the floor, every broker in the country could follow that action trade by trade. With the outbreak of the Erie wars, they had plenty to follow.

By far the most important speculator in Erie was Daniel Drew, who was also a member of its board of directors. Even at the time, Drew's campaigns in Erie were the stuff of legend. William Worthington Fowler, an ardent speculator himself, wrote of Drew that "Erie was like a one-stringed Chinese lyre in his hands, on which he played two tunes: when its price was high, he sang 'who'll buy my Erye? Who'll buy my valuable Erye? Buy it, oh buy!'

"When it was low, he sang 'who'll sell me Erye, who'll sell me worthless Erye? Sell me Erye, sell, sell!'

"And the Street listening entranced to his mellifluous voice, bought it of him at a very high price, and sold it to him at a very low price. Every night Uncle Daniel dreamed of money-bags, and every day his dreams came true. He coined money out of his musical performances on his one-stringed Chinese lyre—Erye."[2]

The naive weren't Drew's only victims. In the fall of 1864, John Tobin and Leonard Jerome moved to corner Erie stock. They borrowed money from Drew to help finance their effort, and he in turn agreed not to sell Erie if it was above a certain price, to make the corner that much cheaper to obtain. The price of Erie reached 102 in early November, but then sagged. By early the following year, it was down to 80. Behind the fall in price was a series of short sales by—who else?—Daniel Drew, who was cheerfully violating his promise to Jerome and Tobin. Next he persuaded a friendly judge to issue an injunction against the Erie paying dividends and then suddenly called in his loan to Jerome and Tobin. They were forced to sell Erie to pay him back.

Total panic in Erie ensued. "Grant and Sherman were pounding at the gates of Richmond," Fowler wrote, "and another stampede now took place" on Wall Street. ". . . They who had bought Erie at 80, and thought it cheap at that, now sold it at 45 and said it was not worth 20. It was offered and sold in blocks of five thousand and ten thousand shares. As fast as it reared itself up, fresh blows threw it back lower than before. It found bottom at 42."[3]

Commodore Vanderbilt, disgusted with such shenanigans, resigned from the Erie board in 1865. He was becoming increasingly interested in the New York Central and by the end of 1867 was that company's president. With his railroad interests now running as far west as the Great Lakes, Vanderbilt began looking at New York railroads from a wider perspective. He realized intuitively that railroads were inherently a volume business. With high capital costs and schedules that meant that trains ran regardless of whether they were empty or full, railroads had to fight for business or go broke. Thus price wars were a common feature of the nineteenth-century railroad industry (as, for precisely the same reason, they are of the deregulated airline industry today). The only way to prevent them were agreements—cartels—among competing railroads.

Three railroads fed the commerce of the Middle West into New York City (along with the still heavily utilized Erie Canal): the Central, the Erie, and the Pennsylvania. With Vanderbilt at the helm, the Central was certain to be well managed and honestly run. The Pennsylvania, under Thomas Scott, was also known to put the interests of its stockholders first. The wild card in the deck was the Erie. As long as the Erie retained its self-interested management, any agreements among the three railroads wouldn't be worth the paper they were printed on. Because of this situation, the Commodore was determined to secure a powerful position on the Erie's new board, to be elected on October 8, 1867.

He had no trouble finding allies, in particular a group in Boston with enough stock to control the election and throw Drew off the board. But Drew, who had known the Commodore well since steamboating days, called on Vanderbilt and convinced him that it would be best if Drew stayed on it. He promised to be Vanderbilt's faithful representative and to keep an eye on the Boston group in turn. As Vanderbilt had been bad-mouthing Drew all over the Street, they devised a face-saving strategy for his change of heart.

Drew was duly defeated for reelection to the board, but the very next day the newly elected Levi Underwood resigned and Drew was elected to replace him. Drew was even given back his old job as treasurer of the Erie, which he had not held since the mid-1850s. Also elected to the board were two men virtually unknown on Wall Street—indeed several of the newspapers misspelled their names. But Jay Gould and Jim Fisk were not to remain obscure for long.

A generation younger than Vanderbilt and Drew, Gould had been born on a farm in upstate New York. Physically he was small and unhealthy. A reporter who covered him closely wrote in his memoirs that "I saw him take the plunge in the Turkish bath at Saratoga. His arms were small, his chest was hollow, his face was tawny and sallow, and his legs! Well, I never saw such a prominent 'bull' that had such insignificant calves. Perhaps—perhaps you could not put a napkin ring over his foot and push it up to his knees; I am not certain."[4] But whatever Gould lacked in physical stature, he more than made up for in brains and determination. All he wanted was to be rich. He would spend his short life becoming exactly that and nothing else.

Jim Fisk, on the other hand, was extraordinarily robust, although even by the lenient standards of the nineteenth century, overweight, and wanted nothing so much as to have a good time in life. "Boldness! boldness!" wrote Fowler while Fisk still lived, "twice, thrice, and four times. Impudence! cheek! brass! unparalleled, unapproachable, sublime!"[5]

Born in southern Vermont and, like Gould, of old New England stock, Fisk was the son of a peddler. When still in his teens, he took over his father's business (hiring his father as an employee) and vastly expanded it. By the time the Civil War broke out, Fisk, now in his early twenties, had sold his peddling business and was working for the Boston dry-goods firm of Jordan, Marsh. With his talents for salesmanship, he successfully negotiated contracts with the federal government. Further, he proved particularly adept at smuggling cotton north through the federal embargo for the firm's use.

At the end of the war, Fisk left Jordan, Marsh, the firm buying out his interest for $65,000, a small fortune at the time. With no experience in the stock market whatever, he opened a brokerage firm at 38 Broad Street, right across from the newly built New York Stock Exchange building. He tried the same tactics that had worked so well for him in Washington with army supply officers and politicians. But Wall Street was not Washington. And while the players there ate his food and drank his champagne, they also took him to the cleaners. He was soon wiped out.

But Fisk quickly bounced back. He negotiated the sale of Drew's money-losing Stonington Line of steamboats for $2,300,000, and Drew was so pleased that he helped Fisk get reestablished on Wall Street, using him as one of his numerous brokers.

When elected to the Erie board, Gould and Fisk apparently met for the first time. They could hardly have been more different. Fowler wrote of Fisk that "he is continuously boiling over with jokes, good, bad, and indifferent,"[6] while Jay Gould's niece described her uncle as "exceedingly quiet. His words were both few and carefully chosen. He was perfectly poised always."[7] But the two were canny enough to immediately recognize that they each had what the other lacked. Together they would make a most remarkable team.

It took Daniel Drew only three months to betray Vanderbilt's trust on the Erie board by joining with other members of the board in a pool to bull the price of Erie upward, exactly the sort of stunt Vanderbilt abhorred. With his undoubted talents in speculation—he was often referred to in the newspapers of the day as "the speculative director"—Drew was placed in charge of the operation. But while the stock reached as high as 79 in January 1868, it then dropped suddenly to 71, signaling that a bear raid was in progress. The newspapers had no doubt whatever who was behind it. "The emissaries of the speculative director," the *Herald* reported, "exerted themselves all day to create a panic, and told more falsehoods than usual about stocks in general and Erie in particular."[8]

Drew had lent money to one of the members of the bull pool—it is not entirely clear whom—so that he could buy Erie on his own. Suspicious, the borrower checked on where the stock he had bought had come from and was horrified to discover that it had come from one of the pool's own brokers. He and the other members of the pool went to Drew and demanded that Drew put the price of Erie up as he had agreed to.

"I sold all our Erie at a profit," Drew responded calmly, "and am now ready to divide the money."[9]

Charles Francis Adams—whose *Chapters of Erie,* written with his brother Henry, is one of the early masterpieces of investigative journalism—explained what Drew had been up to: "The controller of the pool had actually lent the money of the pool to one of the members of the pool to enable him to buy up the stock of the pool; and having thus quietly saddled him with it, the controller proceeded to divide the profits, and calmly returned to the victim a portion of his own money as a share of the proceeds."[10]

Frank Work, who had been placed on the board specifically as Vanderbilt's eyes and ears, may have been Drew's victim in this scheme, and he certainly kept the Commodore fully informed as to what was going on. Vanderbilt was getting nervous. He wanted the Erie to join him and the Pennsylvania in dividing their New York City traffic evenly, allowing everyone to make a profit. But the Erie board promptly defeated the proposal, with only Frank Work voting affirmatively. The majority said that the arrangement was unfair and that the Erie's share of the New York traffic should be larger.

But Vanderbilt recognized the board's action for what it was: a declaration of war. He was determined to control the Erie one way or another. If he could not control it through its directors, he would control it through another means: he would buy it. "Vanderbilt was not accustomed to failure," Adams wrote, "and in this case the sense of treachery, the bitter consciousness of having been outwitted in the presence of all Wall Street, gave a peculiar sting to the rebuff. A long succession of victories had intensified his natural arrogance, and he was by no means disposed even apart from the failure of his cherished plans, to sit down and nurse an impotent wrath in the presence of an injured prestige. Foiled in intrigue, he must now have recourse to his favorite weapon—the brute force of his millions."[11]

But even with his vast fortune, Vanderbilt was undertaking a considerable project. Officially there were 251,050 shares of Erie stock in public hands, but that number did not include a few factors. In 1866, Drew had loaned the company $3,480,000, taking as collateral 28,000 unissued shares and $3 million in the bonds that were endlessly convertible into 30,000 shares of stock and back again. Thus Drew could expand or contract the floating supply of Erie shares by over 10 percent anytime it suited his speculative purposes to do so.

Further, since Drew was now treasurer of the Erie, he was in the perfect position to manufacture even more stock if necessary. Vanderbilt needed to prevent Drew from doing this if he hoped to buy up the floating supply. So he turned to Judge George G. Barnard of the New York State Supreme Court. (Then, as now, in New York's topsy-turvy judicial nomenclature, the Supreme Court is not the top but the bottom court on the ladder.) Barnard, according to Stedman, was "a Tammany Helot, numbered among the Vanderbilt properties."[12]

We forget today just how utterly corrupt American government was in the mid–nineteenth century, and nowhere was it more corrupt than in New York, the country's most populous and richest state. The spoils system ensured that the bureaucracy was both incompetent and venal. That the political clubhouses (Tammany was the most famous of these) had a monopoly on the political machinery needed to get elected ensured that many officeholders would be as well.

So flagrant did the bribery and chicanery become that as early as 1857, the lawyer George Templeton Strong wrote in his diary, "Heaven be praised for all its mercies, the Legislature of the State of New York has adjourned."[13] A few years later, Horace Greeley wrote in the *Tribune* that he did not think it possible "that another body so reckless, not merely of right but of decency—not merely corrupt but shameless—will be assembled in our halls of legislation within the next ten years."[14] Greeley could hardly have been more wrong.

The explosion of business and money on Wall Street only made the politicians greedier. In 1868 the legislature actually passed a bill, duly signed into law by the governor, that, in effect, legalized bribery. "No *conviction*," the bill read, "shall be had under this act on the testimony of the other party to the offense, unless such evidence be *corroborated* in its material parts by other evidence."[15] In that pre-electronic age, this meant that as long as the legislator took his bribe in cash and in private, conviction was impossible. As Hudson C. Tanner, secretary of the New York Assembly before he wrote a tell-all book in the 1880s, explained, "The political cry of 'an honest ballot and a fair count' has been perverted so as to apply more to an honest count of the boodle than an honest count of the ballot."[16]

The judiciary was in little better shape than the legislature. "The Supreme Court," wrote George Templeton Strong, in his diary, "is our *Cloaca Maxima*, with lawyers for its rats. But my simile does that rodent an injustice, for the rat is a remarkably clean animal."[17] The judges in New York State had been elected since the 1840s, and this made them dependent on the political machines. By the late 1860s, *Fraser's Magazine* had to explain to its doubtless bemused English readers that "in New York there is a custom among litigants as peculiar to that city, it is to be hoped, as it is supreme within it, of retaining a judge as well as a lawyer. Especially in such litigation as that now impending [regarding the Erie War], it is absolutely essential to each party to have some magistrate in whom they could place implicit confidence in an hour of sudden emergency."[18]

The businessmen who came of age in the utter governmental corruption of the post–Civil War era, such as Andrew Carnegie, John D. Rockefeller, and J. P. Morgan, would always, and entirely understandably, look upon government as a part of the problem of regulating the marketplace effectively, not part of the solution to it. They would always seek to rely on their own resources to prevent chaos in the marketplace rather than attempt to utilize what was, in fact, the most venal institution in the country. Liberal historians of a later era have almost universally failed to note this fact when discussing the "robber barons."

On January 26, 1868, Vanderbilt prevailed upon Judge Barnard to issue an injunction forbidding the Erie from converting any bonds into stock and forbidding Daniel Drew personally from "selling, transferring, delivering, disposing of or parting with"[19] any Erie stock in his control. Vanderbilt now thought he had Drew thoroughly hog-tied and ordered his brokers to go into the market and quietly begin buying Erie, confident that he would soon obtain control. But the Commodore badly underestimated Drew, who, as the *Herald* explained at the time, "laughs at injunctions."[20]

Drew went right on converting stock and even issuing more convertible bonds, instantly converting them to stock as well. On February 29 he was seen entering the brokerage office of William Heath and Company at 19 Broad Street. "A few moments later," Fowler reported, "that office was resonant with the rustling of fifty thousand shares of fresh, crisp Erie certificates, like the chirping of locusts at noontide in July."[21] The Commodore didn't yet know it, of course, but the floating supply of Erie stock had just increased by 20 percent.

Drew also directed the Erie's loyal upstate judges to suspend

Frank Work from the board, while another judge, sitting in Barnard's district, forbade the Erie board from doing any business *without* Frank Work present. A third Supreme Court judge, named Gilbert, sitting in Brooklyn, ordered the Erie to continue converting bonds into stock on demand. Thus Drew, Fisk, and Gould found themselves in a nearly ideal legal situation. As Stedman explained, "Since they were forbidden by Barnard to convert bonds into stock, and forbidden by Gilbert to refuse to do so, who but the most captious could blame them for doing as they pleased?"[22]

Wall Street went wild. "The whole market hung on one word—Erie," Fowler wrote just the following year. "The strident voice of George Henriques, the Vice President of the Open Board, was heard calling off in quick succession, government bonds, state bonds, Pacific mail, New York Central, then a pause, a shadow rippled across his face and a shiver ran through the hall as he ejaculated in a tone still more strident—Erie! For ten minutes bedlam seemed to have broken loose. Every operator and broker was on his feet in an instant, screaming and gesticulating. The different Vanderbilt brokers stood each in the center of a circle, wheeling as on a pivot from right to left, brandishing their arms and snatching at all the stock offered them. As the presiding officer's hammer fell and his hoarse voice thundered out 'that will do, gentlemen. I shall fine any other offer,' Erie stood at 80. The crowd, leaving the other stocks not yet called, poured into the street, where nothing was heard but Erie. Vanderbilt's brokers had orders to buy every share offered, and under their enormous purchases the price rose, by twelve o'clock, to 83."[23]

And if all that was heard on the Street was Erie, all that was heard at the brokerage house of William Heath & Company was "the rustling of fifty thousand fresh shares, as they dropped from the plump, jeweled fingers of Jim Fisk, Jr."[24] Fisk, enjoying himself thoroughly as always, remarked that "if this printing press don't break down, I'll be damned if I don't give the old hog all he wants of Erie."[25]

The word of the new shares raced through Wall Street at record speed, and the price on the street dropped "like lead" to 71. Vanderbilt was now in trouble, as he had borrowed money on his Erie shares to buy more. Any sign of weakness on his part and Erie could collapse, setting off a general panic in which even his vast wealth could be destroyed. But in his deepest peril he never flinched. He ordered his brokers to keep on buying and they pushed the price back up to 76⅛. At the end of the day the Commodore and his allies held almost two hundred thousand shares of Erie. But was it enough for control? No one, not even the Commodore, had the faintest idea.

Fearing, quite correctly, that the various exchanges would rule the new shares not "good delivery"—effectively rendering them worthless—Drew, Fisk, and Gould hastened to convert the proceeds to cash, draining New York of much of its money supply as they packed $7 million in greenbacks into a carpetbag.

Early on the morning of March 11, Vanderbilt, undoubtedly in a towering rage, sent his lawyers to roust Judge Barnard out of bed. Barnard quickly issued arrest warrants, instructing the sheriff of New York County to put them into effect. Several members of the Erie board, meanwhile, were "holding high festival over their triumphs at the offices of the company at the foot of Duane Street. . . . Uncle Daniel's corrugated visage was set in a chronic chuckle. Jay Gould's financial eye beamed and glittered and the blond bulk of James Fisk, Jr., was unctuous with jokes."[26]

The party spirit evaporated instantly once they heard that the sheriff was on his way. If they were arrested, they knew that the courts would belong to Vanderbilt, and he would have no mercy on them. They had to get beyond the reach of New York law as soon as possible. "In fact," reported the *Herald,* which, like all the other newspapers, was having a field day, "so complete a clearing out has not taken place since the Fenians fled from Dublin on the night of the suspension of *habeas corpus.*"[27]

Within minutes, the policeman walking the beat on Duane Street "observed a squad of respectably dressed, but terrified looking men, loaded down with packages of greenbacks, account books, bundles of papers tied up with red tape, emerge in haste and disorder from the Erie building. Thinking perhaps that something illicit had been taking place, and these individuals might be plunderers playing a bold game in open daylight, he approached them, but soon found out his mistake. They were only the executive committee of the Erie company, flying the wrath of the Commodore, and laden with the spoils of their recent campaign."[28]

Drew, who at age seventy didn't fancy a spell in jail, and several others took the ferry over to Jersey City with the money and the company's books. Fisk and Gould stayed behind. That evening they dined at Delmonico's, New York's fanciest restaurant, with lookouts posted in all directions. Midway through dinner, they learned that the sheriff was on his way. Fleeing Delmonico's, they made their way to the Hudson River waterfront and quickly negotiated with a steamship captain for the use of a boat and two sailors.

The Hudson in those days was always crowded with maritime traffic, and on this moonless night it was also blanketed with fog. The sailors, trying to evade the ferries that were crisscrossing back and forth, soon lost their sense of direction, and the boat was nearly swamped in a ferry's wake. They tried to hail another passing ferryboat, and when it didn't respond, they grabbed hold of the guard surrounding one of the paddle wheels. For a second or two, Gould, Fisk—and the history of Wall Street—were on the edge of disaster before the two men were able to swing themselves aboard and make good their escape to New Jersey.

The two sides of the Erie battle were at a standoff. The Erie directors had $7 million of the Commodore's money while he had one hundred thousand shares of worthless stock. But Vanderbilt had New York, and the directors couldn't come home until they had settled with him. The newspapers, meanwhile, filled their pages with stories about the Wall Street war. *Harper's Weekly* noted that the Erie War "entirely superseded public interest in the impeachment of the President."[29]

The directors set up shop in Taylor's Hotel on the Jersey City waterfront, soon dubbed Fort Taylor by the press. It was indeed fortified by a contingent of policemen from the Erie Railway, men rowing patrol offshore, and even three twelve-pounder cannons. The Erie Railway, with its eastern terminal no longer in Piermont but in Jersey City, dominated the town's economy, and the Erie directors had taken care to shower the local authorities with such perks as free passes. These authorities were naturally eager to help in any way they could.

In New Jersey, power shifted from Drew to Fisk and Gould. Drew, comfortable only in his old haunts, intensely disliked being cooped up in a small New Jersey hotel. And the other directors were only too well aware of Drew's capacity for double-dealing. As early as March 20, the *Herald* was reporting that "Mr. Drew has been kidnaped, not by the New York roughs, but by the directors."

While Drew and the others set up camp in New Jersey, the significant battles were actually being fought in the courts and the legislatures. Barnard appointed one of the Commodore's sons-in-law to be receiver of the proceeds of the stock sale he had previously forbidden to take place at all. An upstate judge then stayed that appointment, Barnard voided the stay, and when the son-in-law declined the appointment, Barnard appointed the Tammany politician Peter Sweeney in his place. Of course, what Sweeney was supposed to receive—the $7 million—was locked up in a New Jersey bank vault, and there was nothing for Sweeney to do. But that did not stop Barnard from awarding him $150,000 of the Erie Railway's money in compensation for his efforts.

Meanwhile, the Erie directors petitioned the New Jersey legislature for a New Jersey charter for the railroad. They feared that the New York courts might give Vanderbilt control of all Erie property in New York State, leaving them a head without a body. The New Jersey legislature, delighted to be able to poke a stick in the eye of its giant and haughty neighbor across the Hudson, rushed to pass the bill and send it on to the governor. They were in such a hurry, in fact, that they even neglected to notice their own interests and were dismayed when Vanderbilt lobbyists showed up in Trenton, ready, willing, and able to bribe them to defeat the bill.

Meanwhile, a bill was submitted in the legislature in Albany to legalize all that the Erie had already done and pretty much allowing it to do as it pleased in the future without regard to the interests of the stockholders. Even Judge Barnard—hardly a stranger to the practice of selling his office—was astonished by the bill's sweeping provisions, calling it "an act to legalize counterfeit money."[30]

Everyone realized the real purpose of this bill: to generate bribes from both sides. The legislators, reported *Fraser's Magazine,* "flocked to Albany like beeves to a cattle-mart. All were for sale, and each brought a price proportioned to his *weight.*"[31]

Jay Gould, who was one of the earliest businessmen to realize the importance of public relations in advancing corporate interests (although, for some reason, he never employed the techniques to improve his own poisonous public image), encouraged the idea that control of the Erie and the New York Central should not be in the hands of the same person, even hands so capable and honest as the Commodore's. He soon had the support of the *Herald* and other papers.

But he also went to Albany with a trunk that was, according to the *Herald,* "literally stuffed with thousand-dollar bills which are to be used for some mysterious purpose in connection with legislation on the subject of the bill now before the Legislature."[32] As soon as Vanderbilt learned of Gould's presence in Albany, he had him arrested and held on $500,000 bail, a sum that Gould produced instantly. Given the money that he was spreading about Albany, that was a small sum. Charles Francis Adams reported that one legislator had received $100,000 from one side to influence the legislation and $70,000 from the other to get out of town, which he did, becoming, in Adams's words, "a gentleman of elegant leisure."[33]

Vanderbilt was also perfectly willing to spend large sums to bribe the legislature, but he quickly realized that doing so might in the end prove a Pyrrhic victory. With public opinion turning sharply against his getting control of the Erie while he controlled the Central, the Commodore—practical as ever—decided to cut his losses. He sent a note to Drew suggesting a meeting. He wanted three things. First, he demanded that the worthless stock he had bought be taken off his hands at a price near what he had paid for it. Second, Richard Schell and Frank Work, his men on the Erie board, had to be fully compensated for all they had lost at the hands of their fellow directors. And third, Drew had to agree to withdraw from all future management of the Erie. What Vanderbilt had always wanted most of all was not ownership of the Erie, but that it be run in a businesslike manner.

The deal was struck on Sunday, April 19. It did not take long for the news to reach Albany. "Suddenly," wrote Adams, "at the very last moment . . . a rumor ran through Albany as of some great public disaster, spreading panic and terror through hotel and corridor. The observer was reminded of the dark days of the war, when tidings came of some great defeat, as that on the Chickahominy or at Fredericksburg. In a moment the lobby was smitten with despair, and the cheeks of the legislators were blanched, for it was reported that Vanderbilt had withdrawn his opposition to the bill."[34]

Legislators who had not yet made a deal with Gould now rushed to his suite in the Delavan House, Albany's leading hotel. "It is said that prices came down wonderfully," the *Herald* reported on the twenty-first. "Those who had been demanding $5,000 were now willing to take anything not less than $100. The great Erie coffers were closed, however. There was no longer any need for votes." The next day, the *Herald* was all mock concern for the legislators, noting that their legal compensation of three dollars a day wouldn't pay the cigar bills of most of them. "What is to be done, then," it asked, "in this extremity for the preservation of the credit of the Solons at Albany?"

When the dust settled, Drew had resigned from the board and the treasurer's job, Frank Work and Richard Schell were paid $429,500 by the Erie to drop their suits against it, and Gould and Fisk were made president and treasurer, respectively, of the railroad. As for the one hundred thousand shares printed up to prevent the Commodore from gaining control, they were artfully unloaded on the market over the next few months in a way designed not to depress the price of Erie. Of course the proceeds of those sales went to Vanderbilt, and the stockholders of Erie saw their equity diluted by 40 percent.

The settlement had cost the Erie about $9 million, about $2 million more than the proceeds of the sale of the watered stock. As Fisk and Gould settled into their new offices, "the first thing we found," said Fisk, "was a very well-dusted treasury."[35] Gould and Fisk began issuing more convertible bonds, most of which were quickly converted to stock. By the end of that year there would be almost four hundred thousand shares of Erie in the market. Gould sold much of this new stock in London, where it would be safely out of the New York market.

Gould, like Drew, found the Erie a perfect platform from which to manipulate the market. He organized a bear trap, inviting Drew to join it by putting in $4 million, although Drew was to be a passive partner. Then to force up interest rates, he began drying up the money supply in New York by writing checks against bank accounts and having those checks certified, forcing the bank to keep the money on hand pending the presentation of the check. He then took the certified checks to other banks, where he used them as collateral on which to borrow greenbacks, further constricting the money supply.

By the end of October the market was becoming more and more volatile, and a new weekly volume record of 647,000 shares was set while Erie stock sank to 38½, half what it had been in the spring. Drew panicked and withdrew from further participation in the pool. In fact he shorted Erie stock on his own to the amount of seventy thousand shares. By Saturday, November 14, Erie stood at 36⅝, and Drew anticipated further declines. But when the Regular Board held its Saturday-morning auction, fully eighty thousand shares of Erie traded, and the price jumped to 52, thanks to Gould and Fisk, who had gone long in Erie and effectively achieved a corner, while unlocking the money supply. Drew's only hope was to hold off disaster until the Cunard liner *Russia* arrived on the twenty-third, with fresh supplies of Erie stock from London.

He tried to use the courts to do so, but was outmaneuvered by Gould and Fisk, who, simply by controlling one of the country's largest railroads, had tremendous influence with the state's judges. When it was all over, Drew had lost $1.3 million, his reputation for invincibility, and his position as a major player on Wall Street. But Drew's days were numbered anyway, for other forces were moving to change Wall Street's ways.

London, still by far the largest securities market in the world, was waking up to the fact that another giant was aborning across the Atlantic. London's market cap at this point was about $10 billion, while Wall Street's was about $3 billion and increasing far faster than London's. Wall Street brokers were increasingly active in the London market, thanks to the new Atlantic cable, in operation since 1866. By 1870, Wall Streeters were running up cable bills that amounted to a million dollars a year. But Londoners were appalled by Wall Street's Wild West ways. The *Times* of London noted that they "seem likely to create distrust as to the possibility of any legal, equitable control being exercised for the protection of investments in American corporations."[36]

Wall Street's brokers, as well, wanted reform. They were in the business for the long term, making their money a little at a time on commissions. The speculators, many of them corporate managers as well, looked only to the next big killing. In response to the out-of-control Erie speculation, the weekly *Commercial and Financial Chronicle,* the *Barron's* of its day, proposed a law that would have required:

(1) That directors shall make no new issues of stock except by and with the consent of two-thirds of the stockholders in interest.
(2) That no new shares shall be issued without first offering them to the existing stockholders, and that all issues shall be made openly and after due notice.
(3) That all stock companies shall keep a record of the amount of their stock outstanding, in the office of some well-known financial institution, at all times open to the inspection of the shareholders, or of parties holding the shares as collateral for loans.
(4) That these requirements shall apply to stock issued in the way of dividends as well as for other purposes.
(5) Any violations of these provisions should be constituted a criminal offense, subject to punishment and fine.[37]

This is, of course, the basis of American securities law today. But in the 1860s it could not be enacted. The federal government did not regard financial markets as part of its mandate, and the New York State legislature was hardly likely to reform a system that supplied its members so handsomely with bribes.

But if state or federal government could not bring about change, Wall Street itself was able to put these reforms in place. The New York Stock Exchange and the Open Board, the two largest organizations on the Street, began moving closer together as they perceived that the interests of their members and their customers in knowing the amount of each company's stock were identical. The brokers who dominated the exchanges were, of course, perfectly happy to make commissions buying and selling dubious stock for the customers' accounts. Lending money on that stock, however, was a different matter altogether. If the number of shares in a corporation could be doubled or halved at any time, how could anyone know the value of an individual share?

On November 30, 1868, the two boards issued identical regulations requiring the registration of all securities sold at their auctions, and thirty days' notice of any new issues. Most companies complied immediately, but the Erie refused. While Gould's coup against Drew was still under way, the New York Stock Exchange sent a delegation to Gould to find out the true situation in Erie. Gould told them, not necessarily honestly, how much stock was outstanding but flatly refused to tell them whether he planned to issue more.

After refusing to comply with the November 30 edict, the Erie was thrown off the two boards. It then briefly appeared at the Mining Exchange, but that board's lease from the New York Stock Exchange did not allow it to trade railroad stocks, and the Erie was soon homeless again. Gould founded the National Stock Exchange to handle Erie. But the exchange attracted few brokers and fewer customers. In 1869, the Open Board merged with the New York Stock Exchange and created a stock exchange large enough to dominate Wall Street. It was soon obvious that the Erie needed the newly merged New York Stock Exchange far more than the exchange needed it.

On September 13, 1869, Gould finally complied with the new regulations and Erie was readmitted to trading on the big board. By that time, the number of shares outstanding was seven hundred thousand, not far from double what Gould less than a year earlier had said existed.

For the first time, with the merger of the two exchanges, it became crucial for major brokers to belong to the exchange. Thus, they, too, had to conform to its regulations, which not only grew in number but were more rigorously enforced. Wall Street was profoundly changed. As the Wall Street writer James K. Medbery explained at the time, "It remains for the brokers of the Stock Exchange to decide whether they will seek the petty profits of a speculation marred by grave faults, or will cast their influence still farther and with more strenuous emphasis against the encroachment of the cliques. The former means isolation. The latter will be prelusive of an expansion in international relations which will make New York imperial, and Wall Street what its pivotal position demands and allows, the paramount financial center of the globe."[38]

The brokers took Medbery's advice. Effective self-regulation of the New York stock market would greatly increase in the next few years. And so would business. Thanks in part to technology, especially the Atlantic cable and the stock ticker, volume would steadily grow. Both the old sit-down auctions of the Regular Board and the continuous auction of the Open Board continued separately after the merger for two years. But in 1871 the sit-down auction was finally abandoned. Seats on the New York Stock Exchange—which had become a salable property right in 1868—became purely symbolic.

Wall Street was finally growing up, but its adolescence wasn't quite over yet.

CHAPTER SEVEN

"The Bulls, Triumphant, Faced Their Foes"

Because gold was then to the world's financial system what the sun is to the solar system, the attempt by Jay Gould and Jim Fisk to corner the metal in the New York market in September of 1869 must rank as the greatest single act of financial derring-do in the history of the Street. Even at the time, Wall Street's severest critics could not help admiring the sheer audacity of it. "Of all financial operations," wrote Henry Adams in 1871, "cornering gold is the most brilliant and the most dangerous, and possibly the very hazard and splendor of the attempt were the reasons of its fascination to Mr. Jay Gould."[1]

At midcentury, gold was legal tender in every major country in the world. Since 1821 the Bank of England had been on the gold standard, and Great Britain was at its apogee as a world power. It possessed roughly 25 percent of world GDP at this time—somewhat more than what the United States has today—and dominated world trade. This financial dominance made the pound sterling the basis of international trade, and the Bank of England the world's de facto central bank.

But because of the Civil War, the United States was not on the gold standard. While the spread between greenbacks and gold had much diminished with the Union victory in 1865, it had not disappeared. Further, an obscure provision of law regarding greenbacks still lingered in the U.S. Code, like an unexploded artillery shell on an old battlefield. When greenbacks had first been issued in 1862, Congress had passed a law requiring that they circulate at par with gold. Legislators soon realized, however, that this provision, due to Gresham's law, would have resulted in the almost immediate disappearance of gold from the money supply, as it vanished into mattresses and safe-deposit boxes.

Congress quickly repealed that provision of the Legal Tender Act. But what they didn't repeal was another provision requiring that contracts that specified payments in gold could be satisfied, at par, with greenbacks. This provision had always been ignored as utterly unfeasible, but its continued existence formed the first element of Gould's scheme.

By 1869 gold trading was averaging $70 million a day in the Gold Room, most of it speculative in nature. Indeed, the margin requirements were so small that the chances of making a fortune—or, equally, of being wiped out—in a few minutes were higher in the Gold Room than almost anywhere else in the world.

The next year Charles J. Osborne of the Gold Exchange Bank testified before a congressional committee chaired by future president James A. Garfield investigating the gold panic that "if a man has a thousand dollars, he can go and buy five millions of gold if he is so inclined."[2] Jay Gould, a little more conservative in his estimates, thought that $100,000 was enough to buy contracts for $20 million in gold. But Gould, who as president of the Erie Railway commanded far more than $100,000 in ready cash, did not think there was $20 million in real gold available to the New York market on any given day. Testifying before Congress the following year, he guessed that there was perhaps $14 million in gold certificates and maybe $3–4 million in gold coin.

The scarcity of actual gold was another element of Gould's audacious scheme. The third was that while the Gold Room was full of speculators, it was also used by respectable merchants in the ordinary course of their business. Because gold was the medium of exchange in international trade, merchants who sold abroad were paid in gold. But time would elapse between when the contract was made and when the gold was delivered. If the price of gold declined, relative to greenbacks, in that period, the merchant would lose money. To prevent such a happening, merchants habitually sold short in the Gold Room an amount equal to the amount they were owed. Thus if the price changed in the interval, they would make in profit in the Gold Room what they lost on their contract, or vice versa. This hedging, as it is called, was and remains one of the principal, indeed vital, functions of any commodities market. But these international merchants, with assets far greater than the speculative riffraff who also operated in the Gold Room and with reputations to protect, were much more vulnerable to someone such as Gould.

So Gould saw his opportunity and decided to take it. With comparatively little money he could buy contracts for gold that amounted to far more than all the gold available in New York. Among his victims would be many of New York's biggest merchants—often necessarily short in the market—who could be squeezed very hard indeed. And, if things did not go as planned, any contracts that Gould made in the Gold Room—which necessarily specified settlement in gold—were unenforceable as law. If necessary, they could simply be repudiated, and in the airy words of Jim Fisk (who joined with Gould only late in the game), "nothing [would be] lost save honor."[3]

There was, of course, one very large problem. The federal Treasury housed more than half the country's gold supply in its vaults. At the subtreasury alone on Wall Street at the head of Broad, more than $100 million in gold was at the ready. Therefore any attempt to corner gold could be broken with the dispatch of a single telegram from Washington. To make sure that this never occurred, Gould had to suborn the United States government into, at the least, benevolent inactivity.

Gould had never met President Grant, but an interview was easy to arrange. Gould cultivated a friendship with Abel Rathbone Corbin, a speculator and a lawyer who, the previous year, had married President Grant's middle-aged spinster sister and was thus at least a quasi-member of the president's family. To obtain Corbin's loyalty, Gould offered to buy for him $1.5 million in gold without Corbin's having to put up a cent. That meant that for every one-dollar rise in the price of gold, Corbin stood to make a $15,000 profit at no risk to himself. (It wouldn't cost Gould much, either, as it could be bought on margin.) Corbin readily accepted the offer, asking only that the gold be put in his wife's name.

When President and Mrs. Grant passed through New York on their way to Fall River, Massachusetts, early that summer, Gould met them at the Corbins' house and escorted them to the pier where the steamboat that was to take them to Fall River was moored. The ship, through no coincidence whatever, was owned by Jim Fisk, who was waiting for them there. Gould, Fisk, and several other New York businessmen accompanied Grant to Fall River, and Gould tried to sound him out on his position regarding gold, but Grant was not very forthcoming. Several times more during Grant's summer travels, Gould managed to be by the president's side, once at the theater—which was owned by Fisk—where his proximity was widely noted.

When the post of assistant treasurer in New York fell vacant, Gould and Corbin convinced the president to appoint General Daniel Butterfield. The assistant treasurer ran the New York subtreasury, and any order to sell gold would have to be executed by him. It was vital to Gould's scheme to have a man under obligation to him in that job.

Butterfield, whose family owned the Butterfield Express Company, a forerunner of American Express, had had a successful Civil War army career and had won the Congressional Medal of Honor. He also won a curious immortality by writing the music to taps, and his statue stands today on Riverside Drive in New York, not far from Grant's Tomb. But shortly after his appointment, Gould made him a loan of $10,000 with no collateral and, it seems, opened a gold account for him with no margin.

Gould and his pool continued to buy gold all summer, but as summer advanced and crops were sold abroad, merchants sold short in the Gold Room to hedge their currency transactions. Under this selling, gold, as high as 140 on July 27, had by August 21 dropped to 131⅝. Regardless, Gould continued to prepare his bear trap. He managed to get the *New York Times* to print an editorial, written by Corbin, that appeared to be a statement of the government's belief that the price of gold should be allowed to rise freely. On September 2, as Grant and his wife passed once more through New York, this time on their way from Newport to Saratoga, the president breakfasted with Corbin, who again pushed the idea that the government should not interfere with the price of gold. Grant, who was an honest if often naive man, agreed to instruct the Treasury not to make any irregular sales of gold without consulting him.

Unbeknownst to the president, Gould was in the back hall listening to the conversation in the dining room.

By the middle of September, the pool held over $90 million in gold contracts, many times the supply available to the New York market as long as the U.S. Treasury did not sell any of its gold. Gould, as we have seen, a master of public relations, floated rumors that everyone in Washington was in on the deal completely. The following year, the head of the arbitration committee of the Gold Room (which settled disputes that arose there) testified that it was common knowledge that "the parties who . . . were manipulating the gold market had in league with them pretty much everybody in authority in the United States, beginning with President Grant and ending with the doorkeepers of Congress."[4] It is a measure of the profound corruption in American government at this time that the rumors that the government itself was a willing party to a conspiracy to corner gold were widely and easily accepted as fact.

By September 15 the price of gold had risen to 138 and the shorts were feeling the pinch as they had to put up the greenback equivalent of their short positions. Gould knew that these powerful men might well be leaning on Secretary of the Treasury George S. Boutwell to narrow the spread by selling Treasury gold. In a rare misjudgment, Gould overplayed his hand. He told Corbin to write his brother-in-law a letter detailing, once again, all the reasons for allowing the price of gold to be dictated by the market (which, under the circumstances, meant by Gould).

Gould had the letter delivered by private messenger to the president, who was now vacationing in Washington, Pennsylvania, a day's trip from New York. (The president, ever naive, had accepted Gould's offer of a private Erie Railway car to take him there.) The messenger delivered the letter to Grant's military secretary and constant companion, General Horace Porter, who gave it to the president. The president read the letter and told the messenger that he had no reply. Porter, curious, asked the president who the messenger was, and Grant was surprised, having assumed that it was just the local postman taking advantage of an opportunity to meet the president.

But when Porter assured the president that the messenger had come all the way from New York, Grant finally realized that he was being bamboozled. He knew that Corbin would never have employed a private messenger just to deliver an already familiar lecture on economics. Grant's wife happened to be writing a letter to Mrs. Corbin, and he instructed her to write, "Tell your husband that my husband is very much annoyed at your speculations. You must close them as quick as you can!"[5]

Gould, having received a telegram from the messenger—"Delivered. Alright"[6]—thought that all was in hand and now convinced Fisk to take an active part in the operation, not for his money but for his histrionic talents. From the start, Fisk had been cautious about an operation he thought risky in the extreme. But once Gould convinced him that Grant was in on the deal, "he joined the movement at once," Garfield reported after the hearings he chaired in the House of Representatives the following year, "and brought to its aid all the force of his magnetic and infectious enthusiasm. The malign influence which Catiline wielded over the reckless and abandoned youth of Rome, finds a fitting parallel in the power which Fisk carried into Wall Street, when . . . he swept into the Gold Room and defied both the Street and the Treasury."[7]

According to Fisk's testimony (a none-too-reliable historical source, to be sure), by the end of that week he held $50–60 million in gold contracts and had recruited his own, separate network of brokers to act for him as necessary. The increased buying had its effect. On Monday, September 20, the price of gold closed at 137⅜. The next day it nudged ahead to 137½. But on Wednesday, when Fisk himself appeared in the Gold Room for the first time, the price shot up to 141½.

That afternoon, Corbin's wife received the letter from her sister-in-law. Corbin, whose stock-in-trade was his access to his brother-in-law, was badly frightened and wanted out. Gould promised him $100,000 if he would shut up and not release the letter. Corbin, caught between titans, did nothing. But Gould realized that the game was up and it was time to bring his scheme to a close as quickly as possible.

While Fisk continued to bull the price of gold upward by his public statements and his public purchases in the Gold Room, Gould became a very quiet seller. But despite Gould's sales, the price of gold moved up again as the more cautious short sellers (who included nearly every important house on the Street) closed out their positions, reaching 143⅛. The volume exploded. Usually about $70 million on an average day, on Thursday, September 23, the Gold Exchange Bank cleared no less than $239 million.

The next morning dawned bright and clear, with the financial district crowded long before the official opening of trading in the Gold Room at ten o'clock. Gould and Fisk had set up a command post in the brokerage offices of William Heath and Company. When the market opened, Fisk instructed his principal broker to buy all the gold that was offered. By ten-thirty General Butterfield at the subtreasury telegraphed Washington that the price of gold had reached 150 and was climbing higher. The scene in the Gold Room was one of frantic excitement, and the *Herald* reported the next day that "it was a desperate battle between two hosts of gamblers, whose minds were quickened by the incessant plots, whose hearts were cold and their greed rapacious. Gold, Gold, Gold was the cry."[8]

The Gold Room, packed with increasingly desperate men, was a bedlam of shouting. The indicator, the clocklike device that showed the current price of gold, moved frantically up and down, trying to keep pace. Many others, in cities across the country, could not. Garfield reported, "The complicated mechanism of these indicators is moved by the electric current carried over telegraph wires directly from the Gold Room, and it is in evidence that in many instances these wires were melted or burned off in the efforts of operators to keep up with the news."[9]

As businessmen in these distant cities, from Boston to San Francisco, gathered around the gold indicators, commerce all but stopped. For two brief, frantic hours, the Gold Room was the scene of virtually the only financial activity in the entire country. Money itself was in thrall. It was not pork bellies or wheat or cotton that Gould and his allies seemed to be on the verge of cornering, it was gold, legal tender throughout the world, the very stuff and symbol of wealth itself.

An eyewitness reported years later in his memoirs that Broad Street "was thronged by some thousands of men . . . coatless, collarless, and some hatless, [who] raged in the streets, as if the inmates of a dozen lunatic asylums had been turned loose. Up the price of gold went steadily amid shouts, screams, and the wringing of hands."[10]

At eleven-thirty, Butterfield telegraphed Washington that the price had reached 158, and a steady stream of shorts were making their way to William Heath's office to settle while they could before the price went higher still.

E. C. Stedman, the poet laureate of the Street, remembered those extraordinary moments in what remains the most famous poem ever written about Wall Street (not, to be sure, that there have been many of them):

> Zounds! how the price went flashing through
> Wall Street, William, Broad Street, New!
> All the specie in the land
> Held in one ring by a giant hand,—
> For millions more it was ready to pay,
> And throttle the Street on hangman's day.
> Up from the Gold-pit's nether hell,
> While the innocent fountain rose and fell,
> Loud and higher the bidding rose,
> And the bulls, triumphant, faced their foes.
> It seemed as if Satan himself were in it,
> Lifting it,—one per cent a minute. . . .

It was the greatest bear panic in Wall Street history, and men who had made comfortable livings for years on the Street faced imminent ruin, for they were short a commodity whose price seemed to be soaring to infinity. But the price of gold was shooting upward not because there was so much buying, but because there were almost no sellers. Gould and his allies were unloading as much as they could privately, while Fisk tried his very best to make it look as though they were still buying.

At eleven-forty Butterfield telegraphed the Treasury in Washington that the price was 160. But Butterfield must have known that Washington was about to act, for his broker, Joseph Seligman, began to sell gold, something he would have done under the circumstances only with insider information.

At that moment, 11:40 A.M., one of Fisk's brokers, Albert Speyers, was shouting that he would buy $5 million in gold at 160 but he found no takers. Over and over he shouted his offer. Then, suddenly, a highly respected broker named James Brown shouted firmly, "Sold!"

In an instant, like a hysteric slapped across the face, the market came to its senses, the psychology of panic broken at a stroke. Within seconds the price of gold fell to 140. Ironically, just at this moment, Butterfield was authorized to sell $4 million in Treasury gold to stop the panic. But it was already over.

Brown had taken a frightful risk to sell short into the teeth of such a market. Anger, apparently, had spurred him to act. As he testified the next year, "We had transactions . . . on our books, running from the time gold was at 133, and we had paid, paid, paid through that infernal combination that was entered into up to 144 and the question arose with us: 'Is this thing to be perpetuated? Are we to stand by and be flayed by this unscrupulous party . . . ?'"

For the rest of the day, Wall Street was "like the vicinity of a great fire or calamity after the climax has passed," the *Herald* wrote the next morning. "A sudden quiet and calm came over the scene. The brokers, hoarse with shouting earlier in the day, were gathered in groups comparing notes and talking in subdued tones. Each few minutes the hammer of the presiding officer called the assemblage to order, and gold was bought or sold 'under the rule' for the account of some defaulting bull or bear."

The financial mess created by the gold panic was never really cleaned up, but more or less swept under the rug. Even whether the Gould and Fisk forces made or lost money is not, and in all probability cannot be, known. The *Herald* was sure they had made a fortune, writing the next day that "Satan sits complacently upon the unholy spoils." But Gould would not settle the last lawsuit generated by the panic until 1877, fully eight years later. Asked at the congressional hearings what had happened to the group's profits, Fisk breezily replied that they had gone "where the woodbine twineth," a phrase that immediately captured the fancy of the country. Woodbine, another name for honeysuckle, was often planted around outhouses to mask unpleasant smells.

Because it was a buyers' panic, Black Friday, as the day was immediately dubbed, had few long-lasting effects on the Street. It is sellers' panics, such as the crashes of 1837 and 1857, that tend to change the nature of the Street. But its effects on the American economy were greater. James Garfield, the soundest of sound-money men, recognized how the gold panic had come about and what was needed to see that it did not recur. "So long as we have two standards of value recognized by law," he wrote in the congressional report, "which may be made to vary in respect to each other by artificial means, so long will speculation in the price of gold offer temptations too great to be resisted."[11] In other words, to prevent another day on Wall Street like Black Friday, the country had to return to the gold standard. It would be another ten years before that was fully accomplished, but it would undoubtedly have been much longer had Jay Gould not given the country so dramatic an example of the consequences of not doing so.

The American economy had expanded rapidly during the Civil War years to meet the demands of the conflict. But it continued to expand after the war as well. Railroad mileage doubled between 1865 and 1873, while the total capital invested in railroads considerably more than tripled. Wheat production, too, doubled in this period. But both farmers and railroads were heavy borrowers of capital, easily adversely impacted by any rise in the cost of money.

Further, the inflation induced by the war and the issuance of greenbacks subsided, allowing the slow deflation that marked the nineteenth-century economy to resume. Steel rails, for instance, the most important constituent in railroad construction, fell in price by nearly 14 percent in the eight years following the Civil War. As both wages and prices fell, producers were forced to expand to keep up cash flow. This gave the American economy a factitious appearance of prosperity, but all the while its underpinnings were rotting.

Deepening the rot were ever greater scandals. The gold panic had been widely perceived as requiring the active participation of the Grant administration, while the so-called Tweed Ring fostered an anything-goes-but-bribe-me-first atmosphere in New York. William M. Tweed was "grand sachem" of Tammany Hall, the leading Democratic clubhouse in New York for over a century, but he was never an all-powerful city boss of the type that flourished in many American cities in the first half of the twentieth century. Instead, thanks largely to the genius of cartoonist Thomas Nast, he became a symbol of the corruption in city government. The infamous "Tweed Courthouse," in fact named the New York County Courthouse, which still stands just north of New York's City Hall, cost more than $14 million to construct. Just how much of that was graft can be seen by comparing it to the Houses of Parliament in London, constructed twenty years earlier. Built to house in unmatched splendor the central political institution of the then richest and most powerful country on earth, the Palace of Westminster covers fully six acres, but cost only $10 million.

But the greatest scandal of this time is known as the Crédit Mobilier scandal. In 1865 the federal government chartered the Union Pacific Railroad to be a link across the Middle West of a transcontinental line. The construction was subsidized by granting the railroad millions of acres of land along the route, land that would become much more valuable once it was accessible by the railroad. To feather their own nests, the management of the Union Pacific set up a construction company with the fancy French name of Crédit Mobilier, then hired this company to construct the railroad. Crédit Mobilier wildly overcharged the railroad to do so, making the stockholders of Crédit Mobilier millions while draining Union Pacific, and thus its stockholders, dry. To make sure there was no interference from Washington, management bribed many members of the Grant administration (including his first vice president, Schuyler Colfax) and Congress. Rather than cash, the Union Pacific executives gave them sweetheart deals, allowing them to buy stock in Crédit Mobilier and pay for it out of the enormous dividends.

Volume on the Big Board, as it could now properly be called, often amounted to fifty thousand shares a day in a single issue, while one-hundred-thousand-share days in total volume became the norm. While the New York Stock Exchange, controlled by brokers, had begun exerting more and more control, Wall Street was still a dangerous and volatile place for the unwary, as fortunes were made and lost in minutes. A westerner named Alden Stockwell, for instance, had gained control of the Pacific Mail Steamship Company and transformed it into a highly profitable operation by bribing officials in Washington to grant it lucrative mail contracts. But only two years later he was wiped out when outmaneuvered by Jay Gould. His fortune lost but not his spirit, Stockwell explained his Wall Street experience to reporters:

> When I came to New York and bought stock by the hundred shares they called me Stockwell. Then I began buying in larger amounts, and they called me Mr. Stockwell. By the time I was trading in thousand-share lots, I was known as Captain Stockwell. They promoted me to Commodore Stockwell when word got around that I had gained control of Pacific Mail. But when Jay Gould got after me and booted me out of the concern all they called me was "that red-headed son-of-a-bitch from the West."[12]

Gould and Fisk remained in charge of the Erie Railway, operating out of the Grand Opera House on West Twenty-third Street, where Fisk staged theatrical productions. The new rules adopted by the exchanges in 1868 had greatly limited the Erie management's ability to manipulate Erie stock on Wall Street. In addition, a majority of the stock was now in English hands. Nonetheless they managed to retain control by the simple expedient of refusing to transfer the stock on the books to the new owners, preventing them from voting. Their stable of well-bought judges, of course, ensured that the New York courts would do their bidding.

And they carried on regular rate wars with the other trunk lines running west. In May of 1870, Vanderbilt cut the rate for shipping cattle from Buffalo to New York City from $120 a carload to $100 and then to $40. The Erie followed suit and then, on June 25, cut the rate to a purely nominal $1 a carload. Vanderbilt, doubtless feeling he could afford such suicidal rates far better than the Erie, also dropped to the new rate.

But after the new rates took effect, the Central was choked with cattle traffic between the two cities, while the Erie had virtually none. Vanderbilt soon found out the reason. Gould and Fisk had bought up nearly all the cattle in the Buffalo market and, shipping them virtually for free on the Central, were selling them in New York for a handsome profit. The Commodore, disgusted with himself for having been so easily taken, vowed "never [to] have anything more to do with them blowers."[13]

Despite this minor humiliation, the Commodore was enjoying himself. He had made the acquaintance of two extraordinary women, Victoria Woodhull and her sister, Tennessee Claflin, who scandalized mid-Victorian society with their activities, which included publishing a newspaper, spiritualism, and, in Woodhull's case, running for president. Vanderbilt, recently widowed, asked the very beautiful Tennessee Claflin to marry him, but—undoubtedly to her deep regret—she could not accept, owing to a long-shed husband she had neglected to divorce.

When Victoria Woodhull approached the Commodore for a loan to open a brokerage house on Wall Street, Vanderbilt, whose keen sense of humor has seldom been recognized, happily obliged. Today it is hard to imagine just how oxymoronic the phrase *lady broker* sounded to the Victorian ear. Few if any women were in any of the professions such as law or medicine at that time, and Wall Street was universally thought to be as unsuitable to women as a battlefield.

The sisters opened an office at 44 Broad Street and were soon doing a brisk business, thanks to the Commodore and to the publicity in the newspapers, which could not get enough of the idea of women buying and selling stocks and bonds. This gave the sisters as many tourists as customers, forcing them to post a sign saying, "All Gentlemen Will Please State Their Business and Then Retire at Once." But the Claflin sisters were not real feminist crusaders and soon tired of the day-to-day routine on Wall Street. Their brokerage, which the rest of Wall Street had treated as a joke, which it basically was, was one of many that did not survive the Panic of 1873, and it would be almost another century before a woman would actually own a seat of her own on the New York Stock Exchange.

Jim Fisk also began to receive attention for activities unconnected to Wall Street. He had assumed the colonelcy of the Ninth Regiment of the New York Militia, providing it, and himself, with snappy new uniforms and the best brass band in the country. He put on major theatrical productions. He organized a major relief effort after the great Chicago fire of 1871, dispatching an Erie train loaded with supplies to the stricken city with all tracks cleared, an action that galvanized the country.

But it was Jim Fisk's love life that got him the most publicity—perhaps the only publicity he did not crave. Although he was married and the marriage was, in its own peculiar way, a successful one, he and his wife lived largely apart. He maintained a house in New York, a few doors down from the Grand Opera House, while his wife lived in a large house he had built for her in Boston. In New York, he could frequently be seen escorting conspicuously beautiful women around town. Unfortunately for him he fell in love with one of them, Josie Mansfield, a large, dark-haired woman, whose full figure was far more fashionable then than it is now. So besotted by her was Fisk that his normal shrewdness deserted him and he failed to see that she was only using him for his money.

He bought a house for her also down the street from the Opera House and soon moved in. His wife, meanwhile, studiously oblivious to her husband's shenanigans, remained in Boston. Mansfield, however, soon fell in love with one of Fisk's business partners, Edwin Stokes, who was as good-looking as he was unstable. The Stokes family had come to New York from England at the beginning of the nineteenth century by chartered ship, and Stokes's uncle lived in great style on Madison Square, then only just beginning to fade as the city's most fashionable neighborhood. But while Stokes had enough money to live well, his family, conscious of his defects, kept him on a short leash.

In 1870, Mansfield told Fisk to move out of the house he had paid for, and he did so. He was still so taken with her that he continued to pay her bills for months, hoping to win her back. Meanwhile, he went after Stokes, who had been helping himself to the cash at a Brooklyn oil refinery he and Fisk owned jointly. A blizzard of suits and countersuits ensued, and the whole sordid mess quickly exploded in the newspapers as reporters flocked to the endless court hearings, at one of which Josie Mansfield testified regarding her relationship with the two men.

Finally, in January 1872, Ned Stokes snapped. He went to the Opera House to confront Fisk and learned that he had left to pay a visit to a friend staying at the Grand Central Hotel, at Third Street and Broadway, then the heart of the city's shopping district. Stokes proceeded to the hotel and actually arrived before Fisk did. When the latter arrived and began to climb the stairs, Stokes appeared above him and shot him twice. The first bullet thudded into Fisk's ample abdomen, knocking him down the stairs. He rose immediately, but Stokes's second bullet struck him in the arm, knocking him down a second time.

Fisk managed to climb the stairs under his own power and hotel personnel took him to a nearby parlor and summoned a doctor. Stokes, meanwhile, made no effort to escape and was soon arrested and taken to the Tombs, New York City's grim—and even more grimly nicknamed—prison. At first it seemed that Fisk might not be seriously wounded, but the first bullet, an autopsy would reveal, had penetrated his intestine in four places, dooming him to peritonitis, then invariably fatal.

Imagine what today's media would make of Donald Trump being gunned down in the lobby of the Waldorf-Astoria by a young member of the Rockefeller family, and you get some idea of the sensation this murder caused in 1872. Within the hour newsboys were on every street corner shouting, "Shooting of Jim Fisk!" Crowds gathered outside the Grand Central Hotel. The superintendent of police sent 250 extra cops to the Tombs to defend it against the lynch mobs that were rumored to be on the way.

Meanwhile, brokers poured into the Fifth Avenue Hotel, uptown on Madison Square, and an informal evening exchange in Erie Railway stock spontaneously formed. While the brokers felt "a kind of sympathy for the man who had been shot down in cold blood in the prime of life," the *Herald* reported, brokers are an unsentimental group. "Erie is sure to go up now," the *Herald* reported one as saying. And it did, opening on Monday morning at 35¼.

But if the brokers were relatively indifferent to Jim Fisk's fate, the ordinary people of the day were not, a fact that astonished the country's moral establishment, who saw only Fisk's antics and his tangled love life. The people saw something else. "They remembered that he had once been a poor, toiling lad who had wrought his success out of hard earnest effort"; the *Herald* noted the next day that "his steps upwards, while decked with the gaudy, semi-barbaric show, were marked by strong traces of liberality and generosity of spirit that threw for the time the faults of his nature in the shade."[14]

Indeed, Fisk had always been extraordinarily generous, and a steady stream of supplicants passed through the Erie offices to ask for, and usually receive, a free pass on the railroad, or money to buy groceries or coal. In fact, the reason he was at the Grand Central Hotel that day was to visit a friend's young widow and her children, whose bills he was quietly paying.

Although Jim Fisk had never donned a uniform that did not belong in a Gilbert and Sullivan operetta, his funeral, thanks to the Ninth Regiment, was the grandest military funeral held in nineteenth-century New York, excepting only those for Lincoln and Grant. One hundred thousand people turned out to watch the procession pass by, and that night smaller knots of people stood along the railroad tracks in the freezing January night to pay their respects as his body was taken home to Brattleboro for burial. A few years earlier he had paid for the wrought-iron fence surrounding the cemetery, although as he jokingly pointed out, he could not see the use of it. "The fellows that are in," he noted, "cannot get out, and those who are out do not want to get in."[15]

Fisk's partner Jay Gould would lose control of the Erie Railway that spring, largely because the Tweed Ring had been broken the previous summer when the *New York Times* began printing endless evidence of its corruption. The judges that had done the Erie management's bidding for so long were now busy saving their own skins (most of them were impeached anyway). Gould, as might be expected of him, managed to make huge profits in the stock of Erie out of the rise that occurred thanks to his ouster. He would go on to enlarge his fortune constantly in Western Union, Southern Pacific, and other companies until, racked by tuberculosis, he died in 1892 at age fifty-six.

The extraordinary decade between the beginning of the Civil War and Fisk's murder had marked Wall Street's entrance onto the world stage as a major financial market. With the sudden death of Wall Street's most conspicuous major player, many of the Wild West aspects that had so characterized Wall Street in these years began to fade. But the Panic of 1873 marked the real end of the era.

Jay Cooke had been the country's most famous and prestigious banker since his success in selling federal bonds to finance the war. While his prestige remained unmatched after the war, his bank, Jay

Cooke and Company, was not as prosperous as it seemed. He still had a major share of the market in government bonds, and interests in several railroads. One of these railroads, however, the Northern Pacific, was a major cause for concern. Although he had sold $100 million in bonds to finance the railroad, the money ran out before it was finished. In 1870, Congress passed a bill giving the line additional government funding and making Cooke the sole agent. Cooke sold more bonds in Europe. (The capital of North Dakota is named Bismarck because Cooke was hoping to attract German investors in the enterprise.) The same public-relations techniques that had worked so well to sell war bonds were now applied to the Northern Pacific. But difficulties persisted. Bridges collapsed, roadbeds washed out. By early 1873 the line was paying its workers in scrip and was deeply overdrawn at the banks. The *Philadelphia Ledger* likened the Northern Pacific to the South Sea Bubble of early eighteenth-century Britain, a financial scheme, half-fraud, half-hope, that had wrecked many families rich and poor alike.

At this time Cooke and J. P. Morgan were jointly marketing a $300-million government bond issue, again mostly in Europe. The actual fee to the underwriters for doing so was a mere $150,000, but the proceeds of the sale did not have to be turned over to the government until the end of 1873. If they could sell the bonds quickly, both Morgan and Cooke would have free use of the proceeds for almost a year. Morgan, then a partner with the Philadelphia banker Anthony Drexel in the firm of Drexel, Morgan and Company, did not need the money. But Cooke was increasingly desperate for it. Unfortunately for Cooke the issue sold slowly. (Morgan has often been accused of deliberately trying to ruin Cooke, but it is not known if the slow sales resulted from a deliberate plan on Morgan's part or just market conditions.)

By September, Cooke's financial situation was grave. With the money supply at its shortest as it always was in the early fall, with Europe notably cool to American securities, with more and more railroads in financial difficulty, and with government scandals continuing to spread, Wall Street seemed to be heading for disaster.

It was. On Saturday, September 13, Kenyon, Cox and Company, Daniel Drew's firm, admitted insolvency and suspended operations. No panic occurred on Monday and Tuesday of the next week, but on Wednesday stocks began declining amid increasing volume, while short selling noticeably increased. Insiders, it appeared, were getting out while the getting was good. The next morning, Thursday, September 18, at 11:00 H. C. Fahnstock, the New York partner of Jay Cooke, announced the suspension of the New York office. Cooke, in Philadelphia, was forced to follow suit shortly thereafter. The most prominent banker in the country was bankrupt.

The news hit Wall Street like a bomb, and the "coal-black steed named Panic" thundered riderless down Wall Street. When the news reached the floor of the exchange, "a monstrous yell went up and seemed to literally shake the building in which all these mad brokers were for the moment confined."[16] Outside the exchange, the *Tribune* reported, "dread seemed to take possession of the multitude."

The next day rumors were swirling through Wall Street that even the Commodore was on the edge of ruin. It was nonsense, of course, as Vanderbilt did not hold his stocks on margin and his holdings were secure. However, numerous brokers and banking houses that were allied with him were forced to suspend operations. Even well-managed and highly profitable companies saw their stocks bludgeoned. Western Union fell from 75 to 54½ on Saturday morning, September 20.

The contagion of fear spread across the Atlantic cable to Europe, and markets there crashed as well, a sign of Wall Street's swiftly growing world influence. The *Herald* thought the hysteria was of the type that brought down empires, and one broker called the crash "the worst disaster since the Black Death."[17]

At 11:00 A.M. on Saturday, the New York Stock Exchange announced for the first time in its history that it would close for an indefinite period. President Grant, the secretary of the treasury, and other officials came to New York from Washington to meet with the city's financial elite to try to figure out what to do. Vanderbilt told them that the cause of the problem was the overexpansion of the country's railroads, much of it financed by federal bonds. "Building railroads from nowhere to nowhere at public expense," he told the newspapers, "is not a legitimate undertaking."[18]

The federal government, severely restricted in its actions by the lack of a central bank, agreed to buy federal bonds on the open market beginning on Monday, thus injecting new money into the financial system. The stock exchange forbade members to trade securities off the floor of the exchange, but most members ignored the prohibition and traded on the curb. The force of the crash eventually dissipated, and within a few days the exchange reported that it would reopen on Tuesday, September 30, and it recovered moderately when it did so. But the effect on the economy as a whole was severe. The prosperity of the Civil War years was over, and it would be six long years of depression before the economy fully recovered. By that time, Wall Street would have matured considerably.

CHAPTER EIGHT

"ALL YOU HAVE TO DO
IS BUY CHEAP AND SELL DEAR"

As always happens on Wall Street after a crash, the Panic of 1873 induced an eerie calm. Volume dried up as prices declined. Rail stocks, still the backbone of Wall Street trading, lost about half their value on average in the years between 1873 and 1878. The price of a seat on the New York Stock Exchange, which had reached as high as $7,700 in 1873, fell as low as $4,250 three years later. (To give those numbers some context, an unskilled workman in the 1870s—at least one lucky enough to have a job at all—would be happy to earn $1,000 a year in wages.) Two hundred and eighty-seven brokerage concerns closed their doors in bankruptcy in these years, and many more disappeared in voluntary liquidation.

And Europeans, as had happened several times before, simply stopped investing in American securities. It is not surprising, therefore, that a German banker stated that American railroad bonds could not be sold in Europe "even if signed by an angel."[1]

But the bottom half of the business cycle, however painful, has its benefits in a capitalist system. For one thing, Europeans, tired of waiting for recovery, began selling their American holdings. Between 1873 and 1879, the value of European holdings of American securities plunged by about $600 million, $251 million in railroad bonds alone. This further depressed prices on Wall Street, of course, but enriched the United States. When European capital built a railroad in the United States, the latter gained a new transportation artery while Europe gained the securities, the interest and any profits that those securities earned. But when the profits, and sometimes even the interest, failed to materialize, the holders dumped the securities on Wall Street, where they were bought up by American investors at greatly reduced prices. Thus the United States ended up with both the railroad *and* its securities.

And when the great engine of the American economy revved up again, the Europeans were back buying American securities. This was not simply a late-nineteenth-century phenomenon. It began, in a sense, with the joint-stock companies that founded many of the American colonies and then went broke, and continued through the late 1980s, when overly sanguine Japanese investors paid top-of-the-market prices for such trophy pieces of American real estate as Rockefeller Center and then lost many of them in default.

But aside from benefiting the home country at the expense of foreign capitalists, depressions also force companies to become more efficient to survive. The excesses that accumulate in times of prosperity are squeezed out of the system, and economic assets tend to move to stronger holders. When conditions improve and the economy starts expanding again, it is much stronger for the bad years.

The American economy began to assume its modern character in the years after the depression of the 1870s, and so, too, did American politics. As late as 1878, not a single industrial company, a company principally engaged in manufacture rather than, say, transportation or communications, was listed on the New York Stock Exchange. Instead the list, fifty-four companies in all, consisted of thirty-six railroads, five coal companies, four telegraph companies, four express companies, three mining firms, one steamship and one land company.

But by 1900 "industrials" were rapidly becoming the dominant stock group on Wall Street, and the United States, which had imported virtually all its steel as recently as 1860, was producing more steel than all of Europe. Carnegie Steel alone had outstripped British production in its entirety.

The industrialization of the United States in the closing decades of the nineteenth century is one of the epic stories of economic history. The reasons for its occurrence are numerous. The Civil War had given a great boost to demand for industrial products, while the high wartime tariffs protected American industrial companies from European competition. And the war had destroyed the political power of the South, allowing the interests of the industrializing North to have priority in Washington.

In addition, a vast pool of labor rapidly formed in American cities, as foreign immigrants poured into the country, and children increasingly left family farms as mechanization decreased the need for farm labor. One of the most rural countries on earth at the turn of the nineteenth century, by 1880 the United States had 25 percent of its population living in cities. By 1900 it was 40 percent.

Meanwhile the railroads, which expanded from 35,000 miles at the end of the Civil War to 164,000 miles in 1890, created a vast market for such heavy industrial products as steel rails, locomotives, coal, and copper wire. Further, the railroads knit the country together into a truly unified market, by far the largest in the world. This in turn made enormous economies of scale possible.

But industrialization on the scale experienced by the United States in the post–Civil War era required more than efficient transportation. It required capital, lots of it, as well. Increasingly, the needed capital could be found only on Wall Street. And the Street in this era was rapidly becoming personified by a single man, J. P. Morgan, who was one of a new breed of men, investment bankers, who came of age in the wild-and-woolly Wall Street of the Civil War era and transformed it into a dominant economic force in the emerging global economy.

J. P. Morgan is the only Wall Street figure of the turn of the century who remains a household name, as familiar as John D. Rockefeller or Andrew Carnegie. Being easily caricatured, Morgan not only epitomized the Street, he came literally to symbolize it as well, appearing in an endless number of political cartoons.

But in fact Morgan's background was not typical of the major figures in Wall Street history. Most Wall Streeters rose to prominence from relatively obscure backgrounds. But Morgan was born an aristocrat. His grandfather, of ancient New England stock, had moved to Hartford, Connecticut, in 1817, just as that city was expanding rapidly. He invested in real estate, steamboat lines, and railroads as the city grew and was one of the founders of the Aetna Fire Insurance Company. His son, Junius Spencer Morgan, was a partner in a dry-goods firm in Hartford for several years before moving to Boston and becoming a partner in the firm of James M.

Beebe & Co., a prominent cotton broker. In 1854, Junius Morgan was invited to become a partner in the London banking firm of George Peabody & Co. Peabody was an American who had lived and worked in London for many years, where he was highly respected for both his integrity and his business acumen. A life-long bachelor, Peabody's charitable contributions were so munifi-cent that Queen Victoria offered him a baronetcy (which he modestly declined), and when he died, his body was returned to the United States escorted by both French and British battleships.

When Peabody retired in the early 1860s, Morgan took over the firm, renaming it J. S. Morgan and Company. Thus from an early age his son was exposed to two influences that were to dominate and characterize his life: international banking at its highest levels and the idea held by his father and Peabody that personal integrity was indispensable to long-term success in that field.

At the end of his life, Morgan was questioned by a congres-sional committee about the workings of Wall Street. "Is not com-mercial credit based primarily upon money or property?" the committee's counsel asked.

"No, sir," replied Morgan. "The first thing is character."

"Before money or property?"

"Before money or anything else," Morgan insisted. "Money can-not buy it. . . . Because a man I do not trust could not get money from me on all the bonds in Christendom."[2]

Morgan never had any doubt what he wanted to do in life. Even as a boy he exhibited a love for the routines of business. At the age of twelve, Morgan and his cousin Jim Goodwin organized a show that they called the "Grand Diorama of the Landing of Colum-bus." Morgan kept precise accounts of all expenses and receipts from ticket sales and afterward prepared a balance sheet of the whole enterprise headed "Morgan & Goodwin, Grand Diorama Balance Sheet, April 20, 1849."[3] Throughout his life he could read ledgers at a glance, spotting even trivial errors made by the trem-bling clerks who held them up for his inspection.

Morgan received an international education in Hartford, Boston, Vevey (Switzerland), and the University of Gottingen in Germany. After a year at Gottingen (where a professor of mathematics unsuc-cessfully tried to convince him to take up mathematics as a career) he moved to New York and took a position as a junior accountant with the Wall Street firm of Duncan and Sherman.

His abilities and his take-charge personality stood out immediately. Sent by his firm to New Orleans to study the cotton business there, he soon spotted opportunity. He bought a shipload of coffee, paying for it with a sight-draft on Duncan and Sherman, although he was not authorized to incur such an obligation. When he received a peremptory telegram from New York to dispose of the coffee at once, he telegraphed back that he had already done so at a handsome profit and was forwarding the check to Duncan and Sherman. This sort of quick, decisive action would characterize Morgan all his life.

In September 1862, Morgan opened his own firm, J. Pierpont Morgan and Company, and quickly prospered in the great boom on Wall Street caused by the Civil War. In 1864, only twenty-seven years old, Morgan had a taxable income of $53,286. (The Civil War income tax act specified that tax returns be public documents, a bonanza for historians.)

In 1871, Morgan formed a partnership with the Drexel firm of Philadelphia. In New York the firm was known as Drexel, Morgan and Company and had headquarters at 23 Wall Street, at the corner of Broad Street. Although the highly ornamented Victorian building was replaced in 1913 by the severely plain present structure, the address has been the headquarters of the Morgan bank ever since, known to Wall Streeters simply as The Corner.

With his connections to the Drexel firm in Philadelphia and his father in London, Morgan prospered from the first. Even in the depression of the 1870s his share of the firm's profits seldom dipped below half a million dollars a year. The London connection mattered most, to both Wall Street and J. P. Morgan, and would make Morgan the most famous banker in the world.

The London and New York markets, the world's two largest, were moving closer together, thanks to the Atlantic cable that had been operating successfully since 1866. And New York was growing up. While the United States would remain an importer of capital for some time, it was beginning to handle foreign bond issues on its own. In 1879 it successfully floated a $3-million issue for the province of Quebec.

And it was in that year that Morgan decisively made a name for himself as an extraordinarily competent banker. When Commodore Vanderbilt died in 1877, he left the vast bulk of his fortune of $105 million—by far the largest fortune in the country—to his eldest son, William H. Vanderbilt. The younger Vanderbilt owned no less than 87 percent of the New York Central Railroad, and he wanted to diversify his holdings. But to dispose of a large chunk of a company as prominent as the New York Central without depressing the market for the stock was no easy task. Morgan took on the job, however, and sold 150,000 shares of New York Central on the London market at the very good price of $120 a share. More, he accomplished the sale so quietly that no notice was taken until it was completed.

Not only was the sale successful, but Morgan now held the proxies of the new English shareholders and sat on the board of the New York Central to represent them. He had become a power in the railroad business and intended to use his new position to bring order to the muddle of American railroading. As we have seen, the American railroad system—if that is the word—had grown chaotically over the previous fifty years. The larger trunk lines had mostly been assembled out of the many small, local lines and often had odd capital and corporate structures as a result.

Railroads were the first economic enterprises to be managed by people who, for the most part, did not own them. Virtually no laws compelled them to act as the fiduciaries for the stockholders of these companies that they in fact were. As a result, managers could, and often most certainly did, act in their self-interest at the expense of both the stockholders and the customers. The Crédit Mobilier scheme is only the most notorious example. And many railroad managers would begin to construct lines that competed with another railroad's for the sole purpose of being bought out by that railroad.

By the mid-1880s, while the nation was prosperous, the railroads were suffering from rapidly declining profits thanks to ferocious rate wars, overbuilding, and poor management. Even the well-managed New York Central and Pennsylvania Railroads were at each other's throat, each building competitive lines in the other's territory. Morgan convinced Vanderbilt to allow him to negotiate a peace settlement. He invited the management of both railroads to come on board his yacht, *Corsair*. The magnificent vessel sailed up and down the Hudson River between Garrison and Sandy Hook until Morgan secured an agreement. The New York Central would acquire the West Shore line, across the Hudson River from its own, and the Pennsylvania would buy the line being built from Harrisburg to Pittsburgh and stop work on it. (The tunnels that had already been bored through the mountains were abandoned, only to be resurrected decades later and utilized by the Pennsylvania Turnpike.)

Morgan's prestige soared on Wall Street and in the business community as a result of the so-called *Corsair* agreement, and much profitable business flowed to his firm as a result. Although a Wall Street banker, not a railroad man at all, Morgan was in the last two decades of the nineteenth century the most influential man in the railroad industry as such companies as the Baltimore and Ohio, the Chesapeake, and the Erie were reorganized and rationalized by Morgan's firm.

Morgan and other investment bankers also greatly increased Wall Street's importance to the American and world economies as they brought an atmosphere of integrity and solidity that had been conspicuously missing earlier on the Street. Most Americans, when they regarded Wall Street at all, thought it little more than a gambling den. Now the Street began to acquire a reputation as a good place to do business. No small factor in this was Morgan's personality and physical presence. At six feet, he was, like Commodore Vanderbilt, well above average height for his generation. Lack of exercise, which he loathed, gave him above average girth as well. But his most impressive feature were his flashing hazel eyes. Edward Steichen, the photographer who took the most famous portrait of Morgan, said that meeting his gaze was like confronting the headlights of an express train. "If one could step off the tracks," one writer paraphrased Steichen, "they were merely awe-inspiring; if one could not they were terrifying."[4]

But if Morgan and his ilk were bringing a new respectability to Wall Street, plenty of its old, raffish ways and eccentrics gave the place color and added to its legend.

Among the more memorable was Hetty Green. Had there been a *Forbes* Four Hundred list when she died in 1916, she would easily have been in the top twenty, and she remains to this day among the forty richest Americans ever, the only woman to make the list in her own right. Her background, like that of her near contemporary J. P. Morgan, was old New England. Her mother had been a Howland, and the Howlands had come on the *Mayflower*. In the early nineteenth century the family built one of the great whaling fortunes of New Bedford, Massachusetts, and Hetty Green inherited a substantial portion of it. She inherited an even larger fortune from her father, Edward Robinson, who had worked for the Howlands and made his own fortune in whaling and then multiplied it on Wall Street. But rich as her family was in money, it was singularly poor in human warmth. Her mother lived most of her life as a voluntary invalid, suffering from mostly nonexistent ailments. Her father cared for nothing but business. The psychological effect of this loveless upbringing would be devastating.

In 1865, when Hetty Green came into her inheritance from her father, her income was in the neighborhood of $300,000 a year at a time when $10,000 a year was enough to live in very considerable upper-middle-class comfort. But for her, it was not enough. No sum could be. For Hetty Green was that great psychological rarity, the genuine miser. She was obsessed not with what money could buy or the power it could be translated into, but with money itself. Merely possessing it gave her immense comfort; parting with it caused great psychological pain.

As a result, Hetty Green would, quite simply, spend anything in profligate abandon—time, convenience, reputation, health, appearance, comfort, friendship, her children's welfare, anything—rather than unnecessarily part with money itself, no matter how trivial a sum. She once spent half a night ransacking a carriage looking for a two-cent stamp that had fallen off a letter. During the hours she spent frantically searching for it, the interest earned on her capital at least equaled an average family's annual income.

But if Hetty Green was nearly incapable of spending money, she was a genius at making it. "I don't much believe in stocks," she once said. "I never buy industrials. Railroads and real estate are the things I like. Before deciding on an investment I seek out every kind of information about it. There is no great secret in fortune making. All you have to do is buy cheap and sell dear, act with thrift and shrewdness and be persistent."[5] Certainly no one could complain that she did not invest thriftily. She once appeared at her bank in New York with $200,000 in bearer bonds—virtually the same as cash—under her arm. She had made her way downtown on a streetcar and her banker admonished her for taking such a risk.

"You should have taken a carriage," he said.

"A carriage, indeed!" responded Hetty Green. "Perhaps you can afford to ride in a carriage—I cannot."[6]

But when her financial interests were directly jeopardized, she could take a cab fast enough. In 1885, her banker of many years, John J. Cisco and Son, was threatened with insolvency. Hetty Green was then living in Bellows Falls, Vermont, her husband's hometown, but even at a distance of two hundred miles, she could seemingly smell a hazard to her fortune. She had over $25 million in securities stored at Cisco—having multiplied her paternal inheritance by a factor of twenty-five in twenty years—and in addition, she had $556,581.33 on deposit at Cisco. In the event of failure, that money would potentially be tied up in bankruptcy for a long time. She wrote the bank instructing it to transfer her deposit to the Chemical Bank.

The bank, knowing that a transfer that large would result in certain failure, refused, informing her that her husband owed the firm over $700,000 and that his collateral, shares of the Louisville and Nashville Railroad, had fallen in value below the point where they fully collateralized the loan. Cisco asked Mrs. Green to make up the difference. Needless to say, she refused, explaining in a letter that her husband's debts were no concern of hers and demanding once more that her assets be transferred. Hastening to New York to attend to the crisis, she even took a cab down from Grand Central to lower Manhattan. But she was too late. On receipt of her second letter, John J. Cisco and Son declared bankruptcy, and its assets were placed in the care of an assignee, Lewis May. Mrs. Green confronted him in his new office in the bank at 59 Wall Street and demanded her money.

May not only refused to turn over her deposit, saying that she was no more than one of some eight hundred creditors of the bank, but far worse, he refused to turn over her securities until she had made good on her husband's debt.

Hetty Green faced her ultimate nightmare. The capital she had husbanded so dearly and enlarged so exceedingly had been snatched from her. In her mind, all that stood between her and a heartless world full of enemies was in peril. It was the crisis of her life and she rose to the occasion.

Half of Wall Street watched through the plate-glass windows of the bank as "the richest woman in the world," as the newspapers were already calling her, fought to regain her fortune and avoid her husband's debts. She wept, she shouted, she threatened, she pleaded in turn. Not until the bank closed five hours later did she leave, only to be back the next morning. The drama continued in such a way for two long weeks, a new tourist attraction in the financial district. Hetty Green was obdurate, vituperative, and emotional. Mr. May was polite, patient, and equally obdurate. He would not part with one dime until her husband's debts were covered.

Finally she wrote out a check for the amount needed to clear up the matter, $422,143.22. Considerably less than 2 percent of her net worth, it was by far the largest check she ever wrote in her life for which she did not receive in exchange something of equal or greater value. Each cent was a drop of her blood. But when the check was written, Lewis May handed over her bonds, stocks, leases, deeds, certificates of deposit, and other proofs of her fortune. She bundled them all into a cab, and with barely enough room for herself, she escorted her fortune down Wall Street to the Chemical Bank on Broadway, where her money, and thus herself, were safe once again.

The struggle over her husband's debts destroyed her marriage, and she and her husband would largely live apart from that point on. But a great deal of genuine affection remained between the two regardless. When he took ill, she would rush to nurse him (she prided herself on her nursing skills), and after he died, she even bought a new dress in which to attend his funeral. For Hetty Green, that was no small token of her love.

Always fighting to avoid being considered a New York resident, which would have subjected her to taxation, Hetty Green began spending much more time in New York to oversee her affairs. She lived in an endless succession of rooming houses and cheap hotels, often under assumed names, to avoid the tax man. But she became a familiar figure on Wall Street in her shabby, old-fashioned black dress, shuffling to and from the Chemical Bank to visit her money. The bank offered her an office, but she declined, fearing the tax consequences, and used whatever desk just happened to be empty. If none was, she would sit on the floor as she read her mail and clipped her coupons. Sometimes she would bring her own lunch, usually oatmeal, which she heated on a radiator.

Wall Street has never been a place for the naive, and the nation's eighteenth president, Ulysses S. Grant, was naive regarding the ways of nearly everything but war. His son and namesake was not much better. But because he was Ulysses S. Grant Jr., known as Buck, he was constantly courted by those who hoped he might be a connection to his father. One of these was Ferdinand Ward.

Ward had come to Wall Street shortly after the gold panic in 1869 and boasted, at best, an indifferent record. He was a clerk at the Produce Exchange and speculated in commodities futures on the side. Soon he was speculating in railroad and other stocks and routinely exaggerating his successes. Most people on Wall Street gave little credence to other people's financial fish stories, but Buck Grant didn't know any better. Trained in the law, he had tried several business ventures, all of which had turned out badly. He took a liking to Ferdinand Ward, who flattered him skillfully. Soon they formed a firm together, Grant and Ward, and were in the brokerage business.

In 1881, when former president Grant and his wife moved to New York City (moving into a house at 3 East Sixty-sixth Street, just off Fifth Avenue), he became a limited partner in the firm. The Grants put up a total of $200,000 in cash when he joined the firm, most of Grant's net worth, and Ward supposedly put up securities of equal value. (They turned out to be worth far less.)

Numerous new brokerage clients, hoping to profit by the connection to the former president and his access to power in Washington, established accounts at Grant and Ward. Meanwhile Ward exploited the Grant name by attempting to borrow money from the Marine National Bank, run by James D. Fish. Fish wrote to

General Grant, who replied, "I think the investments are safe, and I am willing that Mr. Ward should derive what profit he can for the firm that the use of my name and influence may bring."[7]

Fish concluded that the fix was in on government contracts and began to lend Grant and Ward money as well as speculating on his own account with the firm. In turn Ward noised it about that the government was about to give contracts to several companies controlled by Ward. The only problem was that none of this was true. Grant had flatly refused to solicit government contracts, and when he heard the rumors spread about by Ward to encourage people to invest with his firm, he asked Ward for an explanation. Ward simply denied the rumors and claimed that he was engaged in financing the construction of several spurs for the Erie Railway.

But what Ward was actually doing was speculating on Wall Street, and not very successfully. He was using the Grant name to solicit investments from Grant's friends and admirers. He promised them large dividends, which they duly received. But those dividends came largely from capital put in by new investors. In other words, it was a Ponzi scheme.

And like many Ponzi schemes before and since, for a while it worked. As more and more people, including many other members of the Grant family, invested their money in Grant and Ward, father and son got richer and richer (on paper). Buck Grant claimed that he was now worth over a million dollars, and the general figured he was worth at least $2 million, enough in the 1880s to place him among the seriously rich. He started journeying downtown regularly to the Grant and Ward offices, where he would welcome new investors, who were, of course, impressed to meet a national hero and former president.

But Ponzi schemes always collapse sooner or later, of course, and Grant and Ward was no exception. If Ward had been a brilliant speculator, perhaps he might have pulled it off. But he was not, and by May of 1884, he was in desperate straits. Worse, because Marine National Bank was deeply involved, the failure of Grant and Ward would mean the failure of a substantial bank, probably precipitating a serious panic.

Ward knew that if he confessed what he was up to, Grant would not come to his assistance. Grant may have been a fool about money, but he was an honest fool. So Ward fabricated a story. He told the general that it was the Marine National Bank that was in trouble, because of a sudden withdrawal of New York City funds, and that the bank's failure could bring down Grant and Ward with it. He asked Grant to raise $150,000 to remedy the situation. Grant, afraid of a general panic, went to see William H. Vanderbilt, the richest man in the world, for whom $150,000 was nearly petty cash.

Vanderbilt had doubled his father's fortune in the seven years since he had inherited it and was, if not a stellar personality like his father, anything but a fool. Vanderbilt told Grant—who was on crutches because of a fall the previous winter—that he didn't care at all about the Marine National Bank. As for Grant and Ward, Vanderbilt, seldom tactful, told Grant, "What I've heard about that firm would not justify me in lending it a dime."[8] Grant, stunned by Vanderbilt's harsh words, assumed he would be turned down. Instead, Vanderbilt informed him that while he would not loan Grant and Ward any money, "to you—to General Grant—I'm making this loan."[9]

Grant thanked Vanderbilt and hobbled off to his carriage, which took him home. There Ferdinand Ward was waiting for him. Grant turned over the check to Ward, who the next morning cashed it and pocketed the money. On Tuesday, May 6, Grant went downtown to the Grant and Ward office, only to be met by his son, who told him that Marine National Bank, and with it Grant and Ward, had failed and that Ward could not be found.

As news of the failures spread through Wall Street at the speed of sound, crowds gathered. The general stayed in his office for several hours, but when he left, walking as fast as he could on his crutches and with a cigar that had gone out clutched in his teeth, he said nothing. As he passed, everyone in the crowd removed their hats, in tribute to the man who had so mightily helped to save the Union, but could not save himself.

No immediate panic hit the Street, but financial nerves were on edge. The following week John C. Eno, president of the Second National Bank and only twenty-six years old, fled to Canada with $4 million of the bank's money, and that was enough to set off a wave of selling. Several respected houses suspended, at least temporarily, and stocks fell sharply. But the New York Clearing House, used by the banks to handle transactions among themselves, organized a fund to save the sound institutions, in particular the Metropolitan Bank, which was able to reopen in only three days.

The panic soon passed, the underlying national economy quite unaffected. But Grant and Ward and the Marine National Bank were beyond saving. Grant and Ward, it was determined, had assets of $67,174 and liabilities of no less than $16,792,640. James D. Fish was carted off to the Ludlow Street Jail, and after he was apprehended attempting to flee the country, Ferdinand Ward joined him there. (When Fish learned who his new jailmate was, he screamed, "Don't let me get at him. I'll kill the scoundrel!")[10] General Grant was financially wiped out, as were most members of his family. Ward went to jail for ten years for grand larceny.

By June, former president Grant had only about $200 in cash to his name. People began sending him checks (one arrived with a note saying "on account of my share for services ending in April, 1865").[11] Grant had little alternative but to accept them. He turned over his medals and sword to William H. Vanderbilt, who accepted them with the greatest reluctance and donated them to the government. It was a pathetic end for a proud man.

But the failure of Grant and Ward had one fortuitous result. Grant had always resisted writing about the war he had fought in so ferociously, despite numerous remunerative offers from magazine and book publishers. Now he had no choice. He arranged with Mark Twain's publishing company to publish his memoirs for an advance of $25,000—a huge sum from a book publisher in those days. Soon after he began work, he learned that he had inoperable cancer of the throat. Grant knew that he was a dying man and hurried to finish his memoirs so that his family would not be left destitute. He just made it, dying only three days after he finished the manuscript.

When the book was published, it proved a titanic success, selling over three hundred thousand copies and earning the Grant family half a million in royalties. But Grant's memoirs were more than just a best-seller, they were—wholly unexpectedly—a masterpiece as well. Grant never thought he could write. But his fundamental honesty and terse, forthright style produced the finest work of military history of the nineteenth century. Indeed, today, most historians and critics regard the *Memoirs* of Ulysses S. Grant as being equaled in their genre only by Caesar's *Commentaries*.

It is not the least of ironies that Wall Street at its worst would be the force behind the creation of a work of American literature at its best.

CHAPTER NINE

"Have You Anything
to Suggest?"

Wall Street churned after the collapse of Grant and Ward. The depression of the 1870s had ended, but a boom in the national economy did not follow. As a result both volume and seat prices trended downward in these years. Although over 116 million shares had changed hands in 1882, only 69 million did so in 1891. (There were, of course, occasional spurts of activity, and the exchange had its first million-share day on May 5, 1886.) A seat on the exchange, which had cost as much as $26,000 in 1880, could be had for only about $15,000 in 1893.

A terrible panic hit London in November 1889, when Baring Brothers, one of England's most prestigious and powerful private banks, collapsed, after a coup in Argentina made that bank's heavy investments in that country's securities dubious. London investors immediately began unloading American securities, especially those that had been favored by Baring Brothers, and some, such as Santa Fe Railroad, declined by more than half. The old saying on Wall Street that "When London catches cold, New York sneezes" was proving true once again. Fortunately for the New York market, the Bank of England bailed out Baring Brothers to support the London market.

Prosperity seemed to return to America, but it was only an illusion. Gold was moving to Europe as the dollar came under increasing pressure, and volume remained lackluster on the exchange (although when several bear pools culminated on February 20, 1893, volume hit a new one-day record of 1,473,953). Then, on February 25, the Philadelphia & Reading Railroad declared bankruptcy, with debts of more than $125 million, a staggering sum for the time.

After Grover Cleveland was inaugurated for his second term on March 4 that year, the market again appeared to stabilize. Although a Democrat, Cleveland was a sound-money man through and through, and even J. P. Morgan had voted for him. Soon after resuming the presidency, Cleveland convinced a group of Wall Street bankers to take $25 million in notes in exchange for gold, bringing the Treasury gold reserve back up to the legal minimum of $100 million. At the same time, word spread that the balance of foreign trade had swung in the country's favor. Some began to anticipate better times on Wall Street. On April 5, the *New York Times* reported the new mood: "There was an entire change of sentiment in Stock Exchange orders today, and it was accomplished by what appeared to be a preconcerted movement to cover outstanding short contracts all along the line. It is too soon to say that a bull market is upon us, but the figures show that the tendency is toward higher prices. The professional element is still in control, but many orders were executed to-day which were for outsiders who have long been absent from the Street."[1]

The *Times's* crystal ball, however, could hardly have been cloudier. The situation was soon deteriorating rapidly. Some of the smaller houses on Wall Street defaulted in April, and on Monday, May 1, the market began sliding in earnest and on Wednesday endured its worst day since 1884. The next day the National Cordage Company—the so-called rope trust—went into unexpected bankruptcy with debts of $10 million. The company had paid the dividend on the common stock just a few days earlier. The new industrial companies on the exchange fell sharply, but most of the better-run railroads held their values.

In July the bottom finally dropped out of the market. Even the best-managed railroads suffered significant declines. New York Central, which had opened the year at 109, fell to 92 by the end of July. The Pennsylvania declined from 54 to 46, nearly 15 percent. Less profitable lines fared far worse. The Atchison, Topeka & Santa Fe opened the year at 34 and closed it at 10.

The president of National Cordage put his finger on the real problem that was rocking the American economy and thus Wall

Street. "The failure [of National Cordage]," he explained in a newspaper interview, "was entirely due to the inability to get credit, which had never been curtailed before in our history, and the uneasiness due to the general distrust in regard to the silver question and the failure of the Reading Railroad Company."[2]

The silver question. Beneath the relative prosperity of the 1880s an economic time bomb called the Bland-Allison Act had been ticking away. The crash of 1893 was simply the inevitable explosion.

While industrialization brought jobs and wealth to the Northeast, where it was concentrated, and better and cheaper products to consumers everywhere, it had its losers, too, as capitalism always does. As the country, pushed by the Northeast, slowly returned to the gold standard, which it did fully on January 1, 1879, the inflation that had characterized the Civil War greenback era disappeared. It was replaced by a slow deflation. Wheat, at $1.22 a bushel in 1879, dropped to $.89 in 1890. Agriculture, still the bedrock of the American economy, suffered, and farmers blamed the gold standard and the railroads, which gouged prices on the many branch lines where they had monopolies of overland transportation.

Further, farmers, by the nature of the business, are usually debtors, with mortgages on their farms and loans on their crops. But deflation meant that they had to pay back these loans in more expensive dollars than those they had borrowed. The rural parts of the country fought to continue the greenbacks and, indeed, to issue more of them.

The Treasury, as it slowly returned to the gold standard, had stopped minting silver coins in 1873. This so-called "crime of '73" was bitterly resented in the South and West, where farmers and miners dominated politics. When the great silver strikes of the midseventies, such as the Comstock Lode, came in, pressure to remonetize silver increased. Congress, as democratic institutions usually do, tried to please both sides. It required the Treasury to purchase $2–4 million of silver every month at the market rate and turn it into coins at the ratio of sixteen to one. In other words, sixteen ounces of silver, regardless of the market price, were declared by congressional fiat to be equal in value to one ounce of gold. This had the effect of arbitrarily increasing the country's money supply, the classic means of generating inflation.

When Bland-Allison was enacted, in 1878, the sixteen-to-one ratio was approximately the market price of silver. But as the western mines continued to pour out silver in unprecedented quantities, the price of silver began to drop, reaching about twenty to one by 1890. That year Congress made matters worse by replacing Bland-Allison with the Sherman Silver Act, which required the Treasury to buy no less than 4.5 million ounces of silver a month, roughly the whole of the American output. With the face value of silver coins well above the market value of the silver they contained, inflation was inevitable.

But since January 1, 1879, the government had also been on the gold standard, and the Treasury had been legally required to keep $100 million in gold on hand to meet any demand for that metal. With its silver policy inflating the money supply and its gold policy keeping the value of the dollar steady, Congress, in effect, had managed to simultaneously guarantee and forbid inflation.

As anyone who had studied economics anywhere but on Capitol Hill could have predicted, Gresham's law kicked in. Because silver was worth one-twentieth the price of gold in the market, but declared by Congress to be worth one-sixteenth the price of gold when coined, people began to spend the silver and keep the gold. And gold began to trickle out of the Treasury. The country's schizophrenic monetary policy was masked while the government ran huge surpluses throughout the 1880s. But when the crash of 1893 hit, the trickle of gold turned into a flood. With government revenues plummeting, Congress rushed to repeal the Sherman Silver Act, but it was too late. People at home and abroad had begun to lose faith in the soundness of the dollar. They wanted gold. The government issued bonds to buy gold to maintain its reserve, but the metal continued to drain out of the Treasury.

In 1894, as the depression deepened, the Treasury's gold reserve dipped below $100 million once again. In January of that year several Wall Street investment banks underwrote a $50-million issue of gold bonds, selling them to the public and restoring the Treasury's gold reserve to $107 million. No sooner was that gold on hand, however, than it began to drain away once more. By November another $50-million issue, this one handled by Drexel, Morgan, again restored the reserve. But by January 24, 1895, the reserve was down to only $68 million. A week later it was down to $45 million. The country watched in frightened fascination.

President Cleveland tried to persuade Congress to authorize another bond issue to replenish the reserve, but Congress refused. Soon it was possible literally to watch gold flow out of the country, as ships in New York were loaded with the metal bound for Europe, where central banks had redeemed their dollars. The Treasury estimated that $84 million in gold was shipped abroad in the last three months of 1894. Bets were being made on Wall Street as to the exact day when the United States would be forced off the gold standard.

Such a fall from financial grace would have been profoundly embarrassing to the government of any country that was rapidly emerging as a great power. But the United States could suffer more than a loss of face since the federal debt, both principal and interest, was payable in gold. A default on the debt would inevitably send interest rates soaring. With the economy already in deep depression, catastrophe threatened.

But with an inflationary Congress and a sound-money president, the federal government was paralyzed. J. P. Morgan, deeply alarmed, cabled his London office that "we are disposed to do everything [in] our power to avert calamity."[3] Morgan's reputation was a formidable asset for him. In fact, when a broker saw Morgan emerge from the subtreasury at the head of Broad Street with Assistant Secretary of the Treasury William Edmund Curtis, the broker rushed to the floor of the stock exchange. "The Treasury is negotiating a loan!"[4] he shouted. The gathering panic at once began to subside, and the Treasury actually took in $9 million in gold that had previously been withdrawn for shipment abroad.

But the politics of silver and gold continued to exacerbate the situation, and on February 4, Morgan got a letter from the Treasury secretary canceling the negotiations. Cleveland intended to force Congress to allow an issue of bonds to the public. Morgan knew that there was not enough time for that, even if Congress went along. He and August Belmont Jr., who represented the Rothschild interests, rushed to Washington to try to change the president's mind. "Must admit am not hopeful,"[5] Morgan cabled London.

He visited the attorney general at home that evening and

threatened to return to New York the next morning if Cleveland refused to see him. Cleveland reluctantly agreed to meet with him the next morning at nine-thirty, but left Morgan sitting in one corner of the president's office while he conferred with his senior cabinet members. A telephone call informed the secretary of the treasury that only $9 million in gold remained in the Treasury to meet any demands for withdrawal.

Still Cleveland—sound-money man in a free-coinage-of-silver party—was determined to let Congress take the blame for any debacle if it would not authorize a bond sale. But Morgan, finally entering the discussion, told him that he knew of drafts against the Treasury for $12 million and that if they were presented, as well they might be, then the Treasury would default whether or not Congress came to its senses. Something drastic had to be done right then.

Cleveland was silent for a moment, but a shrewd man unfettered by ideology, he knew he had no options. "Have you anything to suggest?"[6] he finally asked. In a very real sense, this was the moment Wall Street emerged as a world power in its own right. The president of the United States, which now had the largest national economy on earth, needed its help.

Morgan rose to the occasion. He pointed out that issuing bonds in the domestic market, even if Congress allowed it, would not work for long, as the gold would simply recycle back to where it had come from, leaving the Treasury even worse off than before. But he and Belmont were willing to raise a new $100-million reserve in Europe that would stem the run on the Treasury's gold. Further, Morgan had devised a means to legally accomplish this that bypassed Congress. In 1862, Congress had passed a law to allow the Treasury to buy coin with bonds as an emergency measure. That authority had never lapsed and could therefore be used in this emergency. Further, Morgan would guarantee that the gold would not immediately drain away to Europe. He made that guarantee entirely on his own, not even consulting August Belmont, who was in the room. It was an extraordinary act of faith in his own reputation, but Morgan was correct in his assessment of the market's reaction.

When the bonds were offered on Wall Street, by Morgan, and in

London, by the Rothschilds, they sold immediately. Equally important, Morgan was able to keep his word that the gold would remain in the Treasury by using the full battery of foreign-exchange techniques, including arbitrage and borrowing pounds in London and selling them in New York to bolster the dollar. Indeed, by June 1895, the Treasury reserve stood at $107.5 million.

The public reaction against Morgan, President Cleveland, Wall Street, and even the Rothschilds was particularly intense in the West and South. Mary E. Lease, a rabble-rousing writer of the day (who earned a place in the quotation books by urging farmers to "raise less corn and more hell"), wrote that Cleveland was nothing more than "the agent of Jewish bankers and British gold."[7] Joseph Pulitzer's *New York World* saw a "Wall Street conspiracy" at work. But the *New York Times* noted, "The admiration of the financial world is turned upon [Morgan's] masterly management of the loan."[8]

Despite the criticism, Morgan's rescue of the dollar changed the economic mood. A recovery began. The following year, William Jennings Bryan, aged only thirty-six, captured the Democratic nomination by promising not to allow mankind to be crucified upon a cross of gold. It was one of the most famous speeches in American history, but his far-less-eloquent opponent, William McKinley, running on a slogan of "Sound Money, Protection, and Prosperity," trounced him in the election.

The 1890s were a period of transition for Wall Street, a time when it began to assume the aspect and the ways of doing business that it would have for the next eighty years. Wall Street banks had established a clearinghouse for checks decades earlier, but a clearinghouse allowing major brokers to transfer securities easily and efficiently was finally established only in 1892. Twice a day runners—usually teenage boys—would carry bundles of stocks and bonds to the clearinghouse and carry back other bundles.

Railroad securities still dominated the Big Board, with about $13 billion worth listed for trading. State bonds made up another $3 billion. But federal bonds, slowly but steadily paid off with the surpluses run up by the high tariff, amounted to only about $700 million. Gaining rapidly were securities coming from the industrial sector. In 1893 they amounted to only about $500 million in market capitalization. But as American industry expanded and consolidated into ever larger companies, the great investment banks financed the creation of the so-called trusts with more and more stock. (The trust form of corporate organization—where a small group of men held the stock of nominally independent but actually subsidiary corporations in trust for the stockholders of the primary corporation—was created by Standard Oil in 1880 to evade out-of-date state incorporation laws. In 1891, New Jersey, looking for tax revenue, became the first state to allow corporations to own stock of other corporations in their own right. Companies, including Standard Oil, rushed to incorporate in that state, and the trust form of organization vanished from the American economy. As one of the great bogeymen of American politics, however, the "trust" is still very much with us.)

Another development that occurred on Wall Street in the 1890s was so fundamentally useful that it is nearly impossible to imagine Wall Street without it: the stock market average. Today, the Dow Jones industrial average is one of the most famous statistics in the world. When people say, "What did the market do today?" that's the number they want. And thanks to computers, you can now watch the Dow Jones go up and down by the second in real time on the various business cable networks.

It is also invaluable to historians of Wall Street, for it is the oldest continuous stock-market average in existence, having been initiated on May 26, 1896. The genius behind this wonderfully simple idea was Charles Dow, cofounder of the *Wall Street Journal*. The *Journal* itself was first published in 1884, one of several newspapers—the *Journal of Commerce,* decades older, is another—that were intended to serve the Wall Street community. The *Wall Street Journal* remained a relatively small newspaper of local distribution until after the Second World War. Then it rapidly grew in both distribution and influence into what it is today, the American newspaper with the largest circulation in the country.

"The stock market," Dow thought, "is in the nature of a barometer which reflects the rise and fall of general conditions."[9] But how to read the barometer? Most newspapers of the day already published closing stock prices, but that didn't tell the reader, in the blink of an eye, how the market as a whole was performing.

Like Fahrenheit's and Celsius's thermometers, Dow's barometer needed a scale. So Dow created two averages, one of railroad stocks—the blue chips of the day—and one for industrial companies, then considered much riskier.

The first industrial average included twelve stocks (General Electric is the only one that is also in the Dow today), and it closed that first day at 40.94. Ironically, Dow created his market index just in time to see the market tank. By August the Dow was down to 28.48, a ferocious 30 percent decline. (The Department of Commerce would show similar bad timing with the gross national product, which it began calculating in 1929.)

But the market quickly recovered when it became clear that McKinley was likely to beat Bryan in the presidential election of that year. Within ten years the Dow Jones had topped 100 and become exactly what Charles Dow had hoped that it would, the Wall Street barometer.

Still another development in the American economy of the 1890s is seldom thought of as having anything to do with Wall Street—modern accounting. But in fact the Wall Street banks and brokerage houses were the main force behind the creation of the modern accounting profession and the imposition of generally accepted accounting principles upon the country's publicly owned companies.

Accounting is as ancient as civilization itself; indeed it was most likely the impetus behind the invention of writing. But accounting did not advance much until the Renaissance, when double-entry bookkeeping appeared in fifteenth-century Italy. Double entry makes it easier to detect errors and allows a much more dynamic financial picture of an enterprise to emerge from the raw numbers. The difference between double-entry and single-entry bookkeeping as financial tools might be analogous to the difference between an electrocardiogram and a stethoscope as diagnostic ones.

Accountancy was among the earliest professions to appear in the New World. In fact, Isabella and Ferdinand put an accountant on board the *Santa Maria* to make sure they got their share of the hoped-for booty. But as most American business enterprises remained small, family-owned affairs, they had little need for outside accountants.

The industrial revolution changed that completely. Railroads stretching hundreds of miles and employing thousands of people were difficult to manage financially. Accountants began devising more and more tools to keep track of the money and to enable managers to see exactly where it was being spent or misspent. The great corporate enterprises created on Wall Street at the end of the nineteenth century were made possible only because of these new accounting tools. (This rapid evolution in accounting continues apace. For instance, cash flow is now considered one of the most important indicators of a company's situation. The very phrase, however, was coined only in 1954.)

The new corporate giants confronted another problem besides keeping their finances in order. As the railroads and other corporations expanded in size, financing far beyond what a single family could supply was often needed. But as stock was sold on Wall Street to raise the necessary money, a widening gulf developed between the interests of the managers of corporations and the owners, the stockholders. The latter wanted timely information that would allow them to evaluate the worth of their holdings and to compare them with other, similar concerns, in order to judge the performance of the managers. The managers, naturally, wanted the freedom to massage the numbers to make them look as good as possible. Far too often this meant parting company with the truth completely and lurching over into fraud.

Worse, publicly traded corporations were not legally required to issue reports at all. When the New York Stock Exchange asked the Delaware, Lackawanna and Western Railroad for information about its finances, it was told, in effect, to buzz off. The "railroad makes no report," it curtly informed the exchange, and "publishes no statements."[10]

Even when a railroad did issue a report, it was often "a very blind document."[11] The Erie Railway, because it had been partly funded by the state, had to give the state an annual report. In 1870, however, Horace Greeley, in the *New York Tribune*, harrumphed that if it was accurate, then "Alaska has a tropical climate and strawberries in their season."[12]

The *Commercial and Financial Chronicle*, another Wall Street newspaper, put its finger on the problem as early as 1870. "The one condition of success in such intrigues," it wrote on May 17 of that year, "is secrecy. Secure to the public at large the opportunity of knowing all that a director can know of the value and prospects of his own stock, and the occupation of the 'speculative director' is gone. . . . The full balance sheet . . . showing the sources and amounts of its revenues, the disposition made of every dollar, the earnings of its property, the expenses of working, of supplies, of new construction, and of repairs, the amount and form of its debt, and the disposition made of all its funds, ought to be made up and published every quarter."

Today, annual and quarterly reports seem so obvious it is hard to imagine a capitalist world without them. In the late nineteenth century the managers, protecting their self-interests as people tend to do, resisted the entire concept fiercely. Henry Clews, an influential broker (and valuable historical source, thanks to his memoirs, *My Fifty Years in Wall Street*), pushed the idea relentlessly and was soon joined by a considerable number of investment bankers and other brokers. When the New York Stock Exchange began to require reports for all listed stocks, the managers had little choice but to comply.

But who was to prepare the reports? The companies' accountants worked for the managers, after all. Independent accountants became increasingly numerous at this time. In 1884, only 81 were listed in the city directories of New York, Chicago, and Philadelphia. Just five years later there were 322. In 1882, the Institute of Accountants and Bookkeepers was formed in New York and began issuing certificates to those who could pass a strict examination. In 1887, the American Association of Public Accountants was organized, the ancestor of today's main governing body of the profession. In 1896, New York State passed legislation establishing the legal basis of the profession and, incidentally, using the phrase *certified public accountant* for the first time to designate those who met the criteria of the law. The legislation, and the phrase, were quickly copied by the other states.

The establishment of independent accountants and generally accepted accounting principles was an unheralded but vital development in the history of free-market capitalism, and it was accomplished almost entirely by the players in the great game.

Government had almost nothing to do with these developments, and indeed, government at both the federal and state levels had yet to adopt these obvious safeguards against phony accounting.

Another change had been taking place on Wall Street during these years, and not one for the better.

As we have seen, Jews had been living in New York since Dutch days. From the beginning, therefore, Jews were an integral part of the New York business community and of its social fabric. To be sure, most Wall Street firms were either Christian or Jewish, but that was largely because these banks and brokerage houses were all partnerships and, often, strictly family concerns. But Jews and gentiles belonged to the same clubs and social institutions. Jews had helped found the Union Club, the city's oldest men's club, in 1836, and many other clubs and organizations. August Belmont Sr., who came to New York in 1837 to handle business for the Rothschilds, changed his name from Schoenberg (which, like Belmont, means "beautiful mountain") and converted to Christianity, but he made no secret of his origins. He married a daughter of the naval hero Oliver Hazard Perry and was completely accepted in the highest reaches of New York society.

But after the Civil War, as Germany changed from myriad petty kingdoms into a more unified state, its Jews, once largely confined to ghettos, were given more and more freedom, including the right to vote, own land, and practice the professions. This led to a rising anti-Semitism in Europe that, unlike the old medieval anti-Semitism, which had been primarily religious in nature, was social and racial instead.

It did not take long for this ugly doctrine to make its way across the Atlantic. Indeed the very word *anti-Semitism* entered the English language only in 1881, coming directly from the German. By the 1890s this prejudicial attitude was quietly fashionable among the younger generation of Wall Street. The new anti-Semitism, however, came to public notice only in 1893, when the young Theodore Seligman was blackballed from the Union League Club, which had been formed during the Civil War when some members of the Union Club had left that organization over its refusal to expel the southern members (including Judah P. Benjamin, who was, successively, Confederate attorney general, secretary of war, and secretary of state—and Jewish).

The Seligmans were among New York's oldest and most distinguished Jewish families, founding members of what would come to be known as Our Crowd. The family firm, J. & W. Seligman, had been one of Wall Street's major players for years (indeed, it still exists), with offices not only in New York but in San Francisco, New Orleans, London, Paris, and Frankfurt as well. More, Jesse Seligman, Theodore's father, was vice president of the Union League Club at the time of his son's blackballing.

Needless to say, the ensuing uproar received extensive coverage in the newspapers. The older members, including Cornelius Bliss, the club's president, and Senator Chauncey Depew (formerly president of the New York Central), had favored the young Seligman's admission. The younger members, those of Theodore's generation, opposed it. Their reasoning, today, seems almost comical. "[Our] opposition," one said, "is not based upon any dislike of particular individuals, but upon the general belief that men of the Jewish race and religion do not readily affiliate in the social way with persons not of their own persuasion."[13]

The elder Seligman resigned immediately from the Union League Club—although the club refused to accept his resignation and carried his name on its list of members for the rest of his life—and so did most of the club's other Jewish members. But the *Times,* referring to the Union League Club's powerful influence in the Republican Party, only noted dryly that "this unfortunate incident would never have been allowed to happen in a year when a campaign fund was to be raised."[14]

Meanwhile, powerful Christian members of the New York power structure, such as J. P. Morgan and the distinguished lawyer Elihu Root (later secretary of state under Theodore Roosevelt, who was himself a member of the Union League), were notably silent on the issue. Soon the other major clubs also stopped accepting Jewish members.

It would be two full generations before this ugly breach began to heal. The Union Club again took in a Jewish member only in 1956, when Judge Harold Medina joined the club.

*   *   *

Despite the prejudice, Jewish houses on Wall Street multiplied in these years and increased in power. While the partners of Christian and Jewish firms may not have visited each other's house, business was business as it has always been on Wall Street. The most powerful Jewish banker on Wall Street at the turn of the twentieth century, and the only banker who could come close to matching J. P. Morgan's power, prestige, and public image, was Jacob Schiff.

Like Morgan, he came from an old and affluent family. Born in Frankfurt am Main in 1847, he could trace his roots back to the 1370s, the oldest known Jewish genealogy in Europe. And also like Morgan, he never had any doubt about what he wanted to do in life. In 1875 he moved permanently to New York, where he soon became a partner in the banking house of Kuhn, Loeb. He quickly joined the family as well when he married Therese Loeb, the daughter of the firm's senior partner. In the 1880s and 1890s, Kuhn, Loeb was nearly as important a force in reorganizing the railroads as Morgan himself. In 1898, Schiff was instrumental in reorganizing the Union Pacific, then controlled by E. H. Harriman.

Harriman had started his career as a runner on Wall Street in 1862, when only fourteen. Small in stature, with a dark complexion and piercing eyes, he reminded many people of Napoleon, a comparison that didn't bother him a bit. In 1870 he borrowed $3,000 from an uncle to buy a seat on the exchange and soon moved into railroads. His father-in-law, William J. Averell, was president of the Ogdensburg and Lake Champlain Railroad, and Harriman used this connection to gain control of the Lake Ontario Southern Railroad in 1881. Harriman, like Commodore Vanderbilt before him, knew how to run a railroad, cutting waste and graft, investing heavily in sound rolling stock and trackage. Within two years he had sold the refurbished line to the Pennsylvania for a huge profit.

He transformed several other railroads, always following his cardinal principle: "The only way to make a good property valuable is to put it in the best possible condition to do business."[15] In 1898 he gained control of the nearly moribund Union Pacific. Still burdened by the malfeasance that had attended its birth in the Crédit Mobilier scandal, the Union Pacific was considered little more than junk. But Harriman inspected it closely and, betting the ranch on the return of prosperity to the Midwestern farm belt it served, nearly rebuilt it. Under his management the Union Pacific became a cash cow.

One historian of Wall Street, John Moody, estimated that one hundred shares of Union Pacific common in 1898 would have cost an investor $1,600. By 1906 the investment, in capital gains and dividends, would have been worth $21,900. The biggest holder of Union Pacific common, of course, was E. H. Harriman, who thus made one of Wall Street's great fortunes.

In 1901, as the prosperity that had returned after the rescue of the dollar in 1895 roared along, Harriman moved to gain control of a major rival and competitor of the Union Pacific's, the Northern Pacific. The Northern Pacific's dominant stockholder was James J. Hill of Minneapolis, builder and master of the Great Northern. Hill had used the Northern Pacific to seize control of the Chicago, Burlington and Quincy, a smaller road that threatened the Union Pacific's territory. When he refused to consider Harriman's interests, Harriman decided to counter the threat of the Burlington by getting control of the Northern Pacific.

Harriman's banker was Jacob Schiff; Hill was a client of J. P. Morgan and Company. So an attack on Hill's interest was an attack on Morgan himself. Schiff was not alarmed at that prospect and had soon managed to quietly buy up a majority of Northern Pacific's outstanding preferred stock (which had equal voting rights with the common). He also held enough of the common to give him an overall majority of the stock. Morgan, who was in Europe, had been caught napping.

When the Morgan Bank finally woke up to what was afoot, a frantic cable was dispatched to Morgan for authority to buy 150,000 shares of Northern Pacific common at the opening of the market on Monday, May 6. The hope was that if Hill could get a majority of the common stock, he could delay things long enough to retire the preferred, which the company could do at its option, and thus keep control. The cost of this operation would be, at a minimum, $15 million, but Morgan cabled back his immediate approval, and the contest between Morgan and Schiff was joined. As the titans battled, of course, everyone else on the Street would have to look out for themselves as best they could.

On Monday morning, Harriman and Hill held between them 630,000 of the 800,000 shares of Northern Pacific. By the close of the market on Tuesday, Morgan had purchased for Hill's account 124,000 additional shares. That left only 46,000 shares in other hands, but volume in Northern Pacific had been a whopping 539,000 shares. The vast majority of these shares had been sold short by speculators who had been looking for a fall in Northern Pacific, whose price had been rising swiftly as Schiff accumulated the stock.

Too late did the shorts realize that Harriman and Hill had between them cornered Northern Pacific. Now desperate to close their shorts while still solvent, they liquidated their other holdings to buy Northern Pacific at ever higher prices. Other stocks and bonds collapsed while panic swept the Street. Morgan's new U.S. Steel, which had been at 54¾ only a few days earlier, skidded on Thursday from 40 to 26.

So great was the demand for Northern Pacific that one broker hired a special train to bring a single certificate for five hundred shares down from Albany. The minor firm of Street and Norton sold three hundred shares to one short for $1,000 a share, ten times what the price had been a week earlier. A floor broker, who had recently returned to the city from the country and took a cab down to Wall Street, was unaware of what was going on and, seeing the uproar at the Northern Pacific post, incautiously admitted that he had ten thousand shares of the common. He was stripped virtually naked on the floor of the exchange as the desperate shorts clawed at him to buy.

By noon on Thursday the panic was threatening to engulf the entire Street in ruin, and J. P. Morgan and Kuhn, Loeb called a hasty truce. Both firms announced that they would buy no more Northern Pacific and would allow the shorts to settle at $150 a share, saving them from ruin. But the results were clear. Kuhn, Loeb had fought the Morgan Bank to a standstill and allowed Harriman to get what he had really wanted in the first place, not control of the Northern Pacific, but attention to his concerns regarding the Burlington. Harriman was soon on the board of that railroad.

The *New York Times* (now in the hands of Adolph Ochs, whose descendants still own it; it was rapidly becoming the paper of record that it has ever since prided itself on being) was disgusted with the whole affair, likening the corner to "cowboys on a spree, shooting wildly at each other in entire disregard of the safety of the bystanders."[16]

But the Northern Pacific corner was the last of Wall Street's great railroad wars, a throwback to the wild and woolly days of the Civil War. It is typical of Wall Street history that two men who epitomized the new Wall Street at the dawn of the new century should also have been its last cowboys.

CHAPTER TEN

"Why Don't You Tell Them What to Do, Mr. Morgan?"

In 1836 the phrase *Wall Street* came to stand for the New York securities market. By the end of the Civil War it represented the American securities market. By the turn of the twentieth century, however, it had come to symbolize much more: abroad it represented the economic power of the emerging American colossus. At home it was a metaphor for the financial power of banks, railroads, and industrial corporations that had developed with extraordinary speed in the years after the Civil War and now, in the eyes of many, needed to be curbed. The left, a word also only then coming into use to signify a segment of American political opinion, had been a rising force since the 1870s. The political struggle between it and "Wall Street" would be the defining divide in American politics for nearly the whole of the twentieth century.

The left—in this century, they would also come to be called liberals, a word that had a nearly opposite meaning in the nineteenth century—were the inheritors of Jefferson and Jackson, champions of the small farmer against the "money interest." As such, they were instinctively anti–Wall Street, just as their forebears two and three generations earlier had opposed the first and second Bank of the United States. But by now the economic situation had changed and farmers were a declining portion of the population. Rising swiftly to supplant them in political importance were the millions of laborers living in cities and working, often under brutal conditions, in the new industries. Jefferson, of course, had never encountered an industrial economy, so the left had to look to European models for ways to oppose the power of capital. Government ownership of "the means of production" never developed a major political following in this country, but government regulation of the economy certainly did. When and how much to regulate has been a major battlefield of domestic economic politics ever since.

The American economy was now so large and, thanks to the rapidly developing railroad net, so integrated, that internal competition forced cost savings and innovation. By 1900 the United States was the foremost industrial power in the world, supplanting Great Britain. It remained a major exporter of agricultural products, especially cotton, wheat, and corn, and mineral products, including two new ones, petroleum and copper. But it also became a major exporter of manufactured goods, which had constituted only 22.78 percent of American exports in 1865. By 1900 they made up 31.65 percent of a vastly larger trade.

Nowhere was this increase more noticeable than in iron and steel, the cutting edge of late-nineteenth-century industrial technology. Before the Civil War, the U.S. exported only about $6 million worth of iron and steel manufactures a year. In 1900 the country exported $121,914,000 worth of locomotives, engines, rails, electrical machinery, wire, pipes, metalworking machinery, boilers, and other goods. Even sewing machines and typewriters were being exported in quantity.

Europe, which had long imported raw materials and exported finished products, became alarmed. In the 1890s books began to appear with such ominous titles as *The American Invaders, The Americanization of the World,* and *The American Commercial Invasion of Europe.* Great Britain, however, found its economic hegemony threatened not only by the United States but also by Germany, which had well surpassed it in production. Because the latter also threatened it militarily, Britain worked to develop closer ties with its gigantic offspring across the North Atlantic. Over the new century these ties would develop into the closest relations between two great powers the modern world has known.

Central to this new relationship was the growing integration of the London and New York markets. Increasingly, Wall Street participated in underwriting foreign bonds as the growing network of telegraph cables under the Atlantic closely united the two great world financial markets. And Wall Street was now very nearly the equal of London, which had dominated world capitalism since the end of the Napoleonic wars. Wall Street's ups and downs were as carefully watched in London, Paris, and Berlin as they were in Washington, Philadelphia, and Chicago. New York remained overwhelmingly the country's leading port, and its banks and other financial institutions dominated the financing of American foreign trade.

And the iron and steel that was the basis of the new industrial economy also transformed the physical appearance of Wall Street for what, at least until now, was the final time. The old six-story office buildings that dated, many of them, from the 1850s were torn down to make way for skyscrapers (a word coined only in 1883), which steel and the electric elevator had made possible and New York's constricted real estate made inevitable. The narrow streets of New York's oldest neighborhood were cast into a world of wide shadows and thin streaks of sunlight that they have known ever since. So alarming did this trend become to some citizens and city officials that construction of the Equitable Building, on Broadway between Cedar and Pine Streets—forty stories tall with no setbacks and filling an entire city block—led directly to the country's first zoning ordinance. As with fast food, Wall Street has been the progenitor of much in American life that has little to do with money.

In 1903 the New York Stock Exchange moved into a new building on the same site as its old building at 8 Broad Street. Far larger than its predecessor, the new exchange featured an imposing classical facade with six Corinthian columns and a pediment with sculpture by John Quincy Adams Ward. Inside, a vast new trading floor, 100 feet wide, 183 feet long, and 79 feet high, accommodated the ever-increasing volume of trading. It remains the site of the stock exchange to this day (although plans are being developed to move it across Broad Street to larger quarters behind the Morgan Bank).

The trading floor, now jammed with electronic displays, was once one of New York's grandest interior spaces with almost daily drama. As the traders rushed to and fro, a sustained, deep noise modulated endlessly between roar and hum, as buyers and sellers—forbidden to use hand signals such as are common on commodities exchanges—made and took bids by open outcry at the various trading posts.

*   *   *

Wall Street bankers were creating the modern American industrial state, and the New York Stock Exchange was where the securities that financed it traded. Although usually viewed as conservative, these bankers, brokers, and industrialists were actually anything but. As the historian Frederick Lewis Allen wrote fifty years ago, "It was [Morgan] and the other fabricators of giant industries, and the lawyers and legislative draftsmen inventing new corporate devices, who were the radicals of the day, changing the face of America; it was those who objected to the results who were conservatives seeking to preserve the individual opportunities and the folkways of an earlier time. You might question the direction in which Morgan was moving; but that he was moving fast, and with a purpose which seemed to him to be to the country's benefit, is certain."[1]

Still, it is no wonder, at the turn of the century, that these activities caused consternation. Morgan had already launched such public companies as General Electric and International Harvester. In 1901 he organized U.S. Steel, which was originally the brainchild of Charles Schwab, president of Carnegie Steel. Astonishingly young for such a position (he had been only thirty-five when Andrew Carnegie gave him the job in 1897), Schwab was honored at a dinner on December 12, 1900, held at the University Club at Fifty-fifth Street and Fifth Avenue. Eighty men were present, including Carnegie, E. H. Harriman, Jacob Schiff, and J. P. Morgan.

Schwab, a gifted public speaker, made the most of his opportunity to influence the cream of America's new business elite. Asked to make a few remarks, he spoke for nearly an hour, during which time he laid out his vision of the future of the American steel industry. The industry was already the world's most efficient, but Schwab told his captivated audience of bankers and industrialists that it could be even more so. If a great consolidation could be arranged, Schwab suggested, so that a single company owned the largest and most efficient mills, economies of scale and specialization would allow it to undersell both British and German companies and to dominate the world market in steel.

Morgan, seated next to Schwab, was deep in thought throughout the speech, an unlit cigar slowly crumbling as he rolled it back and forth in his hand. After the dinner, Morgan took Schwab aside for a few minutes' private conversation. With characteristic dispatch, he resolved to pursue Schwab's vision. Both men knew that Andrew Carnegie was the key to the deal, as he owned a majority of the stock of the largest steel company on earth. So Schwab visited his boss, who was staying at his cottage at the St. Andrew's Country Club a little ways up the Hudson from Manhattan, where Carnegie, a native of Scotland, liked to play golf. Golf, virtually unknown in this country until the 1890s, had exploded in popularity among businessmen and others affluent enough to play an inherently expensive game. (John D. Rockefeller was another early devotee.) It soon became a standard venue for doing business. Over a round of golf (Schwab was careful to let Carnegie win), one of the great business deals in history was forged: Carnegie Steel would sell out to a syndicate to be organized by Morgan for $480 million. Morgan quickly congratulated Carnegie on becoming the richest man in the world. Carnegie, relieved of his business burdens, would spend the last two decades of his life (he died in 1919) giving his fortune away.

The enormity of the deal stunned everyone. The new firm, named United States Steel, was capitalized at $1.4 billion. In comparison, the federal government's budget that year called for only $525 million in expenditures. The entire manufacturing capacity of the United States was capitalized at a mere $9 billion. Even the *Wall Street Journal* confessed to "uneasiness over the magnitude of the affair" and wondered if the new corporation would mark "the high tide of industrial capitalism."[2] A joke circulated on Wall Street—long the joke capital of the planet, although the Internet is now giving it serious competition—in which a teacher asks a student who had made the world. "God made the world in 4004 B.C.," replied the boy, "and it was reorganized in 1901 by J. P. Morgan."[3]

Unease regarding the deal was hardly restricted to Wall Street. Theodore Roosevelt, who assumed the presidency on McKinley's death in the fall of that year, was a firm advocate of more government control over business, to prevent economic power from becoming political hegemony. In 1904, J. P. Morgan was stunned when the Justice Department announced it was suing under the Sherman Antitrust Act to break up the Northern Securities Corporation. This was the holding company Morgan had formed to settle the differences between E. H. Harriman and James J. Hill over the Northern Pacific Railroad. Morgan hurried to Washington, wondering why Theodore Roosevelt had not informed him, as one gentleman to another, ahead of time so that a satisfactory agreement could quietly have been reached.

"If we have done anything wrong," Morgan told the president, "send your man to my man and they can fix it up."

"That can't be done," Roosevelt told him.

"We don't want to fix it up," the attorney general explained, "we want to stop it."[4] And stop it they did.

But while the federal government under Roosevelt moved to increase its regulation of the economy, it still lacked one of the prime instruments for doing so, a central bank. Andrew Jackson had destroyed the country's last central bank, the second Bank of the United States, in 1836, and the country, unique among major powers, had operated without one ever since. The purpose of a central bank is to monitor commercial banks, regulate the money supply, and act in times of panic as a lender of last resort. A banking panic is often called a liquidity crisis. Liquidity, in the financial sense, is a measure of the ease with which one asset can be traded for another. Land, each piece of which is unique, is usually considered the least liquid of investments. Alternatively, cash is the most liquid. The very definition of "money" is any commodity that is universally accepted in trade for every other commodity.

When panic, for whatever reason, begins to creep into an economic system, people begin to convert their assets into more and more liquid form. They sell stocks and bonds and acquire cash and gold. If they begin to fear the soundness of banking institutions, they withdraw their deposits—mere notations in a bankbook—and hoard the cash itself.

Because banks mostly hold deposits that can be withdrawn on demand and lend these deposits out on term loans, they are all, in this sense, perpetually insolvent. If the depositors come to doubt the soundness of a bank and begin to withdraw their deposits, they can quickly drain a bank of cash, forcing the bank to close, at least temporarily. This, of course, makes the depositors of other banks nervous, and the contagion of fear spreads. There are good reasons that the word *panic*, even in its financial sense, is essentially a psychological term, not an economic one. (It also serves to remind us that, fundamentally, "economics" is the study of human beings—in all their unpredictable quirkiness—in the marketplace. Economics can no more successfully be reduced to numbers than can love. And certainly the science of economics would be a lot less dismal if economists would keep this ineluctable fact in mind.)

A central bank, taking a basically sound bank's loan portfolio as security, can provide it with the cash needed to meet any sudden demand, printing the money if necessary and thus aborting the panic as soon as people perceive that their deposits are available. The lack of a central bank was precisely the reason that the periodic panics in the nineteenth century, such as those of 1857, 1873, and 1893, were so much more intense and damaging than were similar panics in Europe. One more would have to be endured to drive the lesson home.

Once the American economy recovered from the terrible days of the early 1890s, it began to expand rapidly, making the early years of the twentieth century times of great prosperity. Government receipts nearly doubled between 1896 and 1907 as exports and imports also doubled, the latter fueling tariff receipts. The Dow Jones industrial average increased by 150 percent in those years, while the profits of the Carnegie Steel corporation, a mere $3 million in the depths of the depression, were over $40 million a year by the time Carnegie sold out to Morgan in 1901.

But all booms nurture the seeds of their own destruction. The gold supply, which on the gold standard ultimately determined the money supply, was not keeping pace with worldwide economic growth and the ever-increasing demand for capital. Further, a series of what in retrospect seem like small wars, such as the Boer War in South Africa and the Russo-Japanese war, placed added strains on the world capital markets as the governments involved had to enter those markets to finance their war efforts. Interest rates—the price of capital—rose steadily, and the more cautious Wall Streeters were openly worried. Even as early as January 1906, Jacob Schiff warned that "if the currency conditions of this country are not changed materially . . . you will have such a panic in this country as will make all previous panics look like child's play."[5]

The economy remained strong, with prices steady and profits increasing, but the market, a leading indicator, began to decline in March of 1907 when prices fell sharply if only temporarily. World markets remained profoundly uneasy. There was a run on the pound, as British gold reserves shrank. Stock markets in such far-away places as Alexandria, Egypt, and Tokyo crashed. In America, many solid companies and respected state and city governments found themselves unable to float new issues.

But the real crisis, when it came, originated not on Wall Street itself, but, as has so often happened in Wall Street history, far away to the west. This time it was the war of the "copper kings" in Butte, Montana.

There had been huge copper strikes in Montana and Arizona just as the new technology of electricity was creating a great new demand for copper. Butte, home of the "richest hill on earth," was producing as much as 300 million pounds of copper a year from mines that had six hundred miles of tunnels. What Butte didn't have was much law and order. The "apex law," passed by the Montana legislature in hopes of spurring production, allowed miners to follow a seam of ore from their property even when it went under someone else's property. Just what constituted the "apex," of course, was fiercely disputed, often with violence, and underground warfare was not uncommon in the dark shafts and endless tunnels beneath Butte.

F. Augustus Heinze, who came from Brooklyn, appeared in Butte in 1889 as an employee of the Boston and Montana Mining Company. Before leaving Butte temporarily to pursue opportunity in Canada, he became intimately familiar with the company's properties. Having made a fortune in Canada, he returned to Butte and began buying mining property. With that mysterious nose for ore characteristic of the born prospector, he often struck serious pay dirt. But he also exploited his knowledge of the local geology, taking advantage of the apex law to strike pay dirt that was the property of the Boston and Montana Mining Company.

But Boston and Montana was now part of Amalgamated Copper, the so-called copper trust. Among the owners and board members of Amalgamated were J. P. Morgan, H. H. Rogers, a high executive at Standard Oil, James Stillman, head of First National

Bank (now part of Citibank), and William Rockefeller, John D.'s younger and far more flamboyant brother. They were not amused by Heinze's brazen expropriation of their property. But they had no easy way to stop him. Heinze had a silver tongue and he soon won the miners—and their votes—to his side. He influenced the election of several judges who were happy to do his bidding and to harm the interests of the giant Amalgamated Copper Company.

Finally Amalgamated decided that it was cheaper to buy this irritating little upstart off than to continue to have their properties in Butte in chaos. They paid Heinze $10.5 million for all his Montana interests—enough, perhaps, to have put him on the *Forbes* Four Hundred list, had there been one in 1905. Heinze decided that having bested the big boys in Butte, he could do so again on Wall Street. He was wrong.

Heinze set up two of his brothers in the brokerage business, buying the firm a seat on the exchange. This allowed him to speculate on the exchange without paying commissions. Together with Charles W. Morse, who had formed the American Ice Company, yet another consolidation of an industry, he began to acquire control of banks as a ready source of funds to aid his speculations still further. Morse controlled the Bank of North America and used that bank's money to gain control of Mercantile National Bank. That bank's assets, in turn, allowed them to gain control of the Knickerbocker Trust Company, one of the largest banks in the city. All that was needed now, Heinze thought, was a suitable speculative vehicle.

Copper stocks were still hot, and Heinze had no doubt that his celebrated success in Butte would give him an advantage in speculating in them. He and Morse set up the grandly named United Copper Company, capitalized at $80 million. The company had few assets, other than the cash the sale of its securities had raised.

Heinze and Morse did not really intend to produce copper, they intended to corner the stock of their own company by purchasing shares and call options, running up the price and inducing other speculators into going short. Once they had a corner, they would exercise their call options and the shorts would discover the trap too late. There was one big problem. H. H. Rogers had neither forgotten nor forgiven what Heinze had done to Amalgamated Cop-

per in Butte two years earlier. And Standard Oil was the most powerful corporation in the world in the first decade of this century,
with an 80 percent monopoly on a product for which demand
seemed only to grow. With hundreds of millions of dollars in financial reserves, Standard Oil was a major financial company as well
as an oil company. Every broker, banker, and journalist on Wall
Street feared it and wanted to be in its good graces.

Heinze and Morse began their maneuvering for a corner in February 1907. In March, as other stocks were taking a beating,
United Copper rose. The market remained uneasy during the
spring and summer, but Heinze and Morse held the price of United
steady. Finally, as the market began to crumble in earnest in October, led by the copper stocks, Heinze was ready to put his plan into
action.

On Monday, October 14, the shorts began to cover, and while all
other copper stocks declined, United shot up from 37½ to 60.
Heinze was sure that triumph was at hand and sent word to his various brokers to exercise his call options. But the brokers were
unaccountably slow to act. Time was of the essence but they daw-
dled about sending out the notices. Further, stories began appearing in the papers about United Copper, questioning its finances.
There is no proof that Standard Oil was involved in either the
delays or the bad press, but few on Wall Street at the time, and few
historians since, have doubted that they were both orchestrated
from 26 Broadway, the headquarters of the Rockefeller empire.

Non–Heinze-and-Morse banks began to call in loans the pair had
taken, forcing them to sell stock at the worst possible time. On
Tuesday morning United sank under the weight of these problems and sank further as large blocks of stock from an unknown
source—but rumored throughout Wall Street to be H. H. Rogers—
were thrown onto the floor. By the end of Tuesday, United had lost
all the gains of the previous day, closing at 36. On Wednesday it sank
to 10. The Heinze corner was gone and with it millions of dollars.

But worse was to come. A run developed on the Mercantile
Bank, and the New York Clearing House, heavily influenced by
Standard Oil, declined to help until Morse and Heinze resigned
their positions. This they did on Friday, October 18. But on Monday, stocks tumbled again and there were further runs on banks,

including the Heinze-controlled Knickerbocker Trust Company, the third-largest trust company in the city.

Bedlam reigned as depositors fought to get to a teller and withdraw their assets from the bank's imposing new headquarters uptown on Fifth Avenue. (The midtown business district, centered on Grand Central Terminal, was just beginning to develop at this time.) Many thought that the Clearing House would have no option but to come to the aid of a bank as large as the Knickerbocker, but it did nothing. On Tuesday, October 22, the Knickerbocker's president bravely opened the doors at the regular hour, hoping the gesture would give confidence to the people that the bank was sound. It didn't work. Within a few hours, they had withdrawn $8 million. By the afternoon the Knickerbocker Trust Company announced its insolvency and closed its doors.

The financial empire of Heinze and Morse was utterly destroyed, and they themselves were as bankrupt as the Knickerbocker. The Standard Oil interests had had their revenge, but now the entire financial structure of the country was threatened by their success. It was a certainty that bank runs would be far worse on Wednesday and that panic would grip the stock exchange.

Unfortunately, there was no central bank, with the power to print money, to handle the crisis. The Roosevelt administration had no choice. It had to turn to J. P. Morgan, the only man with the power and prestige to command the cooperation of all Wall Street. The other major bankers had already pledged to Morgan all possible help. So had the New York Clearing House. John D. Rockefeller pledged $10 million. Now Secretary of the Treasury George B. Cortelyou, who had rushed to New York over the weekend, told Morgan that he was prepared to deposit $6 million in New York banks and that more would be available as needed. With everyone in the country looking to The Corner for help in the crisis, J. P. Morgan and Company, 23 Wall Street, was now the de facto central bank of the greatest economic power on earth.

On Monday, Morgan realized that the Knickerbocker was beyond saving, which is why the Clearing House did not try. But on Wednesday, as Wall and Broad were choked with people and lines of anxious depositors formed outside even the soundest banks, another trust company, the Trust Company of America, was also in deep trouble. At one o'clock that day it had $1,200,000 in cash on hand to meet demands for withdrawal. By 1:20 it was down to $800,000. By 1:45 only $500,000 remained; half an hour later it was down to $180,000.

The president and principal owner, Oakleigh Thorne, rushed over to The Corner and asked for assistance. Morgan turned to his lieutenants and asked if they thought the Trust Company of America was sound. They answered yes. "Then this is the place to stop the trouble,"[6] Morgan said. He ordered money sent to tide the bank over for the rest of the day.

Morgan asked Cortelyou to make deposits of government funds in the trust companies, which were most seriously threatened, but the secretary of the treasury could not, as he had power only to make deposits in national banks. Morgan therefore instructed him to deposit $35 million in those banks and in turn told those banks to lend the money to the trust companies.

The next day, Thursday, the twenty-fourth, brought the stock exchange to Morgan's door. Its officials informed him that unless money could be made available to several leading brokers to meet their obligations, the exchange would have to close, just as it had in 1873. Morgan flatly forbade it to close and summoned the city's leading bankers to his office. In five minutes he raised $27 million to tide the brokers over. Further, he let it be known that any bears found to have tried to profit from the situation by selling short would be "properly attended to."[7] The bears, apparently, decided not to risk having that vague phrase clarified.

That night every important banker in New York City met in Morgan's magnificent private library on East Thirty-sixth Street. As the bankers met in the east room, with its three tiers of glass-fronted cases holding masterpieces of Western literature, Morgan sat in the west room, his office, before the fireplace, playing endless games of solitaire and smoking cigars despite a bad cold.

"Why don't you tell them what to do, Mr. Morgan?" Belle Greene, his librarian and confidential assistant, asked.

"I don't know what to do myself," Morgan answered with his characteristic forthrightness. "But sometime someone will come in with a plan that I know *will* work; and then I will tell them what to do."[8]

THE WALL. Ordered built by Peter Stuyvesant, the wall failed to protect the city and existed less than fifty years, but it earned immortality by giving a name to the street that ran beside it. (Courtesy of Corbis-Bettmann)

ALEXANDER HAMILTON. The most urban and commercial-minded of the Founding Fathers, Hamilton devised a financial program for the new federal government that transformed the country's credit, and, incidentally, gave Wall Street its start as a securities market. (Courtesy of the New York Stock Exchange Archives)

THE BUTTONWOOD AGREEMENT. The ultimate origin of the New York Stock Exchange, the Buttonwood Agreement formed a brokers' cartel. It would be 180 years before the last remnants of that cartel were gone from Wall Street. (Courtesy of the New York Stock Exchange Archives)

WALL STREET, 1798. The fashionable residences of Wall Street were already being taken over by banks and insurance companies. The building on the left was the Bank of New York's first headquarters. (Courtesy of the New-York Historical Society)

THE MERCHANTS' EXCHANGE, CA. 1830. The New York Stock and Exchange Board rented an upstairs room in the Merchants' Exchange. On top of the building's dome was the first of a line of semaphore stations that could transmit opening prices to Philadelphia in about half an hour. It was replaced with the telegraph. (Courtesy of the New York Public Library)

THE GREAT FIRE, 1835. The glow could be seen in Philadelphia. The fire destroyed more than seven hundred buildings, including the Merchants' Exchange. A brave employee managed to rescue the stock exchange's records before the building collapsed. (Courtesy of Culver Pictures)

THE STOCK EXCHANGE, 1850. Sessions of the stock exchange were held in the rebuilt Merchants' Exchange, and the brokers still had actual seats. (Courtesy of the New York Stock Exchange Archives)

SPECULATORS READING THE TICKER, 1872. The Civil War transformed Wall Street in size, and the stock ticker transformed its reach, transmitting prices across the country in seconds. (Courtesy of the New-York Historical Society)

DANIEL DREW. A pious churchgoer on Sundays, there were few tricks Drew would not stoop to on Wall Street the rest of the week. He died broke. (Courtesy of the New York Public Library)

JAMES FISK JR. "Boldness! boldness!" a contemporary wrote of Fisk, "twice, thrice, and four times. Impudence! cheek! brass! unparalleled, unapproachable, sublime!" He played the game with endless zest until murdered in a love triangle. (Courtesy of the New-York Historical Society)

CORNELIUS VANDERBILT. Not interested in the great game of Wall Street, Vanderbilt played it when he had to better than anyone else before or since. He died the richest man in America. (Courtesy of the New York Public Library)

JAY GOULD. As quiet as his partner Fisk was noisy, Gould was, quite possibly, the smartest man ever to play the game. (Courtesy of the New York Public Library)

BROKERS BID FOR ERIE. The "Erie Wars" gave Wall Street some of its most exciting days, but they also showed what rules were needed to run a stable and orderly market. (Courtesy of the New-York Historical Society)

BROAD STREET, 1898. The stock exchange, on the right, had been recently enlarged but was already inadequate. It was replaced in 1903. (Courtesy of the New York Stock Exchange Archives)

WALL STREET LUNCH HOUR, 1880S. The lunch counter—the first fast-food venue—was invented on Wall Street during the Civil War, when the brokers didn't have time to go home for lunch. (Courtesy of the New York Public Library)

HETTY GREEN. The "richest woman in the world," Green lived in mortal terror of being poor and was one of the Street's shrewdest players. (Courtesy of Culver Pictures)

J. P. MORGAN. The epitome of American capitalism at the turn of the twentieth century, Morgan remains Wall Street's most familiar image. This is the famous "dagger portrait" by photographer Edward Steichen. But the "dagger" is only the arm of the chair. (Courtesy of the Pierpont Morgan Library/Art Resource, New York)

WALL STREET, LOOKING EAST, 1880s. The first Morgan Bank building replaced a grocery store in 1871 and was already known simply as The Corner. To be seen walking down the steps with J. P. Morgan was said to make a man's career. (Courtesy of the Museum of the City of New York)

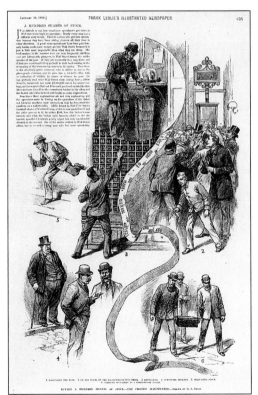

EXPLAINING WALL STREET TO THE PUBLIC, 1890. As American industrialization roared along, the public's interest in Wall Street as a serious financial market increased. (Courtesy of the New York Stock Exchange Archives)

THE WALL STREET JOURNAL.

VOL. 1.—NO. 1.   NEW YORK, MONDAY, JULY 8, 1889.   PRICE TWO CENTS.

THE WALL STREET JOURNAL

PUBLISHED daily, except Sundays and Stock Exchange holidays, at 3.15 P.M.

SUBSCRIPTION Price, $5.00 per annum. Delivered by carrier without charge, to subscribers of our regular news service. Reduced rates to bankers and brokers taking a number of copies for mailing. Postage charged on copies ordered for mailing abroad. All subscriptions payable in advance.

ADVERTISEMENTS 20 cents per line. Special rates to advertisers taking space for one, three, six or twelve months. Advertisements may be changed as often as desired without charge.

DOW, JONES & CO.,
26 BROAD STREET,
NEW YORK.

DOMINICK & DICKERMAN,
Bankers and Brokers,

Average Movement of Prices.

The bull market of 1885 began July 2, with the average price of 12 active stocks 61.49.

The rise culminated May 18, 1887, with the same twelve stocks selling at 93.27.

Prices gradually declined for about a year, reaching the next extreme low point April 2, 1888, the 12 stocks selling at 75.28. The movement since then, counting from one turning point to another, follows:

Last low point	Apr. 2, 1888,	75.28
Rallied to	May 1, "	83.54
Declined to	June 13, "	77.12
Rallied to	Aug. 8, "	85.95
Declined to	Aug. 18, "	83.76
Rallied to	Oct. 1, "	88.10
Declined to	Dec. 6, "	81.68
Rallied to	Feb. 18, 1889,	87.77
Declined to	Mar. 18, "	83.59
Rallied to	June 12, "	91.38
Closed Sat. night	July 6, "	87.71

The Market To-Day.

There is some reason for believing that operators identified with the bear party sent early orders to London to depress Americans in that market as a preparation for the opening here. These orders were faithfully executed, and London at 9.30 was quoted as opening weak and as having become very weak. Prices, however, were only a little below New York closing figures.

London houses were, however, sellers at the opening, and there developed a decided lack of buyers. Lake Shore furnished an illustration. It opened at 101¾ and was then offered down an eighth at a time to 101 where the next sale was made. This temper started a rush to sell out, during the first hour, prices generally went off from ⅜ to 1¾. In St. Paul Mr. Henry Clews & Co. at 19…

Clearings Last Week.

Boston special—The Post's table of clearings shows gross exchanges of 41 cities for the week ending July 6, 1889, $1,127,114,523, against $883,993,314 last year, an inc. of 27.5%. Outside of New York the inc. is 14.2%. New York inc. 37.3%, Boston 27.9, Philadelphia 6.3, St. Louis, 33.6, San Francisco 18, Cincinnati 7.2, Kansas City 27.5, New Orleans 3.1, St. Paul 2, Omaha 39.5, Minneapolis 15.2, Detroit 2, Denver 70.5, Peoria 12.7, Indianapolis 3.9, Ft. Worth 90.3, Wichita 48.4, Chicago dec. 5%, Milwaukee 1.6, Duluth 44.6 and Topeka 4.9.

For the month of June exchanges of 40 cities show an increase of 22.9%. Outside of New York increase 9.3%. New York increase 30.3%, Boston 18.8%, Philadelphia 12.1%, Chicago 0.1%, St. Louis 18.9%, San Francisco 2.7%, Kansas City 0.4%, St. Paul 2.1%, Omaha 20.9%, Denver 26.0%, Peoria 23.8%, Ft. Worth 47%, Topeka 18.4%. Duluth decrease 45.5%.

For 6 months gross exchanges of 40 cities show an increase of 15.8%. Outside of New York increase 11.9%. New York increase 18.2%, Boston 11.8%, Philadelphia 18.9%, Chicago 7.3%, St. Louis 8.5%, San Francisco 1.9%, Kansas City 11.3%, Omaha 19.5%, Denver 38.9%, Peoria 17.3%, Duluth 13.6%, Ft. Worth 31.8%, Topeka 31.4%.

Bankers Exerting Their Power.

Chicago special—It's stated on excellent authority that the Western presidents are getting positive orders from New York and Boston banking houses to settle the Western troubles at the meeting to-morrow. Some sort of plan to take care of C., B. & N. will be considered, and it is believed that if C. B. & N. can be controled, a general settlement will be effected.

Sales of stocks from 12 to 1—Listed 47,426; unlisted 5,454. Total, listed 194,408; unlisted 27,866.

12.40 p. m.—Slayback sold Union Pacific down.

The first bale of cotton from the South was sold at auction in front of the Cotton Exchange to-day and was bought by Henry Clews & Co. at 19…

THE FIRST ISSUE OF *THE WALL STREET JOURNAL*, JULY 8, 1889. The *Journal* remained a small trade paper, little known beyond Wall Street, until after World War II. But as public involvement in Wall Street increased, so did the paper's reach. Today it has the greatest circulation of any daily newspaper in the country. (Courtesy of the New York Stock Exchange Archives)

THE STOCK EXCHANGE FLOOR, 1901. The stock exchange building, constructed only thirty years earlier and enlarged in the 1880s, was already too small to handle the growing trading as the American economy became the largest in the world. (Courtesy of the New York Stock Exchange Archives)

THE FLOOR OF THE NEW EXCHANGE, 1903. Technologically up-to-the-minute, there were five hundred phones around the perimeter to connect the traders with their offices. (Courtesy of the New York Stock Exchange Archives)

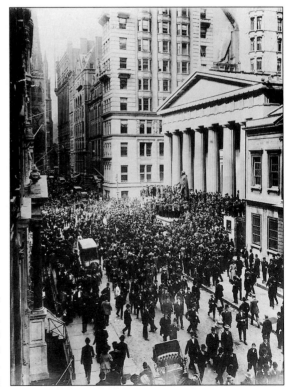

WALL STREET LOOKING WEST, THE DAY OF THE 1907 CRASH. Trinity Church, one of Wall Street's most recognizable symbols, unchanged since 1847, is a block away, across Broadway. (Courtesy of the New York Stock Exchange Archives)

THE CURB MARKET ON BROAD STREET, 1908. Skyscrapers, made possible by steel construction and the elevator, have replaced the old six-story office buildings of Broad Street, but the curb brokers—the spiritual ancestors of today's Nasdaq—didn't move inside until the 1920s. (Courtesy of J. P. Morgan & Co.)

DOUGLAS FAIRBANKS SELLS LIBERTY BONDS ON WALL STREET. One of Hollywood's first great stars, Fairbanks had started off as a Wall Street runner, two decades before World War I transformed the Street. (Courtesy of Culver Pictures)

THE AFTERMATH OF THE BOMB, 1920. Forty people were killed by the explosion; had the bomb gone off a few minutes later, the death toll might have been in the hundreds. The perpetrators were never caught. (Courtesy of the Museum of the City of New York)

WALL STREET LOOKING EAST, 1923. The present Morgan Bank building, far more architecturally restrained than its Victorian predecessor, opened on the Street in 1913, the year that J. P. Morgan died. (Courtesy of the New York Stock Exchange Archives)

CARTOON IN *FORBES* MAGAZINE, JANUARY 1929. The sky was the limit in 1929, until October 24, at least. (Courtesy of the New York Stock Exchange Archives)

VARIETY REPORTS THE CRASH. The 1929 debacle at least produced one of the most famous headlines in the history of journalism. (Courtesy of the New York Stock Exchange Archives)

THE FLOOR, 1930. The floor's old posts—which resembled the street lamps of Broad Street—were replaced in 1930 with horseshoe-shaped posts that could display much more information. (Courtesy of the New York Stock Exchange Archives)

RICHARD WHITNEY. The New York Stock Exchange has long commissioned an oil portrait of each of its presidents. Whitney's, however, was never finished. (Courtesy of Brown Brothers)

CHARLES E. MERRILL. Merrill thought there was money to be made in serving a wider public than Wall Street had had before. By 1950, ten years after its founding, Merrill Lynch was the largest brokerage firm in the world. (Courtesy of UPI/Corbis-Bettmann)

THE NEW ELECTRONIC TICKER, 1966. Keith Funston, president of the New York Stock Exchange points to the electronic display that began replacing the paper tape that year. (Courtesy of the New York Stock Exchange Archives)

THE TRADING FLOOR, 1980s. In 1981, the floor, one of New York City's great interior spaces, was obscured by a cat's cradle of interconnected computer monitors—duplicated in brokerage offices around the world—making the New York Stock Exchange the epicenter of a single global market. (Courtesy of the New York Stock Exchange Archives)

MICHAEL MILKEN. The jury is still out on the extent of Milken's misdeeds, but his creative influence on the Wall Street of the present day is undoubted. (Courtesy of UPI/Corbis-Bettmann)

THE TRIUMPH OF CAPITALISM. On October 31, 1997, the premier of the People's Republic of China rings the bell opening trading on the New York Stock Exchange. (Courtesy of the New York Stock Exchange Archives)

The bankers finally concocted—and Morgan approved—a plan to use clearinghouse deposits as a means of adding liquidity. All member banks maintained large deposits at the New York Clearing House to facilitate settling their transactions among themselves. The bankers decided to use clearinghouse certificates, paying 6 percent interest, instead of cash, to settle these transactions. This freed them to use their clearinghouse deposits to meet any demands for withdrawals at all sound banks. The effect was to increase the money supply—always the key to ending a liquidity crisis—by a then huge $84 million. As people discovered that their banks were prepared to meet any and all withdrawals, they no longer wanted to make them. The panic of 1907 was over.

Praise for Morgan's efforts and success in stemming the panic was immediate. His partner, George W. Perkins, said, "If there ever was a general in charge of any fight for any people that did more intelligent, courageous work than Mr. Morgan did then, I do not know of it in history."[9] Even Theodore Roosevelt, who as recently as August had been railing against the "malefactors of great wealth," now offered unstinting praise to "those conservative and substantial businessmen who in this crisis have acted with such wisdom and public spirit."[10]

No good deed goes unpunished, of course, and many of the left, including the muckraking author Upton Sinclair, accused Morgan of having fomented the panic for his own nefarious ends, and similar calumnies have been echoed over the years by others. Morgan never deigned to respond to such outrageous charges.

The panic of 1907, stopped dead in its tracks, did not lead to a depression as many previous panics had. Prosperity quickly returned. And the panic had one entirely salutary result. That the nation had had no alternative for rescue but to call on the very embodiment of Wall Street power caused even the most ardent opponents of a central bank to realize that it was no longer possible to operate without one. The country's most unfortunate legacy from Thomas Jefferson, after a hundred years of sometimes profound mischief, was at last to be laid to rest.

Still, it took six years to work out the details of what came to be called the Federal Reserve System. Wall Street wanted one bank, headquartered in New York, where, after all, the money was.

Given the politics involved, however, placing the new central bank in the heart of what was often called the "money trust" was never a serious possibility. In the end, twelve banks were established, one in New York, the others in major cities around the country, each with its own governor. The governors were to meet in Washington regularly and take joint action by majority vote.

But the new Federal Reserve was also limited in its reach. National banks, chartered by the federal government since 1863, were required to join the system, and state-chartered banks, far more numerous, were invited to join if they could meet the standards. Most could not, however, and thus the weakest banks, which most needed both the discipline and protection of the new system, were excluded.

The Federal Reserve was also restricted in its actions, especially as to what portions of a bank's loan portfolio it could accept as collateral. It could loan money on short-term commercial loans and agricultural loans, but not on loans backed by undeveloped land or even improved real estate. These two provisions of the Federal Reserve Act would have devastating consequences twenty years hence.

The bill creating the Federal Reserve was signed into law on December 23, 1913, a year that would prove in retrospect to be a watershed year in American financial history.

J. P. Morgan died on March 31 of that year. In just the first twelve hours after news of his death was released, 3,698 telegrams poured in from around the world, from kings, emperors, the pope, art dealers, bankers, and industrialists. Only the deaths of crowned heads have received such attention from the great and the ordinary alike. And people were astonished when his estate was revealed to be only about $60 million (plus another, roughly equal sum in artworks). John D. Rockefeller publicly remarked that this was not even enough to make Morgan "a rich man."

But Morgan, born rich, and in his maturity well able to afford to be ignorant of the costs of operating his yacht—a benchmark of wealth he may or may not have established—had never been greatly interested in accumulating wealth. For Morgan, rationalizing the American economy had been far more important, and the power he had accumulated in doing so had far outstripped the power of mere money. The Morgan Bank would remain the most powerful American bank for several decades to come, but no private American citizen would ever again hold such power and influence as he had had.

Even more significant than Morgan's death, however, was the new political landscape of the country. Theodore Roosevelt had split the Republican Party when he broke with his handpicked successor as president, William Howard Taft, over the latter's cautious approach to public policy. In 1912, Roosevelt bolted the Republican convention, after losing the nomination to Taft, and formed the Progressive Party (known by its symbol, the bull moose). Although the Republicans had been the country's majority party since the Civil War, the result of Roosevelt's action was the election of Woodrow Wilson as president (he was inaugurated less than a month before Morgan died) and to give this first liberal president—liberal in the modern sense—solid majorities in both houses of Congress.

Along with the creation of the Federal Reserve, Wilson and his allies in Congress hastened to enact a personal income tax, signed by Wilson on October 23, 1913. At first it was inconsequential. More a sop to the soak-the-rich wing of the Democratic Party than a serious tax reform, it affected only about 2 percent of American households. But it would have vast consequences.

But if 1913 was a watershed year in American financial history, so was 1914. On June 28 a fanatic assassinated Archduke Ferdinand, heir to the thrones of Austria-Hungary. European politicians, trying to take advantage of circumstances, as politicians are paid to do, bungled the matter and found themselves on the backs of tigers, unable to maintain control of events as the armies of Europe mobilized. What George Kennan called "the seminal catastrophe of the twentieth century" was under way. Neither Wall Street nor the world would ever again be the same.

CHAPTER ELEVEN

"DOES THIS HAPPEN OFTEN?"

Nothing is more troubling to financial markets than uncertainty. Indeed no small part of the reason for their existence is the reduction of uncertainty. They give investors daily, now instant, knowledge of the true worth of their holdings, while futures markets make it possible to lock in profits or reduce risk.

And nothing creates more uncertainty than war, the most unpredictable of all human activities. War between great powers compounds the uncertainty yet again. Thus all who make their livings in markets or depend on them fear war or even the threat of it more than almost anything else. It is ironic, therefore, that in the 1920s and 1930s, a myth arose, propagated by the left. It held that "Wall Street" and the "merchants of death"—the great corporations and their major stockholders—had fomented World War I to increase their profits by selling munitions and financing the war effort.

Political propagandists, of course, have little if any interest in truth, historical or otherwise. But journalists and historians are supposed to. Only a collective amnesia of events on Wall Street in 1914 could have allowed this myth to gain so much credence.

The threat of war in Europe had been growing for years as the great powers jockeyed for political, economic, and colonial advantage. Increasing the instability was that the foreign and military policies of the German empire, by far the strongest military power on land in Europe, were almost entirely in the hands of the mercurial, deeply neurotic, and utterly unpredictable Kaiser Wilhelm II. Each time in these years that a crisis developed, stock markets, unable to predict what the kaiser would do, sank sharply around the world.

In 1912, Serbia and Bulgaria declared war on Turkey, a conflict that threatened to drag in both Austria and Russia and bring about a general conflagration. The reaction was immediate. All the world's stock markets nose-dived. Interest rates rose sharply as the European central banks raised their discount rates. British Consols, the oldest bonds in the world (some date from the mid–eighteenth century and never mature), fell to their lowest point in history. European countries began to liquidate overseas investments, especially American ones, and to repatriate gold. In the period from August to December 1912, usually a time of the year of heavy gold shipments to the United States as the fall crops were exported, only $37 million flowed into the country. In the first six months of 1913, the outflow was fully $63 million.

Further, it was the accepted wisdom that any general European war would be ruinous not only to the economies of Europe but to the American economy as well. In 1910, the future Nobel Peace Prize winner Norman Angell published a best-seller called *The Grand Illusion* in which he argued that the inevitable disruption of international credit that war would cause ensured that any conflict would be entirely avoided or, at worst, speedily concluded. Britain, France, and Germany together had $5 billion in American investments, all of which, it was predicted, would be sold to buy weapons, causing the American stock market to collapse. Interest rates in Europe would skyrocket, dragging American rates along with them; American agricultural exports would sharply decline; and agriculture, still the basis of the American economy in 1914, would go into deep depression, taking everything else with it.

Largely thanks to Angell, popular wisdom had it that such a general war would never come about. One economist, writing in the *New York Times Sunday Magazine* in the early summer of 1914, wrote that "no modern war has been conducted to which the business world as a whole was unalterably opposed, for war must draw its sinews from the money chests of business."[1]

Thus when news reached Wall Street that the Archduke Franz Ferdinand, had been assassinated in Sarajevo by a Serbian nationalist extremist, the market remained calm. European royalty had suffered a steady string of assassinations in the previous decades, and Franz Ferdinand was not much respected in any case. Indeed, the *Commercial and Financial Chronicle* wrote shortly after the event that the assassination "has impressed the political and financial observer, not least of all because of the small degree of consternation with which the world at large received the news. . . . After a day or two of abundant news and comment, the matter seems almost forgotten."[2] Markets had been steady all year and interest rates had been falling. For a few weeks stability reigned. Politicians, brokers, and bankers alike went on vacation. The average daily volume on the New York Stock Exchange that July was a mere three hundred thousand shares.

But the world's political situation grew more perilous toward the end of July. On the twenty-fifth, the British proposed a conference of the powers to settle any questions in the Balkans, where Austria was using the archduke's death as a means of extracting concessions from Serbia. France and Russia promptly accepted, but Germany and Austria did not. Austria was afraid it would be prevented from capitalizing on the situation, and Germany, which is to say the kaiser, was determined to back its Austrian ally.

On Monday, July 27, stocks declined on Wall Street with much increased volume, and the demand for gold also increased. The following day Austria declared war on Serbia, and stock markets around the world fell sharply, while the price of gold soared. Many markets were forced to suspend trading. Volume in New York reached 1,020,000 shares. The following day, as European politicians, ever increasingly aware that the situation was spiraling out of control as the pressure to mobilize their forces grew, desperately sought a way out. But as they did so, more exchanges closed their doors, including those in Vienna, Rome, and most important, Berlin.

The next day, the rush to gold continued, and the dwindling number of stock exchanges that remained open saw panic selling. Volume on the New York Stock Exchange reached 1.3 million shares, the highest since the panic of 1907, while prices crashed, many falling 20 and even 30 percent. General Motors, not yet the country's biggest automobile manufacturer but a leading one, fell almost 34 percent, from 58⅞ to 39. Even Bethlehem Steel, only the country's second-largest steel company but by far its largest producer of the armor plate needed for warships and a major ship-builder, fell 14 percent.

That night the officers of the exchange met to consider closing. Strong arguments existed on both sides. Those who favored keeping the exchange open feared that closing it would only add to the atmosphere of panic and noted that it had stayed open in the dark days of 1907, when banks and brokerages were failing by the hundreds. But others pointed out that in 1907, J. P. Morgan, with his unique prestige and power, had been around to help control events, and that the world's other exchanges had not closed. Now most of them were already closed.

Early in the morning of July 31, the London Stock Exchange announced that it would suspend trading until further notice, the first time it had done so in its long history. Wall Street now had little choice. If the New York Stock Exchange opened for trading, it would be the only major stock exchange in the world to do so. And with the world's markets tied together by a cat's cradle of undersea cables, all the sellers in the world would converge on it. Indeed, the overnight orders to sell at the opening price had been piling into near mountains. The panic was likely to be of a ferocity such as Wall Street had never known. The vast majority of the governors, meeting in emergency session, voted to close and suspend deliveries until further notice. The president of the exchange then walked across the Street to The Corner and checked with J. P. Morgan Jr., now head of the House of Morgan. Morgan spoke with William G. McAdoo, secretary of the treasury, and all agreed that closing, for just the second time in the exchange's history, was the only option.

The banks, however, opened for business as usual, and several throughout the country experienced runs as depositors fled to gold and cash. In the two weeks beginning on Monday, July 27, $80 million was withdrawn from New York banks, $73 million of that in gold.

On the afternoon of the thirty-first, Germany declared war on Russia, and by August 3 all the great powers of Europe were at war. The British foreign secretary, Sir Edward Grey, said on that day, after the cabinet had decided for war, "The lamps are going out all over Europe; we shall not see them lit again in our lifetime."[3] In an economic sense, they have not yet been relighted. The long European economic and financial hegemony over the rest of the world had ended; the American century had begun.

The first problem facing Wall Street was how to get back in business. Investors were unable to buy or sell. Indeed they had no way of determining the worth of their securities. Brokers, meanwhile, were out of business entirely. With seats on the exchange having recently sold for around $80,000, while rent and other bills continued, brokers were desperate to resume trading so they could make money. Proving that where there are willing buyers and willing sellers for any commodity, there *will* be a market, clandestine markets began to spring up almost immediately.

Several curb brokers announced a willingness to buy or sell listed securities for cash, but soon ceased doing so under pressure from the NYSE. Auction markets developed in Boston, Chicago, and Philadelphia that functioned much as had the original Wall Street market under the buttonwood tree 120 years earlier. The prices at those markets, however, at the request of the New York Stock Exchange, were not reported in the newspapers. This prevented them from becoming true stock markets. (It also prevents historians from knowing how prices fluctuated and what size these markets attained. But they appear to have been substantial.)

Soon groups of men appeared on New Street, the narrow street behind the stock exchange, and reports that they were trading securities were investigated by a member of the committee of the exchange that was, curiously, now in charge of *preventing* stock trading in New York. He reported, famously, that there were only "four men and a dog"[4] present on New Street. But the market there was soon in robust operation with as many as a hundred brokers dealing in stock between ten in the morning and three in the afternoon.

Slowly, the exchange brought Wall Street back to full operation. On August 12, limited trading at the clearinghouse was allowed, at prices no lower than they had been on July 30. But this amounted only to a piddling five to seven thousand shares a day. Prices on the New Street market firmed as the weeks passed, and the Curb Market announced that it would resume trading on November 16, the day the New York Federal Reserve Bank was scheduled to begin operations. The Chicago exchange announced that it would open a week later.

The New York Stock Exchange decided to begin trading in bonds on November 28 and some restricted trading in stock on December 12. But only certain issues could be traded, for cash only, with neither short selling nor futures contracts permitted. Bit by bit over the following weeks, the New York Stock Exchange permitted more and more normal activity until, by April of 1915, the market was back to normal operation. It has never again closed for more than a very few days. Today by law the exchange may not be closed for more than three consecutive days, which is why there is a brief session on the Friday after Thanksgiving.

At first, the market was dull, with prices steady and volume moderate. Indeed, the volume on December 30, 1914, was a mere 49,937 shares, the lowest volume of the twentieth century.

The only reason the market had been able to reopen was that the dire predictions of the swift collapse of the world economy in general and the American economy in particular, so widely made in August, had proved spectacularly wrong. By September, the war of movement on the Western front had ceased and the endless agony of the trenches had begun. But the predicted flow of gold out of the United States had also ceased by September. By the end of the year, gold was moving into this country for safekeeping, where much of it has remained ever since, now located in the vaults eighty-five feet below the Federal Reserve Bank on Liberty Street, three blocks north of Wall. Meanwhile American securities began to look more and more attractive to European banks and other financial institutions.

By early September, cooler heads were beginning to notice the real effects of the war on the American economy. The president of the National Association of Manufacturers at that time saw great American opportunities in the war. He boldly predicted that when the war was over, the United States would be the world's leading power and New York its financial capital. He was right.

At first, to be sure, American commerce was severely disrupted. Germany had imported 2.6 million bushels of wheat in the month before the war, but none in August 1914. Cotton exports also fell sharply. With both the White House and the Congress in Democratic hands and the Solid South the dominant region in the Democratic Party, great efforts were made to prevent cotton farmers from failure. Someone even proposed that every family buy a bale of cotton and store it until hostilities ceased. President Wilson himself bought a bale.

But once the Royal Navy had established control of the North Atlantic, demand for American agricultural products rose sharply. This was partly due to a poor harvest in Europe that year. But as more and more European agricultural laborers and farmers were called up for service, poor harvests throughout the war became certain. Further, Russia—a major grain exporter under the czars— was unable to reach world markets, with Germany controlling the Baltic and its ally Turkey the Dardanelles, the entrance to the Black Sea. Between December 1914 and the following April, the United States exported no less than 98 million bushels of wheat, while in the same period a year earlier, it had exported a mere 18 million.

Markets for manufactures in Asia and Latin America, which had been dominated by Europeans, now lay open to American companies, and they moved swiftly to exploit this golden opportunity. And the bottomless demand created by the war for munitions, steel, vehicles, communications equipment, railroad equipment, and ships soon produced a boom in the American economy such as it had not seen since the Civil War.

Until 1914, the largest contract that Bethlehem Steel had ever signed was for $10 million, to supply ships and armor plate to the Argentine navy. But in November of 1914, the head of Bethlehem Steel, Charles Schwab (who had previously headed U.S. Steel), was summoned to London where he was offered a contract by the Royal Navy for guns, shells, and submarines that totaled $135 million. E. I. Du Pont was, during the war, transformed from a large gunpowder company into a chemical-industrial giant. Expanding, well, explosively, Du Pont was to supply the Allies with 40 percent of their munitions. The military contracts Du Pont fulfilled in the four years of war equaled 276 times its average annual military business before the war, and 26 times its total average business.[5] Other companies expanded likewise.

Wall Street, after panicking at the outbreak of war, now found itself in the midst of one of the greatest bull markets in its history.

General Motors, which had recovered from its sharp break in trad-ing on the last day before the closing, ended 1914 at 81½. A year later it stood at 500. American Smelting leaped from 56¼ to 108⅛. Bethlehem Steel, meanwhile, deluged with orders from the Allies, surged from 46⅛ to 459½, having reached as high as 600 during the year.

Germany and the other Central Powers did not have access to American industrial capacity, thanks to the effective blockade of the Royal Navy. Unable to defeat Britain at sea, Germany tried to do so on Wall Street. Charles Schwab held a controlling interest in Bethlehem Steel, and the great bull market of 1915 made his holdings worth $54 million. Representatives from the German embassy in Washington approached Schwab with an offer they evi-dently thought he couldn't refuse: $100 million for his stock. Britain, able to decode and read German diplomatic traffic, quickly learned of the plan and was prepared to make Schwab a coun-teroffer. But Schwab turned the Germans down out of hand and promised the British that their contracts would be fulfilled to the letter. With the help of the Morgan Bank, enough Bethlehem stock was put in trust to assure that the company would not be taken over.

After the war, Admiral Lord Fisher, the father of the modern Royal Navy, wrote in his memoirs, "If any man deserves England's gratitude it is Mr. Schwab."[6] It would appear that greed and fear are, in fact, not the only emotions to be felt on Wall Street. And nothing could more forcefully demonstrate Wall Street's new world stature than that the securities traded there influenced the policies of the warring powers.

In the early days of the war, the U.S. government was strictly neu-tral. The secretary of state, William Jennings Bryan, was deeply isolationist and determined to keep the United States out of the war by enforcing the neutrality laws. This included forbidding loans to belligerent powers, which Bryan deemed "the worst of contrabands."[7] But once economic opportunities resulting from the war were manifest, government policy subtly shifted. Robert Lansing, assistant secretary of state, convinced President Wilson to make a distinction between "loans" and "credits" for the purpose of facilitating purchases in the United States. Bryan, hopelessly a fish out of water in the world of power politics, soon resigned as secretary of state and was replaced by Lansing.

The Morgan Bank, with its extensive relationships in both the British and French banking communities, was soon deeply involved in helping to finance the war efforts of the Allies. On January 15, 1915, Morgan signed an agreement with the British government to become the American purchasing agent for Britain. The first purchase was for $12 million worth of horses, desperately needed on the front to move artillery and supplies. In the spring of that year the bank signed a similar agreement with the French government. At first the bank and the British government did not think that such agreements would amount to that much. Lord Kitchener, British secretary of state for war, thought that $50 million might be on the high side of the final figure. In fact, Morgan would purchase more than $3 billion worth of supplies for Britain before the war ended. That amounted to well over four times federal government revenues in 1916, the last year before the United States entered the war.

With a commission of 1 percent, the House of Morgan made a total of $30 million. And its influence in American industry greatly expanded as a Morgan staff of 175, under Edward Stettinius, scoured the country for needed supplies and arranged for their shipping and insurance.

Morgan, in its capacity as a bank, also helped companies expand to meet the demands of war. By the end of the war the American armaments industry was larger than those of Britain and France combined. Edward Stettinius, whose son and namesake would be Franklin Roosevelt's last secretary of state, is remembered today, rather unkindly, as the father of the American military-industrial complex. But Germany's General von Ludendorff thought he was worth an entire army corps to the Allies.

Although one American in ten was of German ancestry in 1914, public opinion in this country had begun moving toward the Allies almost from the outbreak of the war. German violation of Belgian neutrality and its atrocities in that nation—skillfully exploited by British propaganda—appalled most Americans. But it was the sinking by a submarine of the Cunard liner *Lusitania* on May 7,

1915, that ensured continuing American hostility to the Central Powers.

We who have lived our lives in the shadow of the horrors of the Second World War are inured to civilian war casualties; our great grandparents were not. To be sure, the German embassy had placed ads in the New York papers warning voyagers that a state of war existed between Germany and Great Britain. And the Germans—quite correctly, it turned out—suspected the ship of carrying contraband goods. But few had paid attention, for sinking an unarmed passenger ship was deemed quite beyond the pale. In addition, no one thought the swift liners that covered the North Atlantic route could be attacked by the slow-moving submarines of the day. Only extraordinary luck put the liner dead in the sights of the submarine, whose torpedo sank her in less than fifteen minutes. The death toll was 1,198, including 128 Americans.

Outrage at the event swept the nation. On Wall Street, Jacob Schiff, who, born in Frankfurt, regarded Germany as his native country and still spoke German at home, was shattered. Although, needless to say, he had had nothing whatever to do with the tragedy, he felt it necessary to call on J. P. Morgan Jr. to express his condolences personally. He made his way to The Corner and found Jack Morgan in the partners' room.

But Morgan, instead of responding to this extraordinary courtesy with equal grace, only muttered angrily and left the room, leaving Schiff to make his way out alone. Morgan's partners were stunned, and Morgan himself soon realized that he had behaved poorly indeed. "I suppose I went a little far?" he asked his partners. "I suppose I ought to apologize?"

None of them, apparently, had the courage to state the obvious to Morgan's face, but Dwight Morrow—quick-witted even by the standards of Morgan partners—scribbled a verse from the Bible and handed the note to Morgan. It read, "Not for thy sake, but for thy name's sake, O House of Israel!"[8] Morgan walked over to Kuhn, Loeb and made amends.

Schiff and many of the other Jewish bankers and brokers on Wall Street were often accused of harboring pro-German sentiments. This was only to some extent true. Henry Goldman, of Goldman, Sachs, was ardently pro-German, talking openly of his admiration for Prussia and its orderly ways. But many Jewish firms were not so much pro-German as anti-Russian. Schiff, who had publicly called Russia "the enemy of mankind" for its pogroms against Jews, helped finance the Japanese in their war against Russia in 1904.

It soon became obvious, however, that wherever personal sentiments may have lain, financial interests were with the Allies, who had access to the American market and worldwide commerce. But to win the war, the Allies needed more than matériel. They needed the money and financing to pay for it. By this point, Wall Street and its great banks were the only possible source. Great Britain, whose prewar defense budget had been around 50 million pounds annually, was now spending 5 million pounds *a day* to fight the war.

Although Wilson had acquiesced in the extending of credits to the Allies to facilitate their purchases of American goods, he remained opposed to outright loans. But he was soon persuaded that they were necessary to maintain American exports. Secretary of State Robert Lansing told Wilson that without loans, "the result would be restriction of outputs, industrial depression, idle capital and idle labor, numerous failures, financial demoralization, and general unrest and suffering among the laboring classes."[9] Wilson quickly caved in.

In September 1915, the British sent a delegation to the Morgan Bank to negotiate a loan of unprecedented size. A the turn of the century Morgan had arranged a loan to the British government, to help finance the Boer War, for $100 million, then regarded as a staggering sum. This new loan would be for no less than $500 million.

A loan so vast could not be handled single-handedly by any one bank, even J. P. Morgan and Company. Instead an underwriting syndicate of many banks was needed. In the end the loan would have no fewer than sixty-one underwriters and an additional 1,570 financial firms marketing the loan. But Kuhn, Loeb was not to be one of them. When the chief British negotiator, Lord Reading, the Lord Chief Justice and himself Jewish, called on Kuhn, Loeb, Schiff insisted that not one penny of the loan go to Russia. Reading could hardly accept such a condition, and Kuhn, Loeb would suffer a great loss of prestige and profit because of Schiff's stance. Other Jewish houses were not so adamant. Henry Goldman was forced by his partners to resign from Goldman, Sachs when it appeared that the firm might be blacklisted by London because of his pro-German position.

The $500-million loan of 1915 was but the first of many loans to the Allies before the war ended three years later, and Morgan would finance no less than $1.5 billion of them. But loans and acting as a purchasing agent were not the only source of profit to Wall Street. The British government placed a special tax on dividends from U.S. stocks but allowed holders to pay their income taxes with U.S. securities. Shares in American companies began to pile up at the Bank of England, and the Morgan Bank liquidated fully $3 billion worth, feeding them slowly and skillfully into the New York stock market to prevent any plunge in prices. It is a measure of the war's vast expansive effect on the American economy and the New York stock market itself that it could absorb so great an addition to the supply of stock with hardly a hiccup.

The result was not only vast commissions for the Morgan Bank, but the repatriation of the ownership of American industry. At the beginning of the war, the United States had been the largest debtor nation on earth. Four years later it was the largest creditor. Financially as well as industrially, it was now the world's leading power, and the power of that money flowed, necessarily, through the canyons of Wall Street.

When the United States entered the war, in April 1917, the federal government, too, had to borrow money in unprecedented amounts. The national debt had peaked in 1866 at $2.755 billion and had been falling ever since (and plunging as a percentage of the swiftly rising gross domestic product). By 1916 it was a mere $1.23 billion, 2.54 percent of GDP. When it peaked again in 1919, however, the national debt stood at $25.5 billion, or 30.34 percent of GDP. The bonds that financed this new debt were sold using the same techniques Jay Cooke had used to finance the Civil War fifty years earlier, only with the addition of Hollywood celebrities such as Douglas Fairbanks and Mary Pickford to help sell them. Of course Wall Street, the nation's securities market, burgeoned in power and domain as these new securities were marketed.

By the time the war was over, the United States was the only real victor. Russia was in chaos and soon to fall into the firm grip of the dead hand of communism. The Austrian empire was dismembered. Even Britain and France, nominally victors, were exhausted, their blood and treasure dissipated, their power on the world stage permanently diminished. But the cost in blood to the United States had been only sixty thousand lives in battle casualties (Britain alone, with a much smaller population, had lost over a million men). The American economy was far stronger than it had been before the war. And European nations owed the federal government over $10 billion in addition to their privately held debt.

No part of the American economy had benefited more than Wall Street, which had become the sun around which the world's other financial markets, including London, now revolved. The reason was simple enough; indeed, it was the same reason Willie Sutton gave a few years hence for robbing banks: "That's where the money is."

The sudden end of the war on November 11, 1918, inevitably led to the considerable problems of adjusting to peace. The economy underwent a short, sharp depression beginning in 1920, as war orders ceased and European farm production and nonmilitary manufactures began to increase. The end of the war also produced a new New York tradition. Office workers in the buildings along lower Broadway had thrown ticker tape out of windows during parades as early as the 1880s. But in 1919, Grover Whalen, who served as chairman of the Mayor's Reception Committee from that year until 1953, began organizing ticker-tape parades officially, sending notices to businesses in the area to please cooperate. In 1919, General Pershing and the young Prince of Wales, later the Duke of Windsor, were the first to be honored by having wastepaper rained down upon them.

But Wall Street's most famous decade, the 1920s, began with a quite literal bang. A few minutes before noon on a sunny, warm September 16, 1920, a horse-drawn wagon pulled up on Wall Street beside the Morgan Bank and exploded. Loaded with five hundred pounds of sash weights cut into pieces as well as explosives, the fragments turned into shrapnel, cutting through the air like deadly, invisible flails. Thirty people died instantly, ten more would later die of wounds, and a hundred and thirty were injured. Had the explosion occurred only a few minutes later, when lunchtime crowds would have been surging through the intersection of Wall and Broad, the toll would have been far worse.

The young Joseph P. Kennedy, not yet a power on the Street, was knocked to the ground while strolling perilously close to ground zero, but was otherwise unhurt. Edward Sweet, a millionaire who had owned Sweet's restaurant on the corner of Fulton and South Streets, however, was virtually vaporized. All that was ever found of him was one finger, encircled by his ring. Seward Prosser, president of the Morgan-dominated Bankers Trust Company, barely escaped with his life when one of the sash-weight fragments shot through an office window and missed him by no more than an inch. A young runner was not so lucky. Grievously wounded on the street, he begged passersby to take the bundle of securities he had been carrying so that he would not die with his duty undone.

Awnings, ubiquitous in the days before air-conditioning, burst into flames as high as twelve stories above the ground. Windows as far as half a mile away from the bomb site shattered. A great pall of thick, green smoke filled the area.

Brokers on the floor of the stock exchange, stunned into unaccustomed silence by the blast, surged into the middle of the room as the great windows facing Broad Street vanished into millions of fragments. Then, suddenly realizing their peril from the glass dome above them, which trembled violently but held, the brokers fled once more, this time for the safety of the walls. The president of the exchange immediately fought his way to the rostrum. There he rang the bell, suspending trading within one minute of the explosion.

The windows of J. P. Morgan and Company shattered as well. By some miracle of providence, metal screening had just recently been installed on the inside of the windows, and this alone prevented a bloodbath on the floor of the bank. Still one Morgan employee was dead and another succumbed to injuries the next day. Julius Morgan, the son of J. P. Morgan Jr., was wounded (on the hand, according to the newspaper accounts; on his buttocks, according to his amused partners). Another young banker, William Ewing, was knocked unconscious and awoke to find his head jammed in a wastepaper basket.

Jack Morgan was in England at the time, but four of his senior partners were in conference with a French general when the bomb went off. The thick limestone walls of the bank protected them from injury, but they, like everyone else, were stunned into silence. As the thunderous noise of the bomb melted away, to be replaced by the tinkling of glass, the screams of the survivors, and the moans of the wounded, the French general resumed the conversation, asking politely, "Does this happen often?"[10]

Within minutes the area was swarming with police, firemen, and ambulance personnel, and a huge investigation was launched. The forensics of explosions was not even in its infancy in 1920, however, and all the police had to go on were the pieces of sash weights and two of the horse's hooves, which were found a block away, in front of Trinity Church. Sash weights, it turned out, are all much alike in appearance, and their origin could not be determined. And despite visits to four thousand stables and every blacksmith shop east of Chicago, the horseshoes proved equally untraceable.

In all probability the bomb was the work of anarchists, the final, spectacular outrage, in fact, of the fast-fading nineteenth-century philosophy. After the explosion, the post office turned over to the police some flyers it had found in a mailbox located at the corner of Broadway and Cedar Street, a short walk from Broad and Wall. The mail had been collected from that box at 11:30 and again at 11:58 that morning, two minutes before the explosion. The flyers had been found in the latter batch, placed there almost certainly by someone who knew what was about to happen.

"Remember," the circular said, rather incoherently, "we will not tolerate any longer Free the political prisoners or it will be sure death for all of you." It was signed "American Anarchist Fighters." The circulars were almost identical to some others found after anarchist bombings in New York in 1919, but they led to no arrests.

There was one other major lead. Edwin P. Fischer was a young lawyer, well connected on Wall Street and formerly a nationally ranked tennis player. He also possessed an eccentricity that had more than once gone over the line into outright lunacy. About two weeks before the explosion, Fischer had begun telling friends and acquaintances that a bombing was going to happen on Wall Street, adding disparaging remarks about Wall Street in general and J. P. Morgan and Company in particular. He usually said the bombing would be on September 15 but at least once hit the date right on the money.

Naturally, people had paid no attention until the bomb actually exploded. Fischer was in Canada when it happened, and his brother-in-law immediately went to him and persuaded him to return to the United States. Thoroughly questioned, he was quietly hospitalized for a few months, and no one seriously thought that he had any connection with the bomb. After all, as one friend explained, "No conspirator, after talking to Fischer for ten minutes, would consider letting him into a plot with them."[11] As nearly as anyone can tell, Fischer's warnings were only an instance of that peculiar prescience that so often seems to be nature's gift to the insane.

The bombing of Wall Street in 1920 was, in a sense, a backhanded compliment to the Street's new power as the world's money center. As such, Wall Street, true to form, soon returned to getting and spending, and the bombing was soon largely forgotten. The awnings that had been torched by the explosion were replaced and the glass restored to the windows. But J. P. Morgan and Company decided not to repair the gouges the sash weights had made to its facade. Some of them more than an inch deep, they remain there to this day, the stigmata of capitalism, and one of the Street's minor tourist attractions.

CHAPTER TWELVE

"THE STOCK EXCHANGE
CAN DO ANYTHING"

It is a law of human nature that, absent outside pressure, organizations tend to evolve in ways that favor their elites. This is as true of perk-heavy corporations as it is of boss-ridden labor unions, as true of Congress as it is of Hollywood. But few better examples of this phenomenon exist than the New York Stock Exchange in the 1920s.

After its informal, self-regulating childhood in the 1830s and nearly lawless adolescence in the Civil War era, the stock exchange had worked out the rules and procedures needed to assure an orderly, stable market. Once the exchange had achieved dominance on Wall Street and could enforce these rules, investors were able to search for opportunities there without worrying about being cheated by the very process of investment. Likewise, brokers, at least those with business sense, could expect to make money in the long term.

By 1920 the phenomenal growth of the American economy in the preceding forty years and the accident of a world war fought in Europe had made the New York Stock Exchange the largest and most powerful institution of its kind in the world. But institutionally, it was still much the same as it had been in 1817 when it had come into formal existence. That is to say, it was a private club, operating for the benefit of its members, the seat holders, and not the investing public. And like most private clubs, the New York Stock Exchange was anything but democratic in its internal governance.

Clubs are usually run by a small, self-perpetuating oligarchy among the membership who hold all the major offices and committees. In other words, private clubs are usually run in a manner not at all dissimilar from the governing system of the old Soviet Union, with its general secretary, politburo, and purely nominal elections. In the case of the exchange, the oligarchy was not drawn evenly from across the whole spectrum of the membership. While all the major brokerage houses had partners who owned seats on the exchange, about half the seats were held by specialists and floor traders. But these latter two groups held two-thirds of the seats on the all-important Governing and Law Committees of the exchange.

Specialists make a market in particular stocks, manning the post on the floor where those stocks are traded. Their job is to see to it that a "fair and orderly market" is maintained. Each specialist keeps a book wherein all the orders to buy or sell a given stock are listed, executing those orders when the particular prices are reached. Thus they are in a perfect position to know which way the market is heading and to profit accordingly. In the 1920s, no rules prevented specialists from operating in any way they could for their own profit in the stocks in which they maintained a market, nor prevented them from providing insider information to others and taking a cut on the resulting profit.

The floor traders, on the other hand, traded only for their own accounts. They had two great advantages over the ordinary investors and speculators who increasingly haunted the board rooms of brokerage offices as the decade progressed. Because they had access to the floor itself, they had the latest possible information on how the market, and individual stocks, were moving and could execute trades with lightning speed. And because they paid no brokerage commissions, they could move in and out of stocks and bonds as often as they liked, taking advantage of small swings in price, much as the new "day traders" can do today on the Internet.

Unlike today's day traders, however (at least so far), they could also conspire with each other and with specialists to manipulate the market to their advantage. The reforms of the last three decades of the nineteenth century succeeded in preventing corporations and their officers from manipulating the market to the detriment of the stockholders. But these reforms did not affect the ability of members of the exchange itself to do exactly that.

Pools, wherein several speculators banded together to move a stock up and down, were common. Although so-called wash sales (where brokers reported sales that had not, in fact, taken place) were prohibited, the pools carefully timed sales within the group, called matched orders. These sales could be used to produce a pattern on the ticker (called painting the tape) that would induce outside speculators to buy or sell as the pool wished. When their object had been achieved, they could close out the pool at a tidy profit, leaving the outside speculators holding the bag.

Floor traders were also in a perfect position to stage bear raids, pounding a stock, or the market as a whole, with waves of short sales. Then, because they were right at the heart of things, they could judge better than outsiders when the market was at its bottom and could close out their shorts to maximum profit, just when buyers were beginning to move in to snap up bargains.

It was, at least for the quick-witted and financially courageous, a license to steal. Whom they were stealing from in general, of course, was the investing public at large. But they sometimes stole even from less favored members of the club.

Allan A. Ryan was the son of one of the major financial figures of the turn of the century, Thomas Fortune Ryan. The elder Ryan was born to impoverished Irish parents in western Virginia, but he came to New York in 1870 and by the mid-1880s had left his hard-scrabble origins far behind. That year he teamed up with William C. Whitney and began to take over the local transportation system of New York City, acquiring streetcar franchises, elevateds, and, once it was constructed in the first decade of the twentieth century, the IRT subway system. By 1905, Ryan had acquired a fortune conservatively estimated at $50 million, which he would quintuple by the time he died in 1928. Bernard Baruch called Ryan "lightning in action and the most resourceful man I ever knew."[1]

Ryan began to withdraw from business in 1906, devoting his time to his art collection and his many benefactions to the Catholic Church. In 1915 he turned over his seat on the New York Stock Exchange to his son, who formed Allan A. Ryan and Company. He soon became one of Wall Street's better-known bulls, investing in a wide range of industries and benefiting from the rising tide on Wall Street engendered by World War I.

In 1916 he acquired a controlling interest in the Stutz Motor

Car Company of America, which made the famous Stutz Bearcat, soon to be the automotive emblem of the 1920s. (Interestingly, the company stopped manufacturing the Bearcat in 1920, when the decade had hardly begun. So the transportation icon of the flapper era was, in fact, a used car.) By the time of the acquisition, Allan Ryan was not yet forty and worth, by his reckoning at least, $30 million. That, of course, was a mere trifle compared to his father's vast fortune, but he and his father had become deeply estranged. The cause, while never discussed publicly by either father or son, was apparently that, when the younger Ryan's mother died in 1917, his father remarried less than two weeks later.

In January 1920, Stutz stock, which had been selling for about $100 a share on the New York Stock Exchange, began to rise. By the end of January it was around 120 and, on February 2, suddenly spurted to 134. Then short sellers moved in and began a bear campaign against the stock. Some of these sellers were members of the exchange's inner group, which Ryan, despite his success and his lineage, was not. At the time, Ryan was recovering from pneumonia, but nevertheless, he went down to Wall Street, at first accompanied by a nurse, to defend his interests.

He began to acquire Stutz stock, taking all that was offered. Ryan intended to corner the stock and squeeze the shorts till they squeaked. Rich as he was, he lacked the liquid resources to finance such a large operation, and he borrowed heavily on his other assets and even his personal possessions.

By the end of March it looked as though his goal was in sight. On March 24, Stutz hit 245 early in the trading day and closed at 282. By April 1, it was at 391. Most other holders of Stutz had long since decided to take their profits and run, selling to Ryan, who was for all practical purposes the only buyer. The players of the great game who had shorted the stock at 130 or thereabouts were, however, facing disaster. If Ryan held all the stock, they would have to buy from him and at his price to close their shorts. Still, many of these men continued to sell short, first borrowing the stock from Ryan to sell it to him at ever higher prices. If Ryan had a true corner, this was a suicidal action under the usual rules of the game.

Because he had loaned the stock, Ryan knew who the short sellers were. Most were fellow members of the exchange, but some were also members of important exchange committees, in the inner circle of power. On March 31, Ryan was summoned by the Business Conduct Committee to explain the movements in Stutz. The members of the committee, of course, already knew exactly why the stock was behaving the way it was, and Ryan knew they knew. But he politely explained that the problem was that he and his family now owned all the stock in the company. He had his corner. He also offered a deal: he would supply the stock the shorts needed to fulfill their contracts at $750 a share.

The shorts decided to hang tough. That afternoon, Ryan was informed that the exchange was contemplating delisting Stutz. Ryan would be deprived of a ready market. His answer was to tell the committee that if that happened, the price of settlement would be $1,000, not $750. But curiously, short selling continued in the few minutes of trading left before the market closed at 3 P.M., the sellers again borrowing the stock from the only source available, Allan A. Ryan and Company.

Immediately after the close, however, the reason the shorts were digging themselves still deeper became clear. The Governing Committee of the New York Stock Exchange, the ultimate authority at 8 Broad Street, announced that it had unanimously decided to suspend Stutz from trading. When a reporter pointed out that no rule had been cited for doing so and, indeed, such a thing had never been done before, the stock exchange spokesman merely replied, "The stock exchange can do anything."[2]

Whatever shenanigans have occurred on Wall Street in its two hundred years, there have always been two rules of the game that have rarely been violated. The first is that a deal is a deal. When a buyer and a seller agree, that's that and no matter how the price changes before delivery, the security will be delivered at the agreed price. No free market that operates as quickly and voluminously as a securities market could function if this rule was not rigidly enforced.

At the same time, the exchange can do what individuals must never do, although, to be sure, the power is supposed to be exercised only for the general good. On April 5, it announced that Ryan's contracts were void and that "the Exchange will not treat failure to deliver Stutz Motor stock, due to inability of the contracting party to obtain same, as a failure to comply with contract."[3] In other words, the old adage that "He who sells what isn't his'n / Must buy it back or go to prison" need not apply to the very well connected.

The second rule, equally sacred, is that the privacy of private contracts will not be violated. Neither buyer nor seller will reveal who the other party to a contract is. No businessperson likes to do business with, to use J. P. Morgan's memorable phrase, "glass pockets." The revelation of any one contract to buy or sell might mean the destruction of an elaborate investment strategy.

So sure was the stock exchange that Ryan would not reveal who the shorts actually were in the Stutz corner that the exchange lied freely about it, and a spokesman said with a straight face that the shorts were largely ordinary people of modest means. The idea of little old ladies in Dubuque selling Stutz short in large amounts was so preposterous a tale that few bothered to comment when it appeared in the papers.

Ryan, ignoring the exchange's voiding of his contracts, wrote to suggest that the exchange negotiate with him on behalf of the sellers to save time and trouble. The exchange did not reply. By now all of Wall Street was agog with the contest, and crowds gathered around the broad tape—which carried news reports rather than prices—in brokerage offices across the country to catch the latest statement by one side or the other.

Ryan was no more of a reformer than the next broker. But he knew the value of the role of underdog battling the forces of entrenched power. On April 13 he tendered his resignation as a member of the exchange, writing that "so long as your body is responsible only to itself, and so long as you can make your own rules and regulations . . . so long as you permit men who have personal financial interest at stake to take part in your deliberations, your judgments, and your decisions . . . I cannot with self-respect continue as a member."[4]

Resigning his seat, of course, also freed him from the exchange's rules and, at least in his opinion, Wall Street's code of behavior. Ryan promptly gave a reporter for the *New York World* a list of nine exchange members who, he implied without stating it outright, had sold him Stutz Motor stock and hadn't delivered it.

The nine quickly denied that they or their firms were short the stock, except, perhaps, on account for their clients. Of course a broker is responsible for all his trades, whether he makes them for himself or for a customer.

Talk circulated that the exchange needed outside regulation and that Ryan's father would back him with his vast fortune. The exchange began to backpedal. It issued a statement that its action had been intended only to protect innocent investors, not those who were short the stock. It also suddenly decided that settlement of the contracts was "entirely a matter for negotiation between the parties."[5]

Ryan quickly moved to take advantage of the new atmosphere and called in the stock. In other words, he formally demanded delivery. If it was not forthcoming, then, under exchange rules he was entitled to "buy it in," meaning he could buy from himself the stock which he was owed by others and charge whatever he pleased. The shorts would then have to pay that price or admit bankruptcy and be out of the game.

On April 20, the Protective Committee capitulated. It admitted that it represented no fewer than fifty-eight firms who were short fifty-five hundred shares of Stutz. That figure was far below the reality, of course, but was intended only for public consumption. A mediation committee was organized (made up mostly of bankers who had loaned Ryan the money with which to finance his corner), but they were unable to agree, and Ryan announced that he would buy in the stock at 10 A.M. on April 24. Since Stutz was suspended from trading on the Big Board, he would do so on the Curb, then still located on the sidewalks of Broad Street. Having resigned his seat on the New York Stock Exchange, he was free to trade listed securities on any exchange where he could find a market.

The twenty-fourth was a Saturday, a half day on Wall Street until after the Second World War, and Broad Street was mobbed with people who had come to watch events unfold. The mediation committee was meeting in a nearby law firm and realized that there was not much choice but surrender. But at what price? The fifty-eight shorts each wrote a price on a piece of paper and the prices were averaged. It came to $550 a share for stock that had been selling on January 1 for only $100.

They made their way through the crowd to Ryan's office, and he immediately accepted the figure. The Stutz corner was over, and Ryan had made a profit estimated at from a million to a million and a half dollars.

But the exchange, or rather its oligarchy, wasn't through with Allan Ryan. Rumors continually circulated that it was investigating Ryan for one thing or another. The exchange dragged its feet about selling Ryan's seat, then worth about $100,000, and finally "unaccepted" Ryan's resignation. It charged him with "conduct contrary to just and equitable principles of trade," the gravest charge the exchange could bring against a member. He was invited to a closed hearing to defend himself. Ryan refused with withering scorn: "Your invitation to appear in a star chamber and join you in placing a laurel wreath upon the past and present conduct of your committees and to furnish myself as a sacrificial lamb is respectfully declined."[6] Needless to say, the "trial" went on as scheduled and Ryan was found guilty and expelled from the exchange.

That was not all. The stocks in Ryan's other interests were battered by bear raid after bear raid. Further, the sharp bear market of 1920 got under way, wiping out one-third of the stock exchange values by December. As the prices of Ryan's other stocks dropped, their value as collateral for his loans dropped as well. The banks wanted their money back. But Ryan could repay the banks only if he could sell stock in Stutz Motors, of which he was now virtually the sole owner. And he could do that only if he could find a market for it. The Curb was not nearly able to handle such a large amount of stock. By November, the banks announced that they had taken charge of Ryan's affairs.

He managed to avoid bankruptcy for another year and a half. But on July 21, 1922, he was out of maneuvering room. His petition in bankruptcy listed debts amounting to a staggering $32,435,477 and assets of only $643,533. His Stutz Motors stock was to be auctioned. If it could be sold for more than $50 a share, he would be, at least, solvent. But that was a pipe dream. Its most recent trades on the Curb had been at about 5. In the end, Ryan's shares in Stutz were bought, at $20 a share, by Charles Schwab, one of the few major players on the Street to have stuck by Ryan in his troubles.

The exchange had had its revenge on Ryan, but had paid a terrible price in public reputation. In a different decade, and under utterly different economic circumstances, its arrogance would come back to haunt it. Indeed, the image of Wall Street that would dominate in the public mind until the last two decades of the twentieth century was formed in the early 1920s. (One contribution to that image, if a relatively benign one, was the face of Otto Kahn, a partner in Kuhn, Loeb. When Jacob Schiff died in 1920, Kahn became the firm's dominant partner, making him—also chairman of the board of the Metropolitan Opera for many years—the leading Jewish figure on Wall Street. In the 1930s, his handsome, oval face with its trim but luxuriant mustache was used as the model for the cartoon tycoon in the board game Monopoly.)

Losing money was easy on Wall Street in 1920, even without the powers-that-be out to get you on an unlevel playing field. Indeed, that year saw Wall Street's greatest personal financial disaster, when William C. Durant lost $90 million in less than seven months.

Durant, a natural salesman, had made a fortune in the carriage business when, in 1904, he realized that the automobile was the coming thing in personal transportation. That year he gained control of the Buick Company, then in financial difficulties. By 1908, Durant had transformed it, briefly, into the country's largest automobile manufacturer, turning out 8,820 cars that year, outselling the next two largest companies—Ford and Cadillac—combined.

Durant, ever the optimist, went on a buying spree, acquiring other automobile companies and parts suppliers, folding them, together with Buick, into a new entity called General Motors. But while Durant was a genius at selling, he was a fool at buying, and he often paid too much or acquired companies he shouldn't have bought at all. When recession hit in 1910, General Motors had to be rescued by its bankers, and Durant lost control for five years to a voting trust.

While the bankers rationalized General Motors' structure, Durant went off and founded Chevrolet. Its Model 490, which went on sale in 1915, was a huge success. Only a bit more expensive than the already legendary Ford Model T, it offered more amenities. The marketing of the 490 was the first instance of the mass-class tactic, offering customers affordable status symbols, such as different colors, while Ford offered only a rock-bottom price. General Motors would use mass-class in the next decade to claw its way past Ford and become number one.

The GM voting trust was due to expire that year, and Durant used his new success to buy GM stock and collect proxies from his friends. He also induced the Du Ponts—wallowing in cash, thanks to World War I—to invest as well. The following year Chevrolet bought a majority of GM's stock, and Durant was back in complete control. (The transition from General Motors being owned by Chevrolet to Chevrolet being owned by General Motors would take several years and require numerous complicated securities transactions to effect.)

In the great boom induced by the war, General Motors grew exponentially. In 1918 it manufactured 246,834 cars and trucks, along with much war production. It had nearly 50,000 employees and made $15 million in profits that year. The next year its profits quadrupled to $60 million, while its workforce increased to 86,000 and production to nearly 400,000 vehicles.

In early 1920, General Motors stock split ten for one and stood at about 42. Durant, holding millions of shares, was one of the richest men in the country. But then auto stocks—as the stocks of the companies producing the latest technology so often do—led the market slide that began in April. Durant could simply have waited for the slide to end. Instead, responding to some entrenched psychological need to protect his fellow investors and employees, he obdurately and almost single-handedly tried to support the price. As Alfred P. Sloan, already a major power at GM, put it, "He had about as much chance for success as if he had tried to stand at the top of Niagara Falls and stop it with his hat."[7]

Durant began buying General Motors stock on the open market, using margin to increase his buying power. In those days it was possible to buy stocks on margin by putting up only 10 percent of the purchase price, borrowing the rest from the broker. This could be very profitable indeed if the stock went up. But if it went down, as almost all stocks were doing in 1920, the broker would call for more and more collateral and would sell the stockholder out if the customer didn't deliver it promptly. As always in the great game, risk must equal reward.

By the end of October, GM was down to only 17. By November 10 it was at 14, one-third of its price in April. Durant, rich as he was on paper, was at his limit. Durant was no whiner and kept his troubles to himself. But Wall Street has long had the world's most efficient rumor mills, and General Motors' other major investors, the Du Ponts and the Morgan Bank, pressed Durant to tell them where he stood. Finally, on November 16, he did so, and they were appalled. He had a margin call, due the next morning at the opening of the market, for $150,000 that he managed, just, to meet. But the price declined to 13½ that day and triggered an avalanche of further margin calls that he couldn't begin to handle.

Morgan and the Du Ponts knew that if all of Durant's GM stock was dumped on the market, the results would be disastrous for their own holdings and perhaps for the company as a whole. They had to help extricate Durant from his well-intentioned folly by loaning him the money necessary to allow him to meet the margin calls and then to clear up his indebtedness to the brokers. They managed to prevent what would surely have been a major panic, but Durant lost nearly all his 3 million shares of General Motors as a result, with them becoming the property of the Morgan Bank and the Du Ponts.

Had Durant done nothing to prevent the fall in price of GM stock in the bear market of 1920, he would soon have been among the ten richest men in the world, for by 1926, General Motors stock stood at 210. But Durant did feel a responsibility toward the investors and acted on it as best he knew how. As a result, the founder of the greatest industrial corporation on the face of the earth—with annual sales today that exceed the GDP of all but a handful of nation-states—would end his days managing a bowling alley.

The short depression of 1920–21 soon gave way to renewed expansion. On March 4, 1921, the thoroughly business-friendly Harding administration took office. Andrew Mellon, one of the richest men in the country, was appointed secretary of the treasury, having to resign no fewer than fifty-one corporate directorships to do so. Most of the major political questions facing the nation in the 1920s were economic and financial in nature, and therefore Mellon, who would serve throughout the decade, was extremely influential. The liberal Republican senator George Norris joked, "Three presidents served under Mellon."[8]

Mellon's father, Thomas Mellon, a Scots-Irish immigrant who had come to Pittsburgh with his parents at the age of five, had founded a private bank and soon showed a sure instinct for backing the right entrepreneurial horses, including Andrew Carnegie. He also loaned the young and untried Henry Clay Frick the money necessary to expand his coke company. Frick and Andrew Mellon, who was seven years younger, soon became lifelong friends (each would introduce the other to the woman he would marry). Both developed a passion for art and assembled two of the greatest American collections. Frick gave his to the city of New York, along with his Fifth Avenue mansion, while Mellon gave his to the nation, building the National Gallery to house it.

Andrew Mellon soon demonstrated that he was even better at picking winners than his father, who turned over management of the family bank to him when he was only twenty-seven. The younger Mellon invested heavily in companies that would grow into Gulf Oil and Alcoa.

As secretary of the treasury, Mellon pushed for lower income tax rates and plowed government surpluses into paying off the national debt, which fell by more than a third from its post–World War I high. Government expenditures also fell, from over $5 billion in 1921 to under $3 billion in 1928. But if total government revenues fell, personal income and the gross national product soared in the 1920s. Only $59.4 billion in 1921, GNP was $87.2 billion in 1929, an increase of nearly 47 percent. Per capita income rose from $522 to $716, an increase of more than a third, while inflation was nonexistent.

The boom was fueled by the continuing growth of the automobile industry, which became the engine of the American economy in the early twentieth century, just as the railroads had been in the middle of the nineteenth. And also like the railroad industry, it greatly contributed to the growth of Wall Street. Only 1.26 million cars were on the road in the United States in 1914. In the year 1929 alone the country *produced* 5.6 million. The ancillary industries of oil, highway construction, repairs, glass, steel, and rubber grew apace. Other high-ticket consumer goods, such as refrigerators and washing machines, also proliferated in the 1920s, and electricity consumption doubled in that decade.

And, as so often happens in periods immediately following a great war, the 1920s were a decade of intense self-indulgence, exactly like the years after the Civil War—eat, drink, and be merry was the order of the day. On Wall Street, which at any given time offers a distillation of the nation's mood—if an imperfect and incomplete one—people were determined to live to the fullest, as if to celebrate that they had survived an immense human calamity.

Almost unnoticed—for journalists then as now preferred cities—rural America did not share in the nation's prosperity. The growth of the automobile in the first three decades of the twentieth century was a bonanza for industry, but it was a disaster for farmers. One-third of the cropland of the United States in 1900 was devoted to producing fodder for the nation's millions of horses and mules. As the automobile replaced draft animals, more and more agricultural land was turned over to producing food for humans. The demands of the world war masked the increasing supply in the second decade, but in the 1920s rural income declined as the supply of agricultural products rose far faster than demand.

Further, the automobile also increased the mobility of farm families. The rural banks and stores that they had once had no choice but to patronize now faced competition from larger enterprises in larger towns that were now in reach, thanks to Henry Ford.

The United States has always had more banks than any other country, thanks to the federal nature of American government and the legacy of Thomas Jefferson. But the number peaked in 1921 when there were 29,788 banks in the country, the vast majority of them small, one-branch institutions in rural towns that were heavily dependent on making local agricultural loans. As the 1920s progressed, these banks began to fail in increasing numbers, averaging over five hundred a year by the end of the decade.

But again this festering rural sore in the economy went entirely unnoticed on Wall Street. After all, the Street was in the business of financing industry and trade at the national level. It didn't encounter farmers and local bankers. Its great banking houses dealt not with rural customers, or even their banks, but only with banks in smaller cities.

And Wall Street soared along with the economy as a whole. From 1922 to 1929 (with the exception of 1923), the Dow Jones industrial average was up in every single quarter from the same time the previous year. But in earlier booms, such as the period from 1896 to 1907, when both the national economy and prices on Wall Street had roughly doubled, Wall Street and the underlying economy had tended to be in lockstep. In the twenties, however, Wall Street far outpaced the economy as a whole. GNP rose by less than 50 percent in the 1920s, while the Dow Jones quadrupled.

There were, however, sound economic reasons for some of the discrepancy between national economic growth and Wall Street prices. The fast-spreading use of electric power in the decade allowed worker productivity to increase a whopping 40 percent, while continuing mergers allowed further economies of scale.

In addition, both advertising and the use of credit expanded dramatically in the 1920s, fueling demand. By the middle of the decade the considerable majority of big-ticket items were purchased on credit extended to people of ordinary means. Until the 1920s credit had been the privilege of the rich, although some progressive merchants (such as the Straus family that owned Macy's) had begun offering layaway plans earlier. Credit significantly increased the size and purchasing power of the middle class. Many of these same people had also acquired a taste for capitalism in the war, thanks to the Liberty Bond drives. It wasn't long before they discovered that stocks and bonds, too, could be purchased "on credit," by borrowing from a broker to buy securities on margin.

With a swiftly rising market, dumb luck was easy to come by. By financing 90 percent of an investment, great profits were equally easy. (For instance, a hundred shares of a $100 stock, bought on margin and sold at 120, would yield a return on investment of 200 percent; bought outright, it would yield only 20 percent.) Many of the corporations that issued stock traded on Wall Street were themselves highly leveraged. As long as gross profits kept rising over and above what was required to service their debts, the earnings per share rose far faster, fueling demand for the stock. But when the economy slowed, many of these highly leveraged companies quickly became bankrupt.

While all these factors made the market exuberant in the early years of the 1920s boom, it was not irrationally so. To be sure, fads and fancies caused the uninformed to rush into new types of companies. The Lindbergh flight created a boom in airline stocks, although many of the companies had yet to fly a single passenger.

But all economic booms, however great, tire and end. By 1928, the stresses and strains in the economy were beginning to show. At this point Wall Street began to disconnect from the underlying economy, of which, ultimately, any securities market must be an expression. The great bubble of 1929 had begun.

One of the supreme ironies of Wall Street history is that the Street's most famous calamity might well have been prevented had the Wall Streeter who had run the new Federal Reserve, Benjamin Strong, lived but a few months more than he did.

Born in 1872, Benjamin Strong came from old New England roots. At eighteen he joined Jessup, Paton & Company, a respected private bank in New York, and from there he rose swiftly through the ranks of Wall Street. He married in 1895 and fathered four children, but he was not to know domestic happiness. His wife committed suicide in 1905, and Strong's neighbor Henry Davison, a partner of J. P. Morgan and Company, took Strong's children into his own household. Strong's second marriage was a failure, his wife leaving him in 1916, the same year he contracted tuberculosis.

Lonely and often sick, Strong threw himself more and more intensely into his work, rising ever higher until he became president of Bankers Trust, then dominated by the Morgan interests. He would quite probably have soon achieved the pinnacle of American banking at that time, a Morgan partnership, had he not been persuaded to become governor of the newly created New York Federal Reserve Bank.

The way the Federal Reserve had been set up was not to Strong's liking, of course. Like the rest of Wall Street, he had favored a single bank modeled on the Bank of England and located in New York. Strong felt that the Federal Reserve as it was established by the Wilson administration and Congress would have political thumbs all over it and therefore initially declined when offered the governorship. But Henry Davison insisted he take it, and eventually Strong agreed. He approached the post with the same zeal that had made him so successful on the Street.

Strong had been right that the Federal Reserve Board in Washington would consist largely of political appointees, many of them ignorant of the basics of commercial banking let alone the arcane world of central banking. But that meant they had no choice but to rely on Strong, who had a profound understanding of both. By the 1920s, despite the ever-worsening tuberculosis that was to kill him, Strong was the unquestioned boss of the Federal Reserve, his proposals rubber-stamped by the board.

The age-old crosswinds of banking apply just as much to central banks as to ordinary ones, with the added problem of politics. The dislocations of the war still affected Europe, and Strong, understanding the global nature of modern finance, was anxious to help. To do this, he had to keep American interest rates low so that European capital would stop flowing across the Atlantic. Gold had been moving steadily westward all through the mid-1920s.

But low interest rates, of course, fueled the already booming speculation on Wall Street, because lenders could earn more in the call-money market (used to finance margin accounts) than anywhere else. Borrowers with visions of making a fortune on the Street were notably indifferent to the cost of margin loans, and the call-money rate rose steadily to as high as 20 percent toward the end of summer, 1929. Not just banks were attracted to this market. Bethlehem Steel had more than $150 million invested in the call-money market. Chrysler had $60 million.

But when Strong perceived this speculation was getting out of hand, he moved to stop it, by raising the discount rate (the rate the Fed charged member banks to borrow) three times in 1928, up to 5 percent, a high rate in those days, while beginning a policy of restricting the money supply. "The problem now," Strong wrote at the time, "is to shape our policy as to avoid a calamitous break in the stock market . . . and at the same time accomplish if possible" the recovery of Europe.[9]

The new Fed policies quickly affected the real economy—the one beyond Wall Street—which slowed down noticeably in early

1929. This should have cooled down the Street as well, but it didn't. The market was now operating in a world of its own. Tough action was needed from the Fed to prick the bubble before the calamity Strong had feared came to pass. But Strong was not there to take the necessary action. The previous October, after one last desperate operation to stem his tuberculosis, Strong had died.

The now rudderless Fed did nothing. It kept the discount rate at 5 percent, where Strong had left it. Far worse, it allowed the banks to use the Fed itself to bankroll the increasingly frenzied speculation. Banks that were members of the Fed could borrow at the discount window at 5 percent and lend it to brokers at 12 percent. They in turn loaned money to speculators at 20 percent. Billions moved to Wall Street in this way, and the Fed tried only "moral suasion" to stop it.

Moral suasion is one thing, of course; human nature quite another. As long as it was possible for the banks to make a 7 percent return on someone else's money, they were going to do it. Because call-money loans, in theory, were fully collateralized by the securities purchased, they were considered low risk. As long as the stock market was going up, this was indeed true. And the market did go up throughout the spring and summer of 1929, fueled by dreams of riches. As the *Saturday Evening Post* expressed it:

> Oh, hush thee, my babe, granny's bought some more shares
> Daddy's gone out to play with the bulls and the bears,
> Mother's buying on tips, and she simply can't lose,
> And baby shall have some expensive new shoes![10]

On September 3 the Dow Jones industrial average reached 381.17. It would not see such heights again for fully a quarter of a century.

CHAPTER THIRTEEN

"NOT DICK WHITNEY!"

Stock prices began to drop one day after the market reopened following the Labor Day holiday of 1929. The ensuing decline was sometimes sharp, sometimes gentle, but it was persistent. The sky's-the-limit attitude that had been so pervasive in the summer melted away, replaced by nervousness and whistling-past-the-graveyard statements.

Nothing so marked the sudden change in mood as the so-called Babson Break. Roger Babson was a financial adviser of no great note, and having been a pessimist while the market had sought only optimistic forecasts, his prophecies tended to fall on deaf ears. But on September 5, in a speech to a luncheon group in Wellesley, Massachusetts, he said, "I repeat what I said at this time last year and the year before, that sooner or later a crash is coming."[1] Babson's rather innocent remark was carried on the broad tape at 2 P.M. that day. In an instant, the market nose-dived, with major issues down six to ten points or more by the 3 P.M. close. The volume in the last hour was a fantastic 2 million shares.

Roger Babson's prediction was widely pooh-poohed, but talk of a "technical correction" became common, and the *Wall Street Journal,* still predicting a fall rally, noted that, inevitably, "some stocks rise, some fall."[2] Irving Fisher, professor of economics at Yale, who would earn a dubious immortality for his statement in August that "stock prices have reached what looks like a permanently high plateau,"[3] now opined, less confidently, that he thought the long-term trend was still upward.

The cautious and the perceptive had already been moving out of the market. Rowland Stebbins, a partner of Decoppet and

Doremus, one of the two major odd-lot houses, had become bored with Wall Street and didn't like the smell of things. Besides, he had decided to become a Broadway producer. He sold his seat in August for $640,000. Taking inflation into account, that remains to this day the record price for a seat on the New York Stock Exchange.

Albert H. Wiggin, head of Chase National Bank (which would merge in the early 1950s with the Bank of the Manhattan Company to form today's Chase Manhattan Bank), went further. In July, coolly foreseeing a crash, he quietly went short forty-two thousand shares of the stock he knew best, Chase National Bank. Thus Wiggin—paid $275,000 a year to guide the policies of the bank for the benefit of the stockholders—was personally interested in a fall in the stock. Wiggin and Stebbins were more perspicacious than most, but as the post–Labor Day decline continued, more and more investors decided to head for the exits, and the market drop began to snowball.

On Friday, October 18, the decline accelerated sharply on heavy volume. Matters were no better on Saturday morning. Still the congenitally optimistic were hopeful. The *Wall Street Journal* predicted a rally on Monday, and the ever-sanguine Irving Fisher called it merely a "shaking out of the lunatic fringe."[4] But 6 million shares traded on Monday, a huge volume, and declines far outnumbered advances. On Tuesday there was a rally, but stocks fell again on Wednesday, another 6-million-share day at a time when 3 million was considered heavy volume. Even the most solid, conservative stocks, such as AT&T, showed large losses on the day.

By the morning of October 24, a day almost immediately dubbed Black Thursday, Wall Street was befogged with gloom. Sell orders had accumulated by the thousands overnight in brokerage houses around the country. Prices began to collapse with the opening bell on unprecedented volume. Each decline in prices brought a fresh flood of unmet margin calls, producing further declines and further margin calls. Meanwhile bears hammered stocks mercilessly all morning with more and more short sales. Anxious men and spectators thronged the streets and the steps of Federal Hall at the head of Broad Street. The visitors' gallery overlooking the floor was also filled with people, some screaming, some weeping, until the exchange decided to close the gallery at 11 A.M. By noon, paper losses reached $9.5 billion.

At midday, New York's leading bankers met at The Corner with Thomas Lamont, the senior Morgan partner on hand (J. P. Morgan Jr. was in Europe). Many were still deeply involved in speculation or were also underwriting new issues. If these issues could not be sold, their banks faced mortal peril. To defend the market—and themselves—they agreed to put up $20 million to support prices.

At 1:30 P.M. that day, Richard Whitney, acting president of the New York Stock Exchange, walked onto the trading floor. While the president often appeared at the rostrum above, it was rare, even for an acting president, to appear on the floor itself. Tall and commanding, he strode briskly to the post where U.S. Steel was traded and asked the price of the last sale. He was told it had been at 205, but that the price had fallen several points since, with no takers. "I bid 205 for 10,000 Steel," he announced dramatically.[5] He then went from post to post around the floor, placing similar orders for the bluest of blue chips until he had committed more than $20 million (something on the order of $150 million in today's money).

His tactics succeeded, at least temporarily. The market, in the phrase of the day, had been "taken in hand" by the bankers who had raised the money that Whitney was so conspicuously investing. Short sellers turned into buyers as they closed out their positions and headed for cover. Stocks rallied and the sickening early losses were trimmed. Some stocks actually showed a gain for the day. U.S. Steel, which had opened at 205½ and reached as low as 193½, closed at 206. But the volume that day was 13 million shares, and the ticker did not stop rattling out prices until 7:08 P.M., more than four hours after the market had closed.

Friday saw a further rebound, but on Saturday stocks declined again, although with no signs of panic. Some began to think the worst was over.

On Monday the decline resumed amid a swirl of rumors—nearly all of them untrue—of major players who had shot themselves, of desperate ploys, and new bear pools. Then, on Tuesday, October 29, there was no stopping the avalanche of sell orders. Everyone, from scullery maids to bankers, was a seller that day, it seemed. Many were involuntary sellers, as unmet margin calls caused still more stocks to be dumped on the market to fetch whatever they might. The volume reached a staggering 16 million shares, setting a record that would not be broken for nearly forty years. It is estimated that the nation's tickers spewed forth fifteen thousand miles of tape that day to report all the trades, and they ran more than four hours late.

The *New York Times* that Tuesday morning had written "that the investor who purchases securities at this time with the discrimination that as always is a condition of prudent investing may do so with utmost confidence."[6] But it was the show-business trade paper *Variety* that earned journalistic immortality for its headline afterwards: "Wall Street Lays an Egg."

Stocks rebounded on Wednesday as those with cash moved in to snap up bargains. Among the buyers, it was said, were John D. Rockefeller and Joseph Kennedy. Richard Whitney announced that because the back offices were hopelessly behind in the paperwork, the market would open only at noon on Thursday and then close until Monday.

But Monday saw declines approaching half those of the previous Tuesday, and the fall didn't end until November 13, when the bear market finally ran out of steam, with all the gains of the previous two and a half years gone.

Because the great crash of 1929 seems, in retrospect, to have been followed directly by the Great Depression, it is popularly assumed that the first somehow "caused" the second. That is, of course, not true. The two events were, equally, effects of both economic trends that had been building for years and actions by the federal government designed to address those trends.

Indeed, just as the bull market of the summer of 1929 had ended with the market greatly overbought, the bear market of the fall had left it oversold. Buyers began to move in, and 1929 ended on Wall Street with a new, if subdued, bull market under way. The rise continued until late in the spring of 1930, by which time the market had regained almost half of its losses of the previous fall. As late as June of that year, when a group of clergy visited Herbert Hoover in the White House to urge a public works program,

Hoover told them, "You have come sixty days too late, the depression is over."[7]

The president was as sincere as he was mistaken. For only in the second half of 1930 did what had started as an ordinary economic contraction begin to turn into the greatest economic calamity in the nation's history. The causes of that calamity lay almost entirely in Washington, D.C. First, Hoover had promised during his campaign to provide farm relief by raising tariffs on agricultural products. He called a special session of Congress in the summer of 1929, which soon turned into a special-interest feeding frenzy as everyone pursued an individual agenda and no one looked out for the common good. Every major industry (and many minor ones: tombstone manufacturers, for instance) paraded before Congress demanding protection against "unfair" foreign competition. (Unfair competition, in the peculiar lexicon of protectionism, means foreign competitors who are able and willing to sell to American consumers for less than domestic suppliers can.)

After the crash, the Smoot-Hawley Tariff Bill, as it came to be called after its principal congressional sponsors, developed unstoppable political momentum. Despite a petition signed by over one thousand economists, President Hoover signed the bill into law on June 17, 1930, raising rates sharply on both agricultural and industrial products.

The economists turned out to be right. Other countries immediately imposed their own higher tariffs in retaliation, and world trade collapsed. The United States had exported $5.241 billion worth of products in 1929. By 1932, the figure was a mere $1.611 billion, the lowest exports had been, allowing for inflation, since 1896. Further, the stock market, whose ups and downs in the first half of 1930 had closely tracked the fortunes of the Smoot-Hawley bill in Congress, began a slide that would continue for two and a half years. In contrast, the bear market of the fall of 1929 lasted only two and a half months.

Contributing to the debacle, the Federal Reserve, still essentially leaderless after the death of Benjamin Strong, did nothing as the economy and the market crumbled. Strong had said in 1928 that "the very existence of the Federal Reserve System is a safeguard against anything like a calamity growing out of money rates.

. . . We have the power to deal with such an emergency instantly by flooding the Street with money."[8] But the Fed did no such thing, instead maintaining Strong's anti-inflationary and contractionary policies, keeping money rates far higher than the new conditions warranted. In effect, the Fed continued to treat the American economy for the fever of inflation long after the patient had begun to freeze to death in the greatest deflation in the country's history. The money supply shrank by one-third in these years, while 9,800 banks failed, taking the hopes and savings of millions with them. In addition, the Fed had been unable to help many of its member banks because of the original Federal Reserve law's restrictions on what collateral it could lend on. Many basically sound banks, therefore, followed the unsound ones into oblivion.

Finally, the Hoover administration, true to the traditional policies, tried to balance the federal government's budget in the face of sharply declining revenues and rising expenditures. In 1932, by which time the economy was in virtual free fall, Hoover pushed through Congress the greatest percentage tax increase in American history.

These mistakes are, of course, more easily seen in retrospect, but they were no less disastrous at the time. Unemployment rose to over 25 percent while gross national product fell to barely 50 percent of its 1929 peak. And the stock market, the most reliable leading indicator of the economy as a whole, fell and fell and fell in these years. The corner of Wall and Broad, which had been a hive of human activity all through the twenties, began to take on some aspects of a ghost town.

In the fall of 1932, when matters had reached a crisis, a remarkable thing happened on Wall Street. The interest rate on treasury bills went negative. Treasury bills are the short-term instruments of federal debt, maturing in less than a year. Because they are so short term, they do not pay interest as longer-term bonds do. Instead they are sold at a discount and mature at par. But by October 1932, those who still possessed capital were so fearful of the future that they wanted that capital in the safest possible investment, the short-term paper of a sovereign power. The competition for the limited supply of T-bills pushed the price above par.

Meanwhile, the Dow Jones industrial average sank to 41.22 on

June 8, 1932. This was a fall of 89.19 percent from its 1929 high and barely a quarter point above where it had stood on the very first day of its existence, in May of 1896, when it had closed at 40.94. Annual volume, which had reached 1.1 billion shares in 1929, sank to under 500 million four years later. Seats that had sold for more than half a million dollars could now be had for $70,000.

Such disasters create the need for scapegoats. In this case, the chief scapegoat, of course, was President Herbert Hoover. In 1928 he had carried forty-one states to Al Smith's seven. In 1932, it was Franklin Roosevelt who carried forty-one states, and Hoover only seven. On his inauguration on March 4, 1933, a desperate nation made Roosevelt a virtual dictator—to use the word in its original sense, from the constitution of the Roman republic, as one given total, but temporary, power to meet an overwhelming emergency.

But if Hoover was the nation's chief scapegoat for what had happened during his presidency, Wall Street was a close second. And by no means the least of the reforms that the Roosevelt administration had in mind to prevent another calamity was the reform and regulation of all that fell under the rubric "Wall Street."

A rapidly spreading banking panic was under way as Roosevelt was inaugurated, and virtually his first act as president was to close all the banks until it could be determined which ones were sound, and the exchange closed as well. As banks declared sound reopened one by one, public confidence in them—the sine qua non of successful banking—was restored.

Far more important to Wall Street, however, was a swift series of reforms to the banking, monetary, and securities-trading systems. The Emergency Banking Relief Act of March 9, 1933, gave the president broad powers to control credit, currency, and gold and allowed the secretary of the treasury to call in all gold and gold certificates, which he promptly did. On May 27, Roosevelt signed the Federal Securities Act, the first federal legislation of securities trading in the nation's history. It required that all new issues be registered with the Federal Trade Commission and that certain information be disclosed. On June 5, Congress took the nation off the gold standard and on June 16 passed the Glass-Steagall Act.

Officially called the Banking Act of 1933, Glass-Steagall established the Federal Deposit Insurance Corporation guaranteeing bank deposits up to $5,000 and obviating the motive behind bank runs. (Indeed, there has not been one since at an FDIC bank, which, today, virtually all of them are.) The act also required banks to choose whether they would be depository banks, taking deposits and making loans, or investment banks, which underwrote securities. The great House of Morgan, among many others, had to split into two separate entities, an investment bank known as Morgan Stanley and a depository bank still called J. P. Morgan and Company. Already on the wane, the bank declined still further as a force in world affairs.

The prestige of the Morgan bank and other Wall Street banks had been badly hurt by the hearings of the Senate Finance Committee in 1933, led by chief counsel Ferdinand Pecora. A brilliant lawyer who viewed his job as one of advocacy not investigation, Pecora was a master of the technique of asking technical and loaded questions of people such as J. P. Morgan Jr., who did not have a politician's training in how to avoid answering such questions. The media would then do the rest after Morgan and others gave answers that seemed, inevitably, evasive. But the Pecora Committee uncovered many practices on Wall Street that could not be defended, and this greatly increased the pressure for Washington to regulate the Street. Needless to say, the Street fought any regulation tooth and nail. The point man in this fight was Richard Whitney, who had become president of the New York Stock Exchange after his heroics on Black Thursday. When investigators called on Whitney at his office, he told them, "You gentlemen are making a great mistake. The exchange is a perfect institution."[9] Such rhetoric, of course, did not help Whitney's cause, given the public mood.

Whitney and Roosevelt had both gone to Groton and Harvard, and they met at the White House for forty-five minutes to discuss the future of Wall Street, a meeting at which they had what Whitney described as an exchange of ideas. But if Whitney thought that old school ties might head off federal regulation, he was mistaken. After the president proposed a bill despite Whitney's efforts, Whitney and the exchange decided to reform the most questionable practices on their own. On February 13, 1934, the governors voted to prohibit pools, and to forbid specialists from giving inside information to friends or acquiring options in stocks in which they made a market. Further, Whitney and allies organized a massive campaign to derail Roosevelt's proposed legislation. But it was all to no avail. In some ways the exchange's reforms backfired because they were tantamount to admitting that the stock exchange was not the "perfect institution" that Whitney had claimed it to be.

While not able to prevent it, however, they did succeed in greatly softening the legislation as originally proposed. As first written, the Securities and Exchange Act flatly outlawed numerous specific trading techniques, including short selling. As eventually passed, it merely outlawed "manipulation," leaving it up to a new Securities and Exchange Commission that was to be established to decide exactly what that might mean. The new commission would include Ferdinand Pecora among its members. But the chairman, as proposed by Roosevelt, was to be Joseph P. Kennedy, a typically Rooseveltian choice.

Kennedy came to Wall Street in the early 1920s as a speculator and soon showed himself to be a master of the art. He had learned the business at the brokerage firm of Hayden, Stone in Boston, but on January 1, 1923, set up shop for himself, putting "Joseph P. Kennedy, Banker" on the door of his office in Boston. Kennedy called himself a banker because he liked the sound of it, but his business activities always spanned a much wider spectrum than just banking. It is impossible to trace all of Kennedy's dealings. But the sheer number of stories about him in these early days of his career is impressive evidence of how his contemporaries viewed him. He was accused of rum-running and Mafia ties among numerous other calumnies. How many are true, how many the products of sour grapes, tit-for-tatting, and simple anti-Irish bigotry, will also, of course, never be known. But the whispers continue to swirl about him even now, thirty years after his death.

His first major speculation on Wall Street was in the stock of the Yellow Cab Corporation. One of the frequent bear raids of the day had pushed the stock down from 85 to 50. A principal stockholder, Walter Howey, executive editor of the *Boston American*, had been helpful in one of the political campaigns of Kennedy's father-in-law, former Boston mayor "Honeyfitz" Fitzgerald. To repay the favor and help Howey's position in Yellow Cab, Kennedy went to New York and took a suite in the Waldorf-Astoria, where he had a stock ticker and several phone lines installed. He began using brokers all around the country to buy and sell Yellow Cab stock. Day after day he did little but manipulate the stock until the bear raiders, outmaneuvered by him, quit.

"I woke up one morning, exhausted," Kennedy remembered, "and I realized that I hadn't been out of that hotel room in seven weeks. My baby, Pat, had been born and was almost a month old, and I hadn't even seen her."[10]

As for results, Kennedy simply explained, "Several of us emerged wealthy men."[11] It is safe to assume that Kennedy did not use that phrase lightly. One historian estimates that by the mid-1920s Kennedy had a net worth of $2 million, a considerable fortune by the standards of the day.

Kennedy continued speculating throughout the twenties, and few of the other major players in the great game have had a reputation for pursuing self-interest quite as single-mindedly. Indeed, when a renewed assault on Yellow Cab occurred only a few months after the first one had ended, it was widely thought that Kennedy was now behind the bear raid on the stock he had been so adroitly defending only weeks earlier.

Kennedy, like a surprising number of the most talented Wall Streeters, such as Roger Babson, Albert Wiggin, and Rowland Stebbins, anticipated the crash. And he undoubtedly increased his fortune considerably by vigorously shorting stocks as the market sank into the abyss of the Great Depression. But even as he got richer and richer, his essential pessimism made him wonder if the bottom would ever come. He later remembered thinking that he would have been willing "to part with half of what I had if I could be sure of keeping, under law and order, the other half. It then seemed that I should be able to hold nothing for the protection of my family."[12]

But Kennedy, unlike most speculators, had ambitions that went far beyond mere money. Early on, discerning Franklin Roosevelt as the coming man in American politics, he had assisted Roosevelt in his campaign for governor of New York in 1930 and for president in 1932. Raised on Boston politics—where rewarding the faithful with suitable patronage is a nearly sacred obligation—he fully expected to be named to a high position in the new Roosevelt administration. He told friends he would be secretary of the treasury.

But not only did Roosevelt fail to offer him a cabinet post, he offered him virtually nothing. Finally some of the more centrist members of the administration suggested that Kennedy be named chairman of the new SEC. More doctrinaire liberals thought that would be sending a fox to guard the henhouse. "Mr. Kennedy," *Newsweek* wrote, "former speculator and pool operator, will now curb speculation and prohibit pools."[13]

Kennedy, of course, was far too smart and ambitious to try to profit directly from his position. And he certainly knew where the bodies were buried on Wall Street. Had he chosen to take on the Street directly, the resulting spectacle would surely have been entertaining, but it might not have been good policy. He regarded his job to be not only to restore the confidence of the country in Wall Street, but, equally important, to restore the confidence of Wall Street in the American economy and government. Kennedy's first priority was ending the "strike of capital," in which the great Wall Street banks, and innumerable smaller ones, shell-shocked alike, were refusing to underwrite new issues of securities and to lend money, no matter how good the collateral or how solid the project.

"The New Deal in finance will be found to be a better deal for all,"[14] Kennedy said in his first speech as chairman. He moved adroitly to balance the conflicting pressures on the SEC and quickly established himself as a fair-minded, tough, and efficient administrator, stilling the doubts about him. The Senate, responding to those doubts, had delayed his confirmation for six months to see if he behaved, but then confirmed him without debate or dissent.

Kennedy also helped to strengthen the position of the moderate party on Wall Street, one that was open to reform if it did not go too far or depart from economic reality, such as outlawing short selling. Whitney essentially represented the old guard of the New York Stock Exchange, the floor traders and specialists, who had had things to their liking for decades. The moderates, led by E. A. Pierce, were the brokers who had begun to cater to the new business of small-time investors who had arrived on Wall Street after World War I. Pierce had testified to the Pecora Committee that a certain amount of regulation on stock trading was, in fact, desirable. In part thanks to Kennedy, this group grew in strength, and Whitney stepped down as president of the exchange in 1935, although he was immediately elected to the Governing Committee, which ensured that his faction remained able to block any meaningful reform.

The changed atmosphere in general under Roosevelt—along with Kennedy—helped to end the strike of capital, and business began to pick up at last on Wall Street. The Dow Jones industrial average rose more or less steadily in the early Roosevelt years, tracking what was in fact one of the Street's more notable bull markets. (To be sure, the market was emerging from its lowest point of the century.) Volume also increased, and some firms actually began hiring new employees.

But having established the SEC on a firm footing, Kennedy had no interest in running it day to day. He resigned in September 1935, after fifteen months on the job. He was replaced by James Landis, who was not very aggressive. The third commissioner, William O. Douglas (who would afterward sit for over thirty years on the U.S. Supreme Court), intended to use the previously mostly latent powers of the SEC to force Wall Street to change its ways. He was no radical, however. Instead he was "concerned with the preservation of capitalism."[15] To assure this, Douglas thought, the exchange must be "above suspicion. To satisfy the demands of investors there must be in this great marketplace not only efficient service but also fair play and simple honesty. For none of us can afford to forget that this great market can survive and flourish only by the grace of investors."[16]

Naturally Whitney and the faction he headed saw Douglas as the devil incarnate. With the rising prices and volume on Wall Street, the pressure for reform began to fade, as it always does in bull markets. Had it not been for the return of depression in the autumn of 1937, when all the indices that had been improving steadily, if not dramatically, for the last four years suddenly turned down again, Douglas would have had a much harder time pushing reform through Wall Street than he did. But the renewed depression in turn renewed the pressure for reform. (Economists, probably delighted to have a problem they could actually solve, dubbed the new downturn a "recession" to distinguish it from the larger depression the country was still in. Economic downturns have been recessions ever since, and the word *depression* now applies uniquely to the thirties.) The new contraction also pushed Richard Whitney over the edge.

Whitney had been the most famous broker on Wall Street since his heroics (with someone else's money) during the crash on Black Thursday. He relished the role and had even bought the post where he had purchased the ten thousand shares of U.S. Steel and placed it in the reception room of Richard Whitney and Company (it is now on display at the Museum of the City of New York).

His firm was small, even by the standards of Wall Street in those years, but it had one client of great importance: J. P. Morgan and Company. Whitney's older brother George was a partner of Morgan, and Whitney had their brokerage business. Being known as "the Morgan broker" gave his firm much prestige. But in fact it did not generate much in the way of commissions, as Morgan did little business in the secondary market.

Regardless, Whitney lived a life of splendor, with numerous club memberships, a house on East Seventy-third Street, and a large farm in Far Hills, New Jersey, where he often foxhunted. By the late 1920s he was spending at least $5,000 a month, when $2,500 a year was a middle-class income. He had one big problem: he couldn't afford it. His brokerage house did not yield nearly enough, and to make up the difference he frequently had to borrow from his ever-indulgent brother and from friends and associates. He would, at first, pay these men back quickly, but would often borrow again just as quickly. He also invested in penny stocks of the sort that were traded on the Curb. But like a surprising number of Wall Street professionals, he was a perfect fool where his own investments were concerned. Instead of following the cardinal principle to "cut your losses and let your profits run," Whitney would often throw good money after bad.

In the prosperous 1920s he could play this game successfully, or at least without disaster. But the 1930s were a different story. By mid-1931 his firm had an actual net worth—unknown at the time, probably even to Whitney—of less than $40,000. His personal debts amounted to almost $2 million. Yet he altered his lifestyle not one whit. Instead, he began to steal, from his partners, his friends, his clients, his clubs, his brother, and even his wife. As embezzlements usually do, Whitney's finally unraveled, and November 19, 1937, his world began to fall apart.

He was a trustee of the New York Stock Exchange's Gratuity Fund. Despite its name, the Gratuity Fund was actually a sort of life insurance arrangement supported by the members of the exchange for the benefit of their families. It paid $20,000 to the estate of every member upon his death. To be named a trustee was considered a high honor, and Whitney had been accorded that honor when he retired from the presidency. He had proceeded to loot the fund's assets.

His firm was the broker for the fund, and in March 1937, the trustees decided to sell $225,000 worth of bonds and to purchase other securities with the proceeds. The bonds were duly delivered for sale, but Whitney had never delivered the new securities. In fact, he had never bought them, as he had used the bonds as collateral for personal loans. By November, Whitney had misappropriated well over a million dollars in securities from the Gratuity Fund and had no means to pay it back.

The clerk for the fund, having pressed Whitney for the securities several times only to be brushed off, finally informed the other trustees about the situation at a meeting on November 19, during which Whitney was absent. The trustees voted to ask him to deliver the securities forthwith. But he couldn't. They had gone down the rathole of a typical Whitney investment.

The greatest source of Whitney's troubles dated back to 1933, when, hoping to profit from the coming repeal of Prohibition, he had helped to set up the Distilled Liquors Corporation to distribute a type of applejack called Jersey Lightning. The stock, issued at $15, had briskly risen in the boom for all liquor stocks that the end of Prohibition engendered. It was selling for as much as $45 a share in 1933, before Prohibition was actually repealed. But once a free market in liquor was reestablished, Jersey Lightning had little success and the stock declined in price steadily thereafter. Again, Whitney let his losses run and even increased his investment. By 1937 he, and Richard Whitney and Company, held 134,500 shares.

The asking price by then was $3.50 but the bids were few and far between. Having borrowed on the stock, he had to use more and more collateral to maintain his margin as the price declined. When he ran out of his own securities to use as collateral, he had simply used other people's securities that were in his care.

His back now against the wall, Whitney had no choice but to appeal to his brother George, once again, for help. George, needless to say, was profoundly shocked at what his brother told him, especially about the Gratuity Fund, which amounted, almost literally, to stealing from widows and orphans. George Whitney informed Thomas Lamont, the managing Morgan partner, and the two agreed to help, fearing that any other course of action would result in a scandal that would gravely damage the whole Wall Street community. They lent Whitney enough money to buy the missing securities in the market and deliver them to the fund.

And now, far too late, George demanded that his brother pay a severe price for his folly by withdrawing from business and selling Richard Whitney and Company along with his Distilled Liquors Corporation stock and whatever other assets he might have. George hoped that what was left over after Richard's debts and misappropriations were paid off would, along with his wife's money, allow him to live in decency. George Whitney and Thomas Lamont, of course, did not yet know that Richard had also looted his wife's trust fund. (By failing to inform the authorities of the confession, George Whitney and Lamont were technically guilty of misprision of felony, itself a felony. But that statute is seldom enforced, especially if a relative is involved and no personal gain results. In this case, of course, far from profiting, George Whitney laid out millions on top of the millions he had already advanced and which were now gone forever. Whitney's brother and wife, under no legal obligation to do so, would make good every penny he had stolen.)

No market could be found, however, for either Whitney's firm or his Distilled Liquors stock. His personal expenses undiminished, he continued to hemorrhage money. He also continued to ask friends and, increasingly, acquaintances, for short-term loans, usually $100,000, that he knew he could not repay. Because of his position and prestige, Whitney had little trouble convincing people to agree to these loans.

But Wall Street's rumor mills, ever efficient, began to whisper, and by January it was widely suspected that Richard Whitney and Company was in serious trouble. The SEC was sending a questionnaire to all brokerage firms about their finances, and Howland S. Davis, chairman of the exchange's Committee on Business Conduct, decided to send one to Whitney immediately, even though he wasn't scheduled to receive one until May.

When it was returned, a month later (and a week late), the exchange's comptroller quickly concluded that the answers on the questionnaire were less than truthful and dispatched auditors. They quickly determined that Whitney had been stealing from his customers' accounts. Whitney and Company was bankrupt and the powers-that-were at the New York Stock Exchange now knew it. But Whitney still thought the exchange and its old guard would help him out of his troubles. "I am Richard Whitney," he explained to his successor in the presidency, Charles Gay. "I mean the stock exchange to millions of people. The exchange can't afford to let me go under."[17]

In the old days, that would, quite possibly, have been true. But now, with the SEC steadily expanding its oversight on Wall Street, Gay realized that the stock exchange couldn't afford *not* to let Richard Whitney be disgraced.

On the morning of Monday, March 7, 1938, almost everyone on Wall Street knew that Richard Whitney and Company was bankrupt, so there was little surprise when, at 10:05, the bell was rung suspending trading and President Gay made an announcement to that effect from the rostrum. The reason for the suspension, however, was wholly unexpected: "Conduct contrary to just and equitable principles of trade." In other words, Richard Whitney, Groton old boy, former president of the New York Stock Exchange, broker for the Morgan Bank, and staunch defender of the status quo on Wall Street, was a crook.

Dead silence greeted the announcement at first, followed by "a wild babble of voices" as the brokers reacted.[18] When trading resumed, prices plunged, but then trading almost ceased after noon as brokers lingered at restaurants and bars to discuss what had happened. Perhaps the leftist *Nation* magazine expressed the reaction best when it gleefully reported, "Wall Street could hardly have been more embarrassed if J. P. Morgan had been caught helping himself from the collection plate at the Cathedral of St. John the Divine."[19]

Even Franklin Roosevelt, ever the dyed-in-the-wool eastern aristocrat in social outlook, whatever his politics, was dumbstruck by the enormity of the revelation. "Not Dick Whitney!" he exclaimed when aides informed him of the news. "Dick Whitney—Dick Whitney, I can't believe it."[20]

Events now moved swiftly. On March 10, Whitney was indicted on charges of defrauding a trust set up by his father-in-law for his wife's benefit. District Attorney Thomas Dewey, his political ambitions ill-concealed at best, arrested Whitney personally. On the fifteenth he was again arrested, this time for having misappropriated $153,000 from the New York Yacht Club, of which he was treasurer. He pleaded guilty to both counts and stated that "none of my partners [who were all bankrupted by the collapse of the firm], none of my business associates or connections, in fact no one but myself has or had any responsibility."[21] On March 17, he was expelled from the New York Stock Exchange. On March 25 he filed for personal bankruptcy. On April 8 hearings began before the SEC.

But despite all that had happened to him, Whitney still did not seem to wholly grasp his fate. At the hearings, the hearing officer, Gerhard Gesell, later a distinguished federal judge, asked, "Mr. Whitney, when did you first realize that you were insolvent?"

"I am not insolvent," Whitney replied calmly.

"What do you mean?" asked the understandably astounded Gesell.

"I can still borrow money from my friends," Whitney answered.[22]

Even this peculiar notion of solvency was a pathetic figment of his imagination. At the same hearings, J. P. Morgan Jr. was asked, "Do you know Richard Whitney?"

"I knew him," Morgan icily replied.[23] As far as Wall Street was concerned, Richard Whitney was a dead man.

On April 11, Whitney was sentenced to five to ten years in prison and was taken summarily into custody. He spent the night in the Tombs. The next day he was transferred to Sing Sing. As he passed through Grand Central Terminal—thronged with six thousand people who had come to see him off—handcuffs had replaced the usual gold watch chain across his waist. He boarded the train together with two extortionists, a holdup man, and a rapist. At the prison he was assigned a cell, issued clothing to replace the business suit he had arrived in, and given mop-and-pail duty. That night he dined on baked lima beans, boiled potatoes, tea, bread, and cornstarch pudding.

Meanwhile, on Wall Street, Whitney's disgrace altered the balance of power decisively, and Douglas at the SEC moved immediately to take advantage of the utter disarray of the old guard. Soon the stock exchange had a new constitution, one aimed at furthering its public responsibilities, not just its members' interests. The president became a paid employee, not a member of the exchange itself. More frequent and detailed audits of member firms were instituted. Brokers were forbidden to have margin accounts for themselves if they did business with the public. From now on, the SEC, not the stock exchange, would set margin requirements, a powerful tool for dampening speculation and preventing another bubble such as 1929.

Firm debts were limited to fifteen times working capital. Uncollateralized loans had to be reported to the exchange. Brokerage and underwriting had to be separated. Customers' accounts had to be segregated from firm accounts. To prevent bear raids and pounding the market in panics, short sales could be effected only on an uptick (i.e., at a higher price than the last transaction in that stock).

These reforms would have happened anyway, of course, at least in time. But Richard Whitney's disgrace made it possible for them to happen sooner rather than later. For that, if for nothing else, Wall Street might be grateful to its most famous felon. The reforms that his disgrace made it easier to achieve laid the foundation for a genuine prosperity on Wall Street in the postwar years, a prosperity that would prove far greater, and far more widespread, than anything dreamed of in even the wildest moments of the 1920s bull market.

CHAPTER FOURTEEN

"WALL STREET IS . . . MAIN STREET"

Despite Roosevelt's best efforts, the New Deal did not end the Depression. That was accomplished by the Second World War. In one of the most remarkable developments in economic history, the American economy expanded by 125 percent between 1940 and 1944. With significant exceptions, civilian production continued during these years, but in addition to the civilian production, the United States also produced 6,500 naval vessels, 296,400 airplanes, 86,330 tanks, 64,546 landing craft, 3.5 million jeeps, trucks, and personnel carriers, 53 million deadweight tons of cargo vessels, 12 million rifles, carbines, and machine guns, and 47 million tons of artillery shells.

This fantastic boom in the economy (the unemployed in 1944 numbered a mere seven hundred thousand, 10 percent of the number of unemployed as recently as 1940) was not, however, reflected on Wall Street. Yet the outbreak of war in Europe in September 1939 did not cause a panic such as had occurred in 1914. It was obvious months earlier that war was likely, and the lessons of the Great War indicated that, whatever the tragedy to humanity, it would be beneficial to the American economy. Indeed, the Dow Jones industrial average gained twenty points in the first few days of the war, a major increase at that time. But the rally soon stalled amid fears that Hitler, not facing the threat of a second front thanks to his pact with Stalin, would prevail over France and Britain, who were both relatively weaker than they had been a quarter century earlier. When the great German victories in the spring of 1940 destroyed French power and brought Britain to the brink of defeat, the market began a three-year decline. The Standard & Poor's average had ended 1939 at 12.06. It ended 1942 at 8.67, a drop of more than 25 percent. In April 1942, the Dow Jones closed below 100 for the last time. Significantly these declines came while corporate profits, which had been only $6.4 billion in 1939, soared to $20.9 billion in 1942.

Even worse than the fall in prices, at least from the brokers' standpoint, was that volume began to seriously decline as well. Nineteen thirty-nine was the first year since 1923 when average daily volume on the New York Stock Exchange dropped below a million shares (it had averaged 2.5 million ten years earlier). And that was only the beginning. The average was 954,000 in 1939. The following year it was 751,000. In 1941 it was 619,000, and in 1942 it reached a dismal 455,000. Brokers, with often little to do on the floor of the exchange, would sometimes play baseball, using rolled-up newspapers for bats and crumpled quotation sheets for balls. The Wall Street community of brokers, underwriters, and dealers, which had numbered 5,855 in 1940, had dwindled to only 4,343 by 1947.

Only in 1943, after El Alamein and Stalingrad, did volume pick up, once again averaging a million shares a day that year. But even as victory in the war became more and more certain, the market remained stubbornly mired in the doldrums. The public still had all-too-vivid memories of 1929 and wanted no part of Wall Street. Although per capita disposable income doubled between 1940 and 1945, the public did not invest in stocks. Instead they paid down their automobile and mortgage loans, increased their life insurance, and more than anything, saved. Americans saved $4.2 billion in 1940. Four years later they saved an awesome $35.9 billion, with most of this money going into safe, insured savings accounts and war bonds, not risky Wall Street.

Further, the great majority of economists were predicting the return of depression once the stimulus of war was removed. After all, World War I had been followed by a sharp depression in 1920–21. But the economists, like so many generals throughout history, were fighting the last war. The American economy had been only moderately affected by the First World War, due to just a small number of curbs on civilian production. But the U.S. economy in the Second World War was, in many ways, a centrally planned one. The CEO of the American economy was Donald Nelson, a former executive vice president of Sears Roebuck, who was appointed by Roosevelt as head of the War Production Board. (Roosevelt had originally wanted to call it the War Production Administration, but realized that its initials would then be WPA and knew that that would never do.) It was the job of Nelson and the WPB to determine what was needed to win the war, what raw materials and industrial capacity were available to produce it, and who got what first. By 1945 the WPB was the largest civilian wartime bureaucracy in Washington, with twenty-five thousand employees, and used as much paper every day as a major city newspaper. Hardly a paper clip could be manufactured without its approval.

As a result, new housing, appliances, automobiles, trucks, tires, radios, telephones, and so on, were virtually unobtainable in the war years. This produced a vast pent-up demand that, coupled with the capital accumulated in people's savings accounts and war bonds, fueled a postwar boom, not a bust. When wages and prices were freed from wartime constraints in early 1946, the American economy underwent a virulent inflation as well as a continued expansion.

Still, Wall Street did not fully participate. On December 31, 1949, the Dow Jones average stood at only 200, just twice what it had been in 1940, although the gross national product had nearly tripled and corporate profits had done far better than that. Even the bluest of blue-chip stocks, such as Firestone and Kennecott Copper, were selling for under four times earnings, despite paying 8 to 12 percent in dividends, far above what bonds were paying.

But underneath Wall Street's continued lackluster surface, the seeds of its far brighter future were being sown. That future was powerfully affected by two very different men, Charles E. Merrill and Benjamin Graham.

Charles Merrill, like so many who made their fame and fortune on Wall Street, was from a relatively modest, small-town background. Born in 1885 in Green Cove Springs, south of Jacksonville in what was then the semitropical wilds of northern Florida, Merrill was the son of a doctor and pharmacist. He attended several schools and colleges, including two years at Amherst College, but never graduated. He left school to take a job with his fiancée's father, who was treasurer of a small holding company on Wall Street. Merrill arrived on the Street just in time to experience the panic of 1907 but soon prospered. He worked for several firms before setting up his own, Charles E. Merrill Company, in early 1914.

Merrill, a natural salesman, made friends on Wall Street easily and quickly. But hardly had the new firm opened its doors when the outbreak of World War I put it right out of business with the closing of the exchange. Merrill survived by doing quiet trading in the illicit but tolerated New Street market until the exchange reopened. The following year, Merrill merged his firm with that of a bond salesman named Edmund Lynch, and the name of Merrill Lynch and Company appeared on Wall Street for the first time. (The usual comma between the two names was accidentally omitted in the partnership papers and has been intentionally left out in all the reorganizations and renamings since then.)

By the 1920s the firm was well established and successful. All the same, Merrill was beginning to notice and tentatively exploit a new, untapped source of customers, middle-class families with disposable (thus investable) income who had never before thought of becoming stock owners. He also began underwriting stock issues, especially chain stores such as Kresge, Western Auto Supply, and J. C. Penney. In 1926 his firm underwrote a large issue of Safeway Stores, of which he became a director and a major stockholder in his own right.

As the bull market began to lose touch with the underlying economy in late 1928, Merrill was among the first to sense the impending disaster. So early was he, in fact, that he doubted his own instincts and went to see a psychiatrist—psychiatry had become fashionable among the affluent in the postwar era—fearing he was being irrational. After a few sessions, however, he and the psychiatrist both decided he was very rational indeed. They terminated treatment, and both doctor and patient began selling their stockholdings. Like many brokers, Merrill was largely out of the market by the fall of 1929. Unlike many brokers, however, he had been advising his clients to get out since March of that year.

The following year, as Merrill saw the Depression lasting indefinitely, he decided to get out of the business altogether. He sold his seat on the exchange and sold the firm to E. A. Pierce & Co. He and Lynch both became limited partners of that firm, which was in the forefront of those firms calling for reform on Wall Street. He spent the next few years acting as a consultant to the various chain stores he had helped to underwrite, and in this period he probably began to develop the idea of bringing chain-store techniques to the brokerage business to create a firm of national scope and unprecedented size.

By the end of the 1930s E. A. Pierce & Co. was not doing well and Merrill was invited to return as an active partner and take over the management. In 1940 he agreed. Although Edmund Lynch died that year, Merrill insisted his name be kept, and the new firm was named Merrill Lynch, E. A. Pierce, and Cassatt. The New Orleans brokerage firm of Fenner and Beane soon merged with Merrill's, and the firm became Merrill Lynch, Pierce, Fenner and Beane. (Beane retired in 1958, when Winthrop Smith's name was added.)

Merrill immediately began to create a new type of brokerage business. The smaller firms of the old style were typified by Richard Whitney and Company (except, of course, for the illegalities of its eponymous partner), which had probably fewer than fifty accounts for most of its existence, mostly owned by family and friends. Larger firms of the era had what were then called customers' men to solicit and handle accounts outside the immediate circle of the partners' associates, but these accounts were acquired mostly by word of mouth.

Because customers' men worked strictly on commission, they had a great incentive to encourage their customers to trade frequently, whether that was in their best interest or not. And while many of them were honest, hardworking, and knowledgeable, many others were in the brokerage business only because they were someone's brother-in-law. Their idea of research was to pass on to their customers the latest tips generated by the ever-churning Wall Street rumor mill.

Merrill changed all that. He gave his customers' men (they were later called registered representatives) rigorous training in the basics of the brokerage business and paid them, in the beginning, a straight salary rather than on commission. Merrill also advertised widely beginning in 1948, touting his salesmen's training and expertise. And he realized that one of the biggest obstacles to new customers was the ignorance of the average man in the ways of Wall Street, in the sheer mechanics of buying and selling securities. So in these advertisements, he would also provide a basic course in exactly how to invest in stocks and bonds and what the risks and potential rewards were.

Further, he used advertising to advance his vision of what Wall Street could and should be: a safe place to invest, staffed with honest, competent financial experts. Nearly a century earlier, William Worthington Fowler had written, "The moralist and philosopher look upon [Wall Street] as a gambling den—a cage of unclean birds, an abomination where men drive a horrible trade, fattening and battening on the substance of their friends and neighbors—or perhaps as a kind of modern Coliseum where gladiatorial combats are joined, and bulls, bears, and other ferocious beasts gore and tear each other for the public amusements."[1] Fowler's ruleless Wall Street was long dead and gone by the 1940s, but the image he had helped to create lingered on in the American folk memory because Wall Street had never made any attempt to change it. Merrill did make the attempt and succeeded.

When Harry Truman condemned "the money changers" in one of his campaign speeches in the 1948 campaign, Merrill responded in an ad:

> One campaign tactic did get us a little riled. That was when the moth-eaten bogey of a Wall Street tycoon was trotted out. . . . Mr. Truman knows as well as anybody that there isn't any Wall Street. That's just legend. Wall Street is Montgomery Street in San Francisco. Seventeenth Street in Denver. Marietta Street in Atlanta. Federal Street in Boston. Main Street in Waco, Texas. And it's any spot in Independence, Missouri, where thrifty people go to invest their money, to buy and sell securities.[2]

The new way of doing business was quickly a success, and by the end of the 1940s Merrill Lynch was the largest brokerage house on Wall Street, with a gross income of $45.7 million. By 1960 it was grossing $136 million and was almost four times the size of the second-biggest house on Wall Street, Bache & Co., and about as big as the next four firms combined. That year Merrill

Lynch had 540,000 brokerage accounts and was already known as "the thundering herd."

Merrill's success, of course, forced other Wall Street firms to adopt his practices, and the day of the small, boutique firm in the old style began to end as brokerage firms of national scope quickly spread. The brokerage business of today is, in large measure, the creation of Charles E. Merrill, whose importance as a Wall Street broker is every bit the equal of J. P. Morgan's as a banker.

Another Wall Streeter who helped expand the customer base of the brokerage business was Benjamin Graham. Graham was born Benjamin Grossbaum in London in 1894 (the family name was changed in 1917 when America's entrance into World War I made German-sounding names highly unpopular). Graham's parents were importers of china and bric-a-brac who had immigrated to London from Russian Poland, where his grandfather had been grand rabbi of Warsaw. When Benjamin was a year old, the family migrated to New York and continued in the china importing business.

Graham's father died when he was only nine years old, and his mother struggled to raise her children without him. Graham proved an extraordinarily good student, attending the Boys' High School in Brooklyn—one of New York's premier high schools—and then Columbia University. Math was always his best subject, but he also learned to read no fewer than six languages, including Latin and Greek.

Although offered a teaching job at Columbia, he was enthralled by the numbers abounding on Wall Street. He was drawn especially to the statistics issued by the government and the annual reports of companies whose securities were traded on Wall Street. He quickly realized that they were gold mines of useful information for picking investments. That this seems almost more than obvious today is, in fact, a monument to Benjamin Graham himself, who pioneered the field named only in the 1930s: securities analysis.

Annual reports, of course, had been around since the 1890s. But because bankers had precipitated their creation, these reports tended not to be very forthcoming with information that was of use to investors. Instead they emphasized what was of most importance to bankers, creditworthiness.

Graham soon made a name for himself as someone who could spot value in the numbers. In 1916, the Guggenheim interests decided to liquidate a company called Guggenheim Exploration, then selling for $68.88 a share. Graham noticed that much of the assets of the corporation were in the form of shares of other publicly traded companies, and that even with the most conservative valuation of its fixed assets, the net asset value of each share of Guggenheim Exploration was at least $76.23, indicating a virtually guaranteed profit of over 10 percent. Graham lacked the money to invest himself but he handled the matter for others, taking a 20 percent cut of the profits.

Similarly, in the early 1920s, Graham spotted that the market value of Du Pont stock was no more than the market value of the General Motors stock the Du Pont company owned. (Du Pont was a major shareholder in General Motors until antitrust action forced the company to divest itself of GM stock in the 1950s.) Since Du Pont owned vast other assets besides the GM stock, the market had to be either valuing Du Pont too low or GM stock too high. But which was it?

Graham didn't need to know. He simply loaded up on Du Pont while selling an equivalent amount of GM short and waited for the market to recognize the discrepancy. When it did, Du Pont rose substantially while GM held steady, allowing Graham to close his short at no loss, while making a bundle on Du Pont.

Both of these investments fully illustrate Graham's technique: look for undervalued companies, invest, and wait for the market to catch on. He especially emphasized the primacy of working capital and cash in valuing a company and only then fixed assets such as plant and equipment. He advised being wary of "intangibles" such as goodwill. To Graham, the most important calculation was net current assets, the value of cash and those assets easily converted to cash, minus all current liabilities. If this number was high, then the security had a "margin of safety" that limited any downside risk, while providing an upside potential. The only other thing needed, of course, was patience, a virtue in short supply on Wall Street where, all too often, the measure of eternity is the end of the current quarter.

Graham's reputation as a stock-picking wizard spread quickly, and in 1926 he opened his own investment firm with $450,000 under his management. Just three years later he was managing $2.5 million. Graham consistently beat the Dow Jones in these years, which is a good deal more than can be said for many money managers then and now, and Bernard Baruch offered him a partnership in 1928, which he turned down. Of course, making money in a bull market is easy; conserving it in a bear market is another matter altogether. In 1929 the Dow, thanks to its run-up early in the year, was down only 15 percent, but Graham's fund declined 20 percent. The next year, thinking the bear market was over, Graham pursued an aggressive investment strategy in what turned out to be the biggest mistake of his career. The Dow lost 29 percent in 1930, but Graham's fund was down a staggering 50 percent. But the next year, while the Dow fell by 48 percent, Graham trimmed his losses to only 16 percent.

The market finally hit bottom the following year, and in the oversold conditions typical of the end of a bear market, Graham found countless promising companies that met his criteria for investment. By the end of the decade he had earned back all the money he had lost in the postcrash years. Looking for additional income, Graham began teaching a course at Columbia with the description "Investment theories subjected to practical market tests. Origin and detection of discrepancies between price and value."[3] The course soon became legendary and was often taken by Wall Street professionals as well as by Columbia students.

In 1934 Graham, with coauthor David L. Dodd, published *Security Analysis,* a college-level textbook. In 1949 he followed it with *The Intelligent Investor,* intended for its namesake. Pioneers in the field, both books have been in print since the day they were published, in numerous editions, selling hundreds of thousands of copies each, a remarkable feat in a field where hundreds of books are now published every year, most of them with a shelf life shorter than the latest murder mystery. The reason for this success is easy enough to understand. As Warren Buffett, a pupil and then employee of Graham's, explained, "No one has ever become poor reading Graham."

Charles Merrill and his imitators soon adopted Graham's security analysis as a selling tool and established large research departments—quite unknown until the 1940s—to turn out stock recommendations and market letters. The New York Society of Security Analysts had been founded in the 1930s with only twenty members. By 1962 it had grown to around twenty-seven hundred members.

Although more and more people began to invest in Wall Street in the postwar era, they still numbered fewer than those who had owned stocks in 1929 at the height of the bubble. But far more people owned stock indirectly, thanks to two new developments. Pension funds, designed to supplement Social Security, came into being largely in the 1930s and 1940s as bigger companies became unionized and unions bargained for their creation. Charles E. Wilson, president of General Motors (and later famous for something he never said: "What is good for General Motors is good for the country"), was one of the first to push the idea. The management expert Peter Drucker told him that if the money in such funds was invested in the stock market, in a few years the workers would be the owners of American business. "Exactly what they should be," replied Wilson, whose father had been a strong supporter of Eugene V. Debs.[4]

By 1960 this prophecy was on its way to becoming true as pension funds and unions with assets totaling billions were becoming major players on Wall Street. The Teamsters that year held stock worth $23.5 million; the United Mine Workers Union had $16.4 million invested in Wall Street. In 1961, when the federal budget amounted to less than $100 billion, all noninsured pension funds held $17.4 billion in listed stocks. And by that time pension funds were investing at the rate of around $1 billion a year in stocks and another $2 billion in bonds. In addition, as millions of American families became able to afford the luxury of life insurance, its purveyors, insurance companies, were increasingly major investors on the Street.

Mutual funds, too, were becoming more and more significant. Closed-end funds (in which there are a fixed number of shares that must be bought and sold in the market like other securities) had been around for years, but the first true mutual fund (where shares were bought and redeemed from the fund itself at net asset value) appeared only in 1924 with the creation of the Massachusetts

Investment Trust. Although the mutual funds weathered the crash better than the closed-end funds, they remained relatively unimportant on the Street. Brokers, who earned commissions buying and selling closed-end funds, naturally pushed them rather than the mutuals.

But by 1940 the mutuals, which catered to the small investor by allowing him to invest sums as small as $10, had around $500 million in assets, an amount nearly as large as the assets of closed-end funds. By 1950 they had $2.5 billion invested in them, and a decade later the amount was almost $17 billion and climbing quickly.

As new money and new players impacted the Street, the long shadow of 1929 at last began to fade. One of Wall Street's oldest adages—sell on trumpets, buy on drums—once again proved prophetic. The trumpets that had heralded the victory in World War II had not sparked a real rally. But as the drumbeats of the 1953–54 recession started to be heard, the market unexpectedly took off. The Dow stood at only 264.04 on September 30, 1953. A few days earlier, *U.S. News and World Report* had written that "stocks today, on the average, sell for about eleven percent less than eight months ago. Investors, seeing prices fall in the midst of great prosperity, are mystified."[5]

But in January 1954, after President Eisenhower promised a balanced budget (which he didn't manage to actually deliver), the market at last began to move strongly upward. The gross national product that year dipped from $365.4 billion to $363.1 billion, while the Dow Jones rose 125 points. It reached a new post-depression high on February 13, when it closed at 294.03, its highest since April 1930. By June it was at 330. By the first week in December, it finally smashed through the 1929 record of 381.17 that had stood for twenty-five long years.

This turned out to be the signal that the market had been waiting for, and the Eisenhower bull market took off with a roar. Stock prices far outstripped dividends, which rose only about 35 percent in the decade of the 1950s. Indeed stock prices often outstripped corporate earnings as well. General Motors rose from a high of 32⅞ in 1954 to one of 55⅞ in 1960, but its earnings rose only from $3.02 a share to $3.35.

Besides the attenuation of fears generated by the 1929 crash, two other forces drove the new bull market. The first was simple supply and demand. The money pouring into pension and mutual funds and insurance companies had to be invested somewhere. And the supply of securities did not rise as quickly as the demand for them. The number of listed issues on the New York Stock Exchange actually fell between 1953 and 1959, from 1,532 to 1,507. The total number of shares rose only from 3.2 billion to 5.8 billion, while stock prices considerably more than doubled.

The second reason was that the market was, in many ways, only catching up with economic reality. With a few minor interruptions, the market had been lagging behind the rapidly expanding postwar American economy. As one economic historian put it, "The Eisenhower bull market was solidly based on Truman prosperity."[6]

But a bull market it certainly was. People who had nothing to do with the Street began following it. Radio and television personalities offered stock tips. Walter Winchell was perhaps the best known of these, and his touted stocks would usually leap momentarily before returning to the obscurity from which he had plucked them.

And volume, the sine qua non of all bull markets, increased sharply. The total volume in 1954, 573 million shares, was the greatest since 1931, and the average daily volume topped 2 million for the first time since the bottom of the Great Depression in 1933. By 1959, annual volume surpassed 1 billion shares for the first time.

For the rest of the decade and beyond, the Dow kept rising. But the Dow, while then as now the most frequently noted barometer of the stock market, actually understated the bull market of the 1950s and 1960s. Complaints about the Dow have been commonplace almost since the day it was born. For one thing, it is "price-weighted" rather than "market-weighted." This means that the high-priced stocks in the average count for more than the low-priced ones, regardless of their market capitalization (the price of their shares times the total number of shares outstanding). The average is calculated this way because, in 1898, Charles Dow needed to be able to make the calculations quickly, with paper and pencil. Another cause for complaint is that only thirty stocks are in the average, while tens of thousands of stocks are traded every day on Wall Street.

And these thirty stocks have changed over the years. General Electric, as noted earlier, is the only stock that was in the original Dow that is in it today. Some companies were removed because they collapsed into bankruptcy or merged with other companies. Some were removed because the keepers of the flame at Dow Jones thought others would represent the American economy better. This sort of changeover has had no small effect on the Dow and on the history of the stock market, especially in the postwar era.

In 1939, for instance, IBM, then a manufacturer of business equipment and tabulating machines, was removed from the Dow to make room for AT&T, which, except for its Western Electric subsidiary, wasn't an industrial company at all. But in the next forty years, until IBM was readmitted to the Dow in 1979, AT&T's stock price merely doubled, an unimpressive performance to say the least. Meanwhile, IBM became one of the legends of Wall Street, splitting its stock no less than twenty-nine times in those forty years while its price increased a staggering 22,000 percent.[7]

Thus, had the powers-that-were at Dow Jones simply left well enough alone, the stock market would have recovered its 1929 high, crossed a thousand, and begun its climb into the stratosphere much sooner than it officially did. And the actual history of the stock market would have been altered as well, for the players in the market would have reacted differently to the very different readings Charles Dow's barometer would have provided them.

While Wall Street's reforms of the 1930s, Charles Merrill's new-style brokerage, and the Eisenhower bull market had given the Street an entirely new image, crooks were still to be found. They always will be. One of the more memorable of these was Anthony De Angelis, known as Tino, whose larceny led to a major change on the Street.

De Angelis was a speculator in the commodities markets, especially those in cotton and soybean oils and in the meal that was a by-product of this oil production. In 1962 he tried to corner the market in these oils, weaving a complicated web of speculation to do so. He bought vast quantities of oil on both the spot and futures markets and stored this oil in a tank farm he owned in Bayonne,

New Jersey, just across New York Bay from lower Manhattan. To help finance his speculations he sold warehouse receipts for this oil, mostly to a subsidiary of American Express called the American Express Field Warehousing Company.

American Express, in turn, sold the warehouse receipts, implicitly guaranteeing them. At some point American Express sent inspectors to De Angelis's tank farm to see that everything was in order. It wasn't. The tanks were mostly empty, for De Angelis had sold not just the warehouse receipts for the oil, but the oil itself.

On Tuesday, November 19, 1963, De Angelis's Crude Vegetable Oil Refining Company filed for bankruptcy. But that was only the beginning. De Angelis had used two major brokerage houses, Williston and Beane, and Ira Haupt and Company, to handle his speculations in salad-oil futures, and both were now in mortal peril. The next morning the New York Stock Exchange suspended both firms from trading until their condition could be ascertained.

In the 1920s the failure of a brokerage firm was largely the concern of its partners and its relative handful of customers. But Ira Haupt had nearly twenty-one thousand customers, who had $450 million in securities and $5.5 million in cash on deposit at the firm. Many of the securities were in "street name," meaning that while owned by the customers, they were registered in the name of the firm to facilitate trading or to act as collateral for margin accounts. In bankruptcy, securities that are in the customers' names are relatively quickly returned to the owners. But those in street name can be tied up for months and even years.

Williston and Beane had another nine thousand customers, with similar amounts at risk. With the suspension, all these assets were suddenly unavailable to their customers. The solvency of American Express, a major bank as well as a travel company, was also at risk.

Customers at other brokerage houses began demanding their securities and cash deposits, and something resembling an old-fashioned bank run began. Although neither the New York Stock Exchange nor its member firms were obligated to bail out the customers of the two firms, they were compelled to act out of enlightened self-interest, for other firms could be rendered temporarily insolvent if too many of their customers withdrew their securities and cash. And if Wall Street didn't do something, the Securities and Exchange Commission most certainly would, further curtailing the independence of the Street.

On Friday morning, Merrill Lynch and Walston and Company, another brokerage house, announced that they had offered Williston and Beane a loan of $500,000 to allow it to meet the exchange's capital requirements and reopen. Merrill Lynch also said it was prepared to take the firm over if need be, which, in fact, it would later do. Williston and Beane was able to reopen about noon on Friday, November 22. Ira Haupt, however, remained in serious jeopardy.

Keith Funston, the president of the exchange, called a conference of bankers to consider what to do about Ira Haupt. But before they could meet, news of President Kennedy's assassination in Dallas crossed the wires and Wall Street plunged into a far greater panic than anything promised by the salad-oil scandal. The Dow Jones plummeted 24 points in only half an hour on volume of 2.6 million shares before the market could be closed, shortly after two o'clock.

While the nation mourned its dead president, Keith Funston worked to arrange an orderly liquidation of Ira Haupt and Company. On Monday, November 25, an agreement was reached. The exchange would assess its members $12 million to make Ira Haupt's customers whole, and the banks who were creditors of Haupt's would defer $24 million owed them. Then the firm would be liquidated, its assets used to pay back the exchange and the banks. Anything that was left over would then go to the firm's partners.

The next morning, Tuesday, the exchange reopened for the first time since Friday afternoon. The news of the exchange's action—the first time in its history it had assumed responsibility for a member firm's failure—and the apparent orderly transition of power in Washington combined to cause the greatest one-day increase in the Dow in history, 32.03 points. (American Express as well acted with responsibility. It could have allowed its subsidiary to go into receivership and leave those who had bought the warehouse receipts from it holding the bag. But American Express made good its subsidiary's obligations.)

A year later the exchange announced the establishment of a special fund of $10 million (plus a $15-million line of credit) to handle any future similar events. The new fund was a major change in the way that Wall Street did business and a recognition that Wall Street had collective interests that transcended individual-firm interests. In that way it was strikingly similar to the reforms of the late 1860s, when the newly merged New York Stock Exchange and Open Board of Brokers had curbed the excesses of the era of unbridled speculation, and the 1890s, when the investment banks had imposed annual reports and independent accounting on corporate management. Adam Smith's invisible hand had once again moved the Street in the right direction.

On February 28, 1964, the Dow closed over 800 for the first time, and there seemed to be no end to the great bull market that had begun more than a decade earlier. The Dow would close the year at 874.13, a 14.6 percent gain for the year. Seats were selling for well over $200,000, and volume was higher than it had been since 1929. The exchange announced the introduction of a new ticker, one capable of pumping out nine hundred characters a minute and handling 10-million-share days. It would be the last major advance in a technology that had done more to advance the reach of Wall Street than any other in the previous hundred years. A new technology, the digital computer, already in the back offices of every bank, insurance company, and large brokerage house, would soon do to the ticker what the telephone had done to the telegraph.

In the latter part of the 1960s, however, the bull market stalled out, below the once nearly mythic 1,000 mark on the Dow. The average reached 1,000 intraday for the first time in 1966, and would reach it intraday four more times, before finally closing above 1,000 for the first time in 1972, fully six years later. But while the market rise stalled, the volume did not. It averaged 6.2 million shares in 1965 and 7.5 million in 1966. In 1967 the slowest day of the year saw a volume of 5.9 million shares. That was 695,000 more shares traded than on the *busiest* day as recently as 1960. In 1968, the daily volume record that had been set on October 29, 1929, finally fell after nearly forty years. It should have been a cause for celebration. After all, volume is mother's milk to brokers.

But it was not, for by the late sixties Wall Street was drowning in paper. Fails—trades that are recorded differently by buyer and seller so that delivery cannot be effected until the matter is straightened out—were rising alarmingly. In December 1968, no less than $4.1 billion in securities simply could not be accounted for at all.

No one knew it at the time, of course, but it was the beginning of the worst period on Wall Street since Herbert Hoover was in the White House.

CHAPTER FIFTEEN

"It's Time We Put In a Good Word for Greed"

As the great bull market of the fifties and early sixties stalled out, power was shifting again on Wall Street. Some of the changes were mostly symbolic. In 1967, Muriel Siebert became the first woman to own a seat on the New York Stock Exchange, ninety-eight years after Victoria Woodhull had opened a brokerage using Commodore Vanderbilt's money. Three years later Joseph L. Searles III became the first black. A far more important power shift, however, concerned institutions and the men (and they still mostly were men) who ran them. These men were the new stars of the Street. In the 1920s men such as Jesse Livermore and Joe Kennedy, acting strictly in their own self-interest, had gotten the headlines in stories about Wall Street. In the late 1960s, Fred Carr and Gerald Tsai were the talk of the Street. Fred Carr managed the Enterprise Fund, a mutual fund that in 1967 increased in value by 117 percent while the Dow increased by only 15 percent. Gerald Tsai made a name for himself as a stock picker at Fidelity Capital. When he left in 1966 to open his own mutual fund, called the Manhattan Fund, he hoped to attract $25 million in initial capital. The public rushed to give him no less than $270 million to invest for them.

But individual investors were becoming relatively less important on the Street as they turned over more and more capital to the institutional money-managers. In the 1960s, the number of individual investors more than doubled. But the share of trading on the Street by individual investors was falling relentlessly. In 1961, individuals accounted for 51.4 percent of all trading on the New York Stock Exchange, while institutions were responsible for 26.2

percent, and member firms did the rest for their own accounts. In 1969, however, institutions did 42.4 percent of the trading while individuals accounted for only 33.4 percent.

Beyond the increased number of individual investors and the rapidly increasing portfolios of the institutions, the steadily rising volume was in large part due to the greatly increased number of turnovers in those institutional portfolios. As more and more attention was paid to the star money managers, the greater the pressure became for "performance" and the shorter the time horizon became to achieve it. In 1955, mutual funds had turned over on average only about one-sixth of their portfolios in a year. By 1969 an annual turnover of half a portfolio was normal. With the institutions trading in blocks (defined as trades of ten thousand shares or more), it is little wonder that volume spiraled upward. Seats, which had sold for $270,000 in 1966, were going for half a million two years later, a price (ignoring inflation) not seen since the late 1920s.

But Wall Street simply wasn't prepared to cope with the scope of the new volume, and the back-office mess that resulted forced the New York Stock Exchange to drastically curtail hours to give member firms time to catch up with the paperwork. In the spring of 1968 the exchange decided to close on Wednesdays and remained closed on that day until January 1969, when five-day trading resumed but with shortened hours. Regular trading days did not return until May 4, 1970.

Brokers made considerable investments in computers at this time in an attempt to cure the problem. But computers in the late sixties remained large, difficult to use, and expensive. In the early sixties, securities trading was still conducted almost entirely by voice and on paper. Orders to the floor came by telephone to clerks who wrote them down for brokers to execute. Brokers in turn recorded executed trades and handed them back to the clerks. The stock ticker still disseminated the latest prices to brokers' offices around the country, spewing out endless miles of tape as volume rose relentlessly.

In 1965 the ticker was finally hooked up to an electronic display board, allowing an entire board room to read the tape simultaneously. But this considerable advance in communications had one curious side effect. As more and more brokerage offices converted to electronic display, less and less tape was on hand to throw out windows for ticker-tape parades. By now they were far too deeply embedded a New York tradition to be abandoned, so the Sanitation Department now delivers scrap paper to offices the day before a parade and then expensively sweeps it all up again afterward.

After forty years of discussion, a central securities depository, which greatly reduced the amount of paper that had to be physically shuffled all around Wall Street, was finally instituted in 1969. But it was a drop in the bucket compared to what was needed. Despite the ever-increasing volume, the back-office chaos and the costs incurred in trying to solve the problem were impacting brokerage profits. Smaller houses, especially, began running into trouble. The exchange at this time lacked authority to force a firm to stop going after new business if it was unable to handle what it currently had, unless its capital fell below requirements or it broke other specific rules. The exchange could only urge prudence.

In January 1968 the relatively small firm of Pickard & Co. was liquidated when it was unable to cope with the volume it was trying to handle. An investigation revealed that it had been involved in many irregularities—including selling unregistered securities and churning accounts (trading securities in customers' accounts for the purposes of generating commissions). The firm's thirty-five hundred customers, however, were made whole by the Special Trust Fund the exchange had set up after the Ira Haupt collapse in 1963. The Pickard collapse attracted little notice outside the Street. But by August of that year the exchange had thirty-five firms under various restrictions "designed," wrote *Fortune* magazine, "to prevent the sort of overload that did in Pickard."[1]

Even well-established firms were affected. Lehman Brothers agreed not to open additional branches or hire any new salesmen. Paine, Webber (which was not among the thirty-five) voluntarily ended advertising and increased minimums for margin accounts.

The need for additional capital finally broke the back of opposition to allowing members of the stock exchange to sell stock to the public. On the theory that the partners should be personally liable for any failure up to the full extent of their assets, member firms of the New York Stock Exchange had been required to be partnerships until the 1940s. At that time, they were allowed to take corporate form, but only with the stock privately held. A rule change in 1970 made it possible to sell stock to the public—precisely the way every other industry had raised capital on Wall Street since the 1790s—and in 1971, Merrill Lynch became the first New York Stock Exchange member to have its stock listed on the New York Stock Exchange.

The election of a Republican administration in 1968 did not cause much of a rally on the Street. Richard Nixon had no choice but to continue the tight-money policies the outgoing Johnson administration had introduced to combat the increasingly virulent inflation caused by the guns-and-butter policies of Vietnam and the Great Society.

The discount rate, upon which all other interest rates are essentially predicated, had been at 4 percent as recently as October 1967. By early 1969 it stood at 5.5 percent and was raised in April to 6 percent, a level not seen since the fateful year of 1929. The Dow Jones closed 1968 at 943.75. But it fell to 801.96 by the end of July, a 15 percent decline, the biggest in almost a decade.

The uncertainties of the day—inflation, Vietnam, college and urban unrest—caused the institutions, now the backbone of Wall Street, to become more cautious, and volume declined slightly from its earlier feverish pace. On August 11, 1969, volume was a mere 6,680,000, the slowest in two years.

The effect of declining prices, which impacted the value of securities held by brokerage firms as capital, and slowing volume growth, which reduced revenues, devastated some of the weaker firms on the Street. On October 22 the small house of Gregory & Co. was suspended from membership on the exchange, and the Special Fund had to disperse $4 million to its customers. In 1970, the Dow continued to decline in the "Nixon market," imperiling still more and larger firms.

McDonnell & Co. was one of the rising stars of Wall Street in the late 1960s, expanding rapidly and hoping to become the next Merrill Lynch. But in late 1969 it began a precipitous retrenchment, closing offices and firing brokers. The *Wall Street Journal* reported that the firm was in serious trouble, but McDonnell & Co. denied it. The *Journal*, however, was right, and in March 1970, McDonnell & Co. closed its doors in the biggest collapse since Ira Haupt. An SEC investigation revealed fraud, hopelessly inadequate record-keeping, and systematic account churning to generate commissions.

That McDonnell's troubles had been revealed by a newspaper, not the NYSE or the SEC, naturally caused people to wonder who was minding the store. But Robert Haack, president of the exchange, assured the press that the top twenty-five firms on the exchange were all in compliance with capital requirements. Unfortunately, that proved to be untrue, and some of those firms were in serious difficulty. Bache & Co. had lost $9 million in 1969. Hayden, Stone, which had ninety thousand customer accounts, had been fined by the exchange for rule-breaking and was in violation of the capital rules.

The $30 million that the exchange had squirreled away beginning in 1959 to build a new facility was transferred to the Special Fund to be ready to handle the collapse of a major house. But more than one major house was imperiled and the resources of the exchange and its members were limited. To lessen the possibility of a major panic should a big house fail, Congress created the Securities Investor Protection Corporation, modeled on the Federal Deposit Insurance Corporation, which had been set up in the 1930s to end runs on banks.

Hayden, Stone, the largest firm in deep trouble, survived the spring by borrowing $12.4 million from a group of investors in far-off Oklahoma. McDonnell & Co. and three other firms were liquidated in an orderly manner. One prominent Wall Streeter remarked, "If someone had told me a year ago that we could have four New York Stock Exchange firms in liquidation at one time . . . I wouldn't have believed it."[2]

The Dow continued to drop. On May 26, 1970, it reached 631.16, fully one-third below its year-end close and below where the Dow had stood on Kennedy's inauguration nine years earlier. This proved the bottom of the first Nixon bear market, however. Indeed the market rallied sharply for the rest of the year, closing at 838.92. The carnage would have been far worse if not for institutional commitment to the stocks with the largest market capitalization, many of which were represented in the Dow.

The "nifty fifty" were the top fifty stocks held by the major institutions, sometimes in huge amounts. Morgan Guaranty (J. P. Morgan and Company had merged with the Guaranty Trust Company in 1959), for instance, held over $2 billion in IBM stock. It would have been impossible for these institutions to dispose of such large blocks of stock without knocking the price down disastrously, and thus the value of their own shares. Indeed so many institutions were holding large blocks of such a relative handful of stocks that they tended to help support the prices of the nifty fifty when any of them came under selling pressure. Polaroid, with flat earnings over five years and a dividend that paid under 1 percent, maintained a P/E ratio of one hundred while many less fashionable companies with solid growth and good dividends could be had for six times earnings.

Brokerage firms continued to close or be suspended. Hayden, Stone, the capital from Oklahoma already exhausted, was saved only by vigorous arm-twisting to get creditors to agree to a new plan. Merrill Lynch took over Goodbody & Co., the fifth-largest brokerage house in the country, with 225,000 accounts.

By the time the dust settled, the New York Stock Exchange had intervened directly in the operations of two hundred member firms, more than half the number that dealt directly with the public as retail brokers. One hundred and twenty-nine firms either went out of business or were merged or taken over. As some firms vanished and others tightened their belts and began to see the benefits from investment in technology, the number of people employed in the securities industry in New York began to decline. In January 1969, 105,200 people worked on Wall Street. By April 1974, the number was down 28 percent to 75,000.

By the end of 1970 the newspapers and newsmagazines were full of stories that Nixon, beset by inflation, stagnation, and Vietnam, would be a one-term president. But presidents have powerful levers to affect the economy, and Nixon used them all, including price controls and cooperation from the Federal Reserve. By 1972, as the next presidential election was drawing near, the economy seemed to be in better shape than it had been in some time, and the Dow Jones industrial average bumped up once more against the 1,000 ceiling that had been impregnable since 1966, when it first crossed it intraday. After the election, in which Nixon carried forty-nine states, the Dow finally closed over 1,000, reaching 1,051.70 on January 11, 1973.

But the prosperity, or rather the illusory appearance of it, that had characterized 1972 vanished in 1973. With the price controls removed, inflation immediately took off again, reaching levels not seen since the immediate postwar years. As a result, interest rates also climbed sharply, devastating the bond market. And the Watergate scandal broke open in April 1973, adding further uncertainty to an economy that already had plenty of it. In the summer of 1973 meat shortages appeared here and there in the country. And in October the Yom Kippur War precipitated an oil crisis, when Arab states imposed an embargo on the United States and the price of oil skyrocketed. Long lines formed at gas stations around the country.

The Dow quickly fell back below 1,000 and by the end of the year was down below 800, a 25 percent drop from its January high. This time, the nifty fifty declined sharply as well. In 1974, the year Nixon was forced to resign, the Dow plunged to 577.60 in December. In fact, the virulent inflation of 1973–74 masked an even steeper decline in the market averages. The Wall Street writer Andrew Tobias, in an article entitled "The Bulls of Wall Street (Both of Them)" in *New York* magazine, wrote that if greed and fear are the only emotions known on Wall Street, "I think it's time we put in a good word for greed."[3]

In the rampant inflation, banks began offering an alternative to investing in Wall Street that increasing numbers of people decided to take advantage of: certificates of deposit. With the sky-high interest rates of the time, the certificates paid far better than most stocks or bonds and with no risk of capital losses. The mutual funds that had grown so relentlessly since the end of World War II saw that growth diminish and in many cases stop altogether as the value of their shares dropped sharply in the bear market.

The upheavals of the late sixties, the back-office crisis, the failing houses, and now the worst bear market since Herbert Hoover had been president made Wall Street a deeply unfashionable place by the early seventies. It seemed old-fashioned, a leftover from an earlier era. Talk of its imminent demise, not heard since the early 1930s, was heard again, long and loud now. A good measure of how low the image of Wall Street—as a place to invest or to work—had fallen was the price of a seat on the New York Stock Exchange in the early 1970s. A seat, which had cost as much as half a million in 1969, could be had for only $130,000 a year later. By the bottom of the 1974 bear market, seats were selling for $65,000. That was only two and a half times the price of a taxi medallion—a license to operate a taxicab in New York City—the number of which, like seats on the exchange, was strictly limited.

But as has so often happened in the history of Wall Street, technology—this time assisted by a timely shove from the SEC—came to the Street's rescue. Far from being in its last days, Wall Street's ultimate triumph was nearly upon it.

As the power of the institutional money-managers grew, their opposition to fixed commissions grew as well. Fixed commissions had as long a history on Wall Street as stock trading itself. Indeed, nearly the whole point of the Buttonwood Agreement of 1792 had been to fix them. "We the Subscribers," it began, "Brokers for the Purchase and Sale of Public Stock, do hereby solemnly promise and pledge ourselves to each other, that we will not buy or sell from this day for any person whatsoever any kind of Public Stock, at a less rate than one quarter per cent Commission on the specie value."[4]

While the New York Stock Exchange held a virtual monopoly on trading stocks and bonds of the major corporations—a monopoly it held from 1869 until after the Second World War—the customers, however big or small, could do little about this price-fixing. But Wall Street was never the monolithic establishment the metonym implies. The banks, major insurance companies, the Curb Exchange, the over-the-counter market, and the regional exchanges located outside of New York altogether each had diverging interests.

Even the membership of the New York Stock Exchange was not monolithic. The commission houses—brokerage firms that dealt with the public—had one set of interests; the specialists, who facilitated trading on the floor, quite another. The commission houses wanted to be able to buy or sell wherever they could get the best price. The specialists, naturally, wanted trading restricted to the floor of the NYSE.

The over-the-counter market was an entirely informal network of brokers who made markets in various stocks that were not listed on any exchange. They would offer to buy or sell these stocks at prices that might change at any time, making their profit on the spread between the buy and the sell prices. The OTC operated over the telephone and Teletype networks that had long bound the national financial community together. And many of them were not members of the New York Stock Exchange—they were, in effect, the new curb traders, now doing their business by telephone rather than on the street itself. They were perfectly free to trade any stocks they pleased. Because they usually had lower costs (and no exchange fees), they could sometimes offer better prices for listed securities than could be found on the floor.

The major brokers, of course, wanted to take advantage of these better prices, and indeed the law required them to. Federal securities laws mandated that brokers seek out the best price for a stock. But the NYSE specialists had rammed Rule 394 through the Board of Governors in 1955. It forbade member firms from buying or selling listed securities off the floor, "except as otherwise specifically exempted by the Exchange."[5] In other words, federal law compelled brokers to seek out the market offering the best price, while exchange rules forbade them from doing any such thing.

But the mutual funds and other institutions most certainly could. Trades that might have gone to the New York Stock Exchange began drifting away to the regional exchanges and OTC market, the so-called Third Market. The percent of trades in NYSE-listed securities in the OTC market increased 185 percent between 1955 and 1962, although even then it amounted to only about 5 percent of all trading in these securities. But still, some of the OTC firms were becoming as large as major members of the New York Stock Exchange. The unheralded Weeden & Co. traded $900 million worth of securities in 1961. The New York Stock Exchange struck back by removing the tickers from two OTC firms, knowing they couldn't do business without the quotes from the exchange floor. In 1962, the Supreme Court ruled this illegal.

If quotes from the floor were, in effect, public property, then individuals as well as institutions might begin trading listed securities in the OTC market. In other words they would buy from and sell to dealers who made markets in particular stocks rather than in the auction guided by specialists on the floor.

The regional exchanges in such cities as Cincinnati, Philadelphia, and San Francisco that had more than a century before been reduced to securities backwaters by Wall Street and the telegraph, and were since limited to trading mostly in local stocks, also began vying for a part of the institutional business. They were more than willing to adjust their rules in order to succeed. The NYSE forbade anyone who wasn't principally engaged in the securities trading business—brokerage—to own a seat. The regionals abandoned such a rule in the late sixties to encourage institutions to trade on their exchanges. NYSE brokerage houses also bought seats on regional exchanges to do business there that they were not allowed to do on the New York Stock Exchange.

By 1967 the dollar volume of trading at the NYSE was down to 78 percent of total trading on the nation's stock exchanges. But the exchange had already begun to budge from its strict rules. The previous year, under pressure from the SEC, it had adopted Rule 394(b), which finally allowed members to deal with OTC firms in listed securities under specified conditions. The exchange also allowed volume discounts on commissions, although the commission schedule itself remained fixed. But the trend continued, and by 1970 the president of the exchange, Robert Haack, in a widely reported speech, said that somewhere between 35 and 45 percent of all trades of ten thousand shares or more were now taking place off the floor of the New York Stock Exchange. The American securities market was fragmenting, and unless something was done, that trend would continue.

Haack had been a compromise candidate for president of the New York Stock Exchange and bore little resemblance to former presidents. For one thing, most of his career had been outside New York. He was born in Milwaukee in 1917, had joined the Midwestern brokerage firm of Robert A. Baird & Co. after World War II, and by the early 1960s was deeply involved with the National Association of Securities Dealers, being named a governor of that organization in 1961. After NASD rewrote its constitution, which called for a paid president, he was appointed to that post.

Another difference with past NYSE presidents was that Haack

was a liberal Democrat. He even played golf regularly with the chairman of the SEC at that time, Manuel Cohen. The major brokerage houses such as Merrill Lynch, much more amenable to the change than many others on the Street, thought he would make an excellent NYSE president. But the others, increasingly alarmed by the OTC market, thought hiring Haack was like hiring the enemy's general. The big brokerage houses prevailed, and Haack was given a five-year contract as president. But those who feared change had been right to fear Haack. His 1970 speech before the Economic Club of New York, one of the most important policy statements in Wall Street history, proved that.

Robert Haack proposed a solution to the NYSE's problems. "Notwithstanding my own previous personal and strong support of fixed minimum commissions," he said, "I believe that it now behooves our industry leaders to rethink their personal judgments. . . . I personally think [the industry] might well consider fully negotiated commissions as an ultimate objective."[6]

Haack also said, "Whatever vestiges of a private club atmosphere still remain at the New York Stock Exchange must be discarded."[7] This was a bit like the pope suggesting that the Catholic Church might want to think about reconsidering priestly celibacy and transubstantiation. The membership of the exchange was, initially, fiercely opposed. But the pressure for both reforms continued to grow.

By as early as 1972, when Robert Haack left office, the speech had already proved prophetic. When he left, the last aspects of the private club disappeared. The offices of president of the exchange—a paid employee and not a member—and chairman of the Board of Governors, who was a member, were merged. The Board of Governors itself, which had had thirty-three members, all members of the exchange, became the Board of Directors, with twenty-one members, including the chairman. Ten of these were securities-industry leaders and ten were representatives of the public. The board, to emphasize its new character and the institution it represented, began holding occasional meetings outside of New York.

The New York Stock Exchange, a nonprofit corporation since 1941, still technically belonged to its members. But in fact, it was now the premier institution of the securities industry and played a role somewhat similar to the role the Federal Reserve played in the banking industry.

The power of the specialists was broken, and the movement toward fully negotiated brokerage commissions, led by the SEC and the institutions, slowly grew and soon became irresistible. On May 1, 1975, almost 183 years after the Buttonwood Agreement, fixed commissions ended on Wall Street. They would end in London a few years later, but they linger on in many of the world's other exchanges, most significantly Tokyo. But the early ability of the New York Stock Exchange to compete for business by using the revolutionary idea—at least in the brokerage industry—of offering lower prices would be a powerful tool for retaining and extending its lead as the world's largest and most powerful exchange.

The end of fixed commissions was not the only major change occurring in 1975. That year the highly liberal Congress elected in the wake of the Watergate scandal passed the Securities Acts Amendments. It was the most important legislation to affect Wall Street since the 1930s, for it mandated the establishment of a national market system, linking together the nation's exchanges and the Third Market.

These links, in fact, were already well under way by the midseventies. The first was called AutEx, dating to 1969, which at first linked together 140 subscribers. Seventy-five of these subscribers were institutions, not brokers, and it was meant to handle institutional block trades. A system of keyboards and television screens knitted together by telephone lines, AutEx by the end of 1970 was said to be handling an average of fifteen block trades a day, worth $5.2 million.

Far more important was the Nasdaq (National Association of Securities Dealers Automated Quotation System). Planning had begun in the late 1960s. The system, more sophisticated than AutEx and other similar systems because it utilized computers from the first, formally began operations on February 5, 1971. More than eight hundred dealers initially subscribed to Nasdaq, and it provided information on twenty-four hundred unlisted securities.

Nasdaq centralized information on unlisted securities and allowed separate market makers to compete, narrowing spreads between buy and sell and making it easier for traders to be confident they had reliable information. Within a year Nasdaq volume was averaging 8 million shares a day, more than the American Stock Exchange, the traditional number two on Wall Street, and the regional exchanges combined. It also began offering selected listed securities. When trading in these securities on the Nasdaq system increased rapidly, the NYSE grew alarmed.

The second revolution of the 1970s was technological. Digital computers had been around since the 1940s. But through the 1960s they were the size of refrigerators, were kept in special air-conditioned rooms, where they were tended by men in white coats who spoke a language quite unintelligible to others. Then, in 1971, Intel marketed the first microprocessor. The microprocessor is essentially a computer on a chip of silicon. After the onetime expense (admittedly huge) of design and engineering, an endless number can be manufactured at a trivial cost for each.

The microprocessor made the computer cheap, and the price of computing power has not stopped dropping since it was introduced. And no major industry made quicker or more intense use of computer power than the securities industry. Only ten years after the microprocessor was introduced, the trading floor of the New York Stock Exchange was transformed. The huge room—one of New York's great interior spaces—had been largely unchanged in appearance since it opened for business in 1903, but in 1981 a truss of steel girders and cables was installed above the floor to hold a myriad of TV monitors and electronic readouts that have only become more complex in the eighteen years since. They are linked to every major brokerage firm and securities market on the earth.

To a stranger the torrents of pixels pouring out of these displays is utterly bewildering; to traders, however, they are information, the lifeblood of any market. The ancient rule that a market can never be any larger than the area in which information passes instantaneously holds just as true today as it did in 1792. And today that information is simultaneously displayed in every brokerage office, bank, and insurance company on earth. It is also seen and acted upon by a rapidly growing number of "day traders," members of the public who can now move into and out of particular securities dozens of times a day, just as the floor traders of the 1920s were able to do.

And the displays are by no means limited to the trading on the floor of the New York Stock Exchange itself. After Congress mandated a true intermarket system in 1975, the NYSE and its rivals started working on the Intermarket Trading System, or ITS. This system began operation in 1978. It linked together nine markets—the American, Boston, Cincinnati, Midwest, New York, Pacific, and Philadelphia Stock Exchanges, the Chicago Board Options Exchange, and the Nasdaq, producing a consolidated tape for all NYSE-listed securities, regardless of where the trades actually took place.

The rule that the best prices are usually to be had in the biggest market still applied. In the 1840s the telegraph had allowed this law of financial gravity to make New York not just the largest stock market in the country but the dominant one. In the 1970s the ITS and computer technology did exactly the same. The NYSE had been losing market share in its listed securities in the late sixties and early seventies as its old system made it hard for it to compete. Now the business that had drifted away from the Street flowed back into it. By the late 1980s, there were really only two securities markets in the United States, the NYSE for listed securities—major, highly capitalized, and widely held companies—and Nasdaq for smaller, unlisted stocks. There are conspicuous exceptions, however; Intel and Microsoft are both on Nasdaq, not the Big Board. Today the volume of the Nasdaq often exceeds that of the Big Board, but the market value of the stocks traded on the NYSE far exceeds Nasdaq's market cap.

But if Wall Street had gotten its act together, so to speak, in the midseventies and begun to meet the future, the national economy had not. Inflation, after abating somewhat in the middle years of the decade, soared during the Carter administration to levels not seen since the Civil War when the federal government was printing money to pay its bills. Interest rates rose still higher, choking off investment. Gas shortages once more appeared as the government, to curb the runaway inflation, tried selected price controls. But they proved just as ineffective as peacetime price controls had always proved before.

In this troubled atmosphere, as the Dow Jones traded within a range established a decade before, Wall Street had a last reminder of a long-ago era, a corner in precious metals. Corners, which had abounded in the nineteenth century on Wall Street, had become rarer and rarer as the twentieth century progressed. The size of the market capitalization of stocks listed on the Big Board made corners there difficult to achieve as the cost of accumulating the necessary stock became prohibitive. The last real one, involving the stock of Piggly Wiggly, the Southern grocery chain, occurred in 1923. Although not specifically forbidden by SEC regulations that began in the 1930s, the regulations regarding stock-ownership disclosure made them for all practical purposes extinct on the New York and other stock exchanges.

The commodities markets were a different matter, however. In 1980, the brazen attempt to corner silver by two of the country's richest men, the Texas oilmen Nelson Bunker Hunt and his brother William Herbert Hunt, provided the Street with some of its most exciting days in recent times.

Silver, unlike gold, has numerous industrial uses, especially in the photographic and electronic industries (silver conducts electricity better than any other metal), so a strong demand for the metal exists even apart from its monetary uses. But because silver *was* used as money, the U.S. government had long fixed the price at $1.25 an ounce, an echo of the old sixteen-to-one ratio with gold. While the United States had gone off the internal gold standard in 1933, it remained on the silver standard that dated back to the era of William Jennings Bryan. Silver coins contained nearly their face value in the precious metal, and the Treasury issued one-dollar silver certificates that could be redeemed for the precious metal. By the mid-1960s the federal government found it could no longer maintain this policy because demand for the metal was growing swiftly while world production lagged.

The United States was forced off the silver standard. The Treasury recalled the silver certificates and reduced or eliminated the silver content of coins. (In a textbook example of Gresham's law, the old silver coins, which had circulated freely before the new so-called sandwich coins appeared, vanished from circulation nearly overnight.) In the early 1970s, Bunker Hunt thought he saw opportunity in silver. In 1971, President Nixon severed the last link between the dollar and precious metals when he ended the external gold standard, in which foreign governments could exchange dollars for gold at a fixed rate, created under the Bretton Woods agreement. With inflation rising swiftly, partly as a consequence, gold and silver were likely to increase in value relative to the dollar.

It was still illegal at that time for Americans to hold gold in bullion form, so Hunt began to buy silver. Being one of the richest men in the world, he bought it on a massive scale and almost single-handedly doubled the price in 1974 from $3.27 to $6.70 an ounce. And, unlike nearly all modern commodities traders, he took physical delivery, removing the silver from the marketplace.

By 1979 the Hunt brothers had accumulated a vast hoard of silver, estimated at as much as 200 million ounces, just about the amount of silver that was thought to be in the floating supply. With the silver available for trading rapidly dwindling, the price ratcheted upward all through 1979. Tiffany was even forced to temporarily close its silver department to reprice everything sharply upward.

As the year ended, short sellers disappeared from the silver market, adding to the Hunts' already massive buying pressure as they covered their positions. In early January 1980, the price of silver reached $50.06 an ounce. Gold and platinum also soared to prices that have never been seen since, thanks partly to inflation and partly to the spillover of the approaching corner in silver. The Hunts' silver hoard was worth—on paper—$10 billion. The first great Wall Street corner in nearly sixty years seemed to be at hand.

But the problems that have plagued all would-be cornerers plagued the Hunts as well. They had borrowed hundreds of millions to buy the silver on margin, using the metal they held as collateral. With the prime rate at over 19 percent thanks to the galloping inflation of those years, the interest expense, even for the Hunt brothers, was awesome. Further, as with the gold corner of 110 years earlier, the U.S. Treasury could always break the corner at will. The government held massive quantities of silver both in the form of bullion and in unreleased silver dollars.

Finally, with the price of silver more than ten times what it had been only a decade earlier, many mines that had been closed for years because they could not be worked profitably could now be worked very profitably indeed and reopened. In addition, huge amounts of silver began coming out of attics and basements. The metal content of the old silver coins was now worth much more than the face value or even the numismatic value, and people sold them while the selling was good. Meanwhile, tens of thousands of American families decided that this was the perfect time to turn Grandmother's ugly, long-unused tea service into ready cash. No one knows how many tons of Victorian silverware were melted down and joined the floating supply.

With the amount of silver in the market increasing, and the Hunts by now virtually the only buyers, the price of silver began to crumble. The Hunts were forced to borrow more and more money to prop it up, straining even their enormous resources to the utmost. The nation's leading banks and brokerage houses were strained as well, for they had lent the Hunts more than $800 million, equal to about 10 percent of all the bank lending in the country in the previous two months.

By March 1980, the price of silver was below $40 an ounce and falling fast. Then on March 27, the corner collapsed when the Hunts were unable to meet a margin call. Their brokers, in deep jeopardy themselves, began to sell them out, and panic reigned on Wall Street. The stock market plunged while the price of silver lost half its value in a single day, closing at $10.82. By the time "Silver Thursday" was over, the Hunt brothers had taken a billion-dollar bath.

Fast action by the major banks and the Federal Reserve prevented the panic from turning into a disaster for the entire financial system of the country, however. The next day stocks rallied sharply and the Street quickly returned to normal. But for the Hunt brothers, things never returned to normal. The bankers rescheduled their debts, allowing them to pay them off over ten years. However, it was all predicated on the price of silver at least remaining stable. And in the 1980s, as inflation subsided, mining soared, and demand stagnated, the price declined steadily. The Hunt brothers' financial position followed right behind the price of silver. In 1987 they were forced into bankruptcy.

By then Wall Street was a very different place.

EPILOGUE

Wall Street remains very much in the economic era that began with the election of Ronald Reagan in 1980, and the end of that era is nowhere in sight. Thus the last two decades are more properly the province of journalists than historians. While it is already clear that both Wall Street and the federal government have learned the economic lessons of the past, it is less clear if they have learned the lessons of the present. There already are several.

The reforms instituted by the New York Stock Exchange in the 1970s and the massive investment in communications by the entire Wall Street community prepared the Street for the economy of the 1980s and 1990s. The intermarket trading system and Nasdaq were developed to handle stocks, and the Telerate system was established in 1969, to allow bank bond-trading departments to keep close track of bond prices. It soon became the electronic market for U.S. Treasury bonds, which were increasingly bought by foreign governments and investors as well as Americans. In 1973 the British news agency Reuters instituted a service called Monitor Money Rates, which allowed global currency traders to operate twenty-four hours a day.

Meanwhile the cost of being part of a global market had fallen drastically. In 1950 a total of a million overseas phone calls originated in the United States, each one placed by an operator and most arranged in advance. Due to increasing prosperity and falling prices, that number had climbed to 25 million by 1970. But as the microprocessor replaced operators and satellites greatly increased capacity, the cost plummeted and the number of calls exploded. In 1995, no fewer than 2.821 billion overseas phone calls originated in the United States. To put that another way, for every overseas call made in 1950, nearly three thousand were being made only forty-five years later.

The great majority of these calls did not even involve human beings. Rather they were made by computers to other computers to transfer massive amounts of data nearly instantly. The result was the complete globalization and integration of the world's financial markets in only a few years.

Sovereign governments were not prepared for the new information economy, however. The political leaders of countries with weak currencies had railed against speculators ever since the end of the gold standard. During the Suez crisis of 1956, the future British prime minister Harold Wilson coined the phrase "the gnomes of Zurich" to attack Swiss bankers who were speculating against the British pound. But by the 1980s the power of the gnomes—by no means geographically limited to Zurich—had grown enormously.

In 1981, when France elected a socialist government, the new president, François Mitterrand, attempted to implement a traditional socialist agenda, including the nationalization of the banks and increased taxes on higher-income earners. He quickly learned that he did not possess the power to make such a program stick. The global currency market—traders pursuing their self-interests in New York, Tokyo, Hong Kong, London, and elsewhere, but operating as a single, integrated market—brought so much pressure on the French franc that Mitterrand had to back down. France, one of the world's great powers since the sixteenth century, was humbled by a mere market. By the end of the decade, nearly all of the world's socialist regimes were abandoning socialism—which tries to substitute bureaucrats for free markets—and adopting capitalism.

Since the French failure to control its own currency, the world's leading currencies have been controlled not by the old gold standard but by the international-currency-market standard. It is not a coincidence that the inflation that so bedeviled the 1970s has largely vanished, although not painlessly.

The Carter administration proved itself unable to deal with the extraordinary inflation of the late seventies—by far the worst the nation has ever experienced in peacetime—and saw the purchasing power of the dollar erode by as much as 12 percent a year. Pushed by inflation into higher and higher tax brackets, while real incomes stagnated, the American electorate made Jimmy Carter the first one-term elected president since Hoover and elected Ronald Reagan in his place. Reagan, unlike Carter, was willing to endure what was necessary to end the inflation: a deep recession.

Backed by the Reagan administration, Paul Volcker, chairman of the Federal Reserve, applied the brakes hard. He sharply increased the discount rate, which in turn caused most other interest rates to rise. The 1950s and 1960s New York real estate investor William Zeckendorf, famous for his creative financing, once said that he would rather "be alive at twenty percent than dead at the prime rate." But by the early 1980s the prime rate itself was at 20 percent.

That pushed unemployment above 10 percent for the first time since the Great Depression, sent corporate profits plunging, and the Dow plummeting by about 20 percent, to below 800, a figure it had first reached on the upside fifteen years earlier. Newspapers and television nightly news were filled with stories of Reagan being a one-term president, too.

But once the inflationary pressures had been reduced, the Fed was able to cut the discount rate in the summer of 1982. The market, as usual a leading indicator, experienced a major buyers' panic in August of that year and began to climb sharply. The Dow once more closed over the 1,000 mark in 1982, for the third time, never again to close beneath it. Indeed, the Dow began a rise that, with one brief if spectacular exception, has been continuing ever since. It hit 1,500 for the first time on December 11, 1985—a 50 percent climb in three years—and hit 2,000 barely a year later, on January 8, 1987. Only six months later still, on July 17, 1987, it hit 2,500, a Dow Jones number almost beyond imagination only ten years earlier.

Many felt that such a swift rise in so short a time was scarily reminiscent of the late 1920s, and prophecies of a sharp correction, even a crash, were increasingly heard. But more than just memories of 1929 were behind these forecasts. Interest rates were rising again. Nippon Telephone and Telegraph, the Japanese telecommunications monopoly, was planning an immense $35-billion stock offering that fall, and Japanese investors were selling

U.S. securities, especially Treasury bonds, in anticipation of it. The selling pressure on bond prices drove interest rates on treasuries over 10 percent. With a return that high on the safest of all possible investments, many began to question buying stocks at price-earnings multiples averaging as great as twenty-three to one.

The market peaked on August 25, 1987, at 2,722.42. Then, as troubling news items compounded (the continuing rise in bond yields, a threat by Treasury Secretary James Baker to let the dollar fall against other currencies, a large trade deficit, an Iranian missile hit on a U.S.-flag tanker in the Persian Gulf, and more), the market began to slide. By October 16, when it fell 109 points, the biggest one-day drop in its history, it had fallen 17.5 percent to 2,246.74.

On Monday, October 19, the extent to which financial markets had become globalized was fully revealed. Smaller Asian markets, such as Hong Kong and Singapore, which were the first to open, fell heavily. London followed. Then the biggest market of all, Wall Street, opened. Half an hour after the New York opening, so great was the imbalance between buy and sell orders that only twenty-five of the five hundred stocks in the Standard & Poor's 500 index had been able to begin trading. Indeed, in many cases there simply were no buy orders.

The futures market at the Chicago Mercantile Exchange acted synergistically with Wall Street, as panic selling on one caused further panic selling on the other. Rumors that the SEC was about to close the market caused further panic, as investors rushed to sell while they could. By the time the market closed at 4 P.M., the Dow Jones was down 22.6 percent on volume of 608 million shares, twice the volume record that had been set the previous Friday and more than six times normal trading volume. Two large, old, and respected firms, E. F. Hutton and L. F. Rothschild, had failed, as had more than sixty smaller firms.

The situation was eerily reminiscent of 1929. In that year, the market peaked on September 3 and then fell 21.6 percent over the next few weeks. In 1987 it peaked on August 25 and then fell 17.5 percent. In 1929 the market fell 23 percent over the two days of October 28 and 29. In 1987 it fell 22.6 percent in one day. In both years, respected, if not celebrated, analysts—Roger Babson in 1929, Elaine Garzarelli of Shearson Lehman in 1987—had predicted catastrophe. In 1929, margin calls and short selling had compounded the decline. In 1987 computer-program trading and funds managed by traders using a theory called portfolio insurance—an economic oxymoron that supposedly eliminated risk while protecting reward—battered the market.

It is little wonder then that the press and many far more attuned to the ways of Wall Street anticipated a new Great Depression. Sir James Goldsmith, the legendary British financier, had recently liquidated much of his holdings expecting a crash. He now compared his prescience to "winning a rubber of bridge in the card room of the *Titanic*."[1]

But it didn't happen. The next day, while the market fell sharply in the morning, it steadied at noon and then rallied sharply. Afterward, the market recovered its old high in only two years and reached 3,000 on April 17, 1991. Today, only twelve years after the event, the crash of 1987 is nearly forgotten. Why?

There are numerous reasons, but let three suffice. The first is that in 1929 a large percentage of the individuals playing the market had most of their assets at risk. Once the crash came, these people who had felt rich and spent accordingly now felt—and often were—poor, dragging the economy along with them as they sharply curtailed their spending. But in 1987, investors were much more diversified, with a far higher percentage of their net worth in assets other than securities, especially real estate. Painful as the crash had been, it didn't render them broke.

The second reason was the sharply differing response of the president to the event. In 1929, Hoover had taken great pains to assure the public, over and over, that Wall Street was a good place to invest. This backfired, making people only more wary. But Ronald Reagan said little regarding the crash, and his laid-back, these-things-happen-from-time-to-time attitude was reassuring to the public. Meanwhile the White House quietly jawboned several large companies to announce that they were taking advantage of the circumstances to buy back some of their own stock. The action of these companies was far more influential than any promises the president might have made.

But the most important reason was that the Federal Reserve, unlike in 1929, acted the way a central bank is supposed to act in a panic. Paul Volcker had recently retired as chairman and been replaced by Alan Greenspan. Greenspan, then by no means the iconic figure he has since become, knew exactly what to do. Benjamin Strong had put it succinctly sixty years earlier when he wrote that "the way to deal with such an emergency instantly [is] by flooding the Street with money,"[2] and that is exactly what Greenspan did. The morning of Tuesday, October 20, the Fed purchased large quantities of government securities, which had the effect of creating about $12 billion in new bank reserves. This in turn caused the Fed funds rate (which determines short-term interest rates) to fall by three-quarters of a point, a huge one-day drop. With liquidity restored, the panic quickly ended. It was the first time an American central bank had acted to prevent a panic from becoming an economic disaster since Alexander Hamilton had in 1792. Just possibly, the ghost of Thomas Jefferson has finally and permanently been exorcised from the nation's markets.

As always in a boom, new people and new ideas flooded into Wall Street in the 1980s. The plethora of new jobs there largely masked the loss of employment in New York's other major job centers, such as manufacturing, and made the city's tax base dangerously dependent on Wall Street. The price of a seat on the New York Stock Exchange rebounded from its awful low of $65,000 in 1974 and by the middle of the 1980s reached over a million dollars, a new high if inflation is ignored.

Just as Commodore Vanderbilt and Jay Gould epitomized the 1860s and Jesse Livermore and Joseph Kennedy the 1920s, so a few of these new traders became symbols of the 1980s, two in particular, Ivan Boesky and Michael Milken. Boesky, the son of a Detroit bar owner, had come to the Street in 1975, but his career only really took off with the return of prosperity after 1982 and the development of the LBO, or leveraged buyout. Investment banking firms had traditionally made money by taking private companies public, buying the stock from the holders at one price and offering it to the public at a higher one. LBOs reversed this, making money by taking public companies private. To do this, they would float bonds to buy up a controlling interest in the stock and then use the company's cash flow to finance the debt. The secret of the successful LBO was accurately forecasting the company's cash flow, the measure of how much debt it could support.

Boesky made his money by becoming a risk arbitrageur, a new Wall Street phenomenon. By acquiring stock in a potential takeover target early, he could sell at a handsome profit when the deal came to pass. There was just one problem: if the deal did not get completed, he was left holding the bag. When Gulf Oil's takeover attempt of Cities Service failed in 1982, Boesky lost $24 million. To improve his odds, Boesky began developing a network of bankers and brokers willing to supply him with insider information, including Martin Siegel at Kidder Peabody and Dennis Levine at Drexel, Burnham, Lambert, both old and respected firms.

A strong argument can be made that nothing is wrong with insider trading as long as it does not breach a fiduciary duty. But it has been illegal—if never precisely defined—since the 1930s. But Boesky's form of insider trading was not even close to defensible. He paid for secret information with suitcases full of cash. On November 14, 1986, the SEC announced that Boesky had confessed to numerous violations of securities law and was cooperating with the authorities. He went to jail for more than three years.

Michael Milken was a different matter altogether. The son of an accountant, Milken has a brilliant analytical mind. Like J. P. Morgan of a hundred years earlier, he could read and grasp a balance sheet at a glance. Reared in Los Angeles, he went to work in 1970 for Drexel, Burnham, Lambert, a firm that had, in fact, once been associated with J. P. Morgan as Drexel, Morgan and Co. It is a measure of just how globalized Wall Street had become by the 1980s that the most important force operating in the market for much of that decade lived not in New York but Los Angeles, rising at four in the morning to be at his office for the opening of the market.

Milken specialized in what are, unfortunately, called junk bonds. These are bonds with much higher yields than those issued by governments and blue-chip companies. Their yields are higher, of course, because they are regarded as riskier. Some junk bonds are so rated because the issuing companies are in deep trouble and their debt is priced by the market accordingly. But Milken argued that these bonds often made good investments because the yield more than compensated for the higher risk involved. Milken also realized that junk bonds could be used to finance new companies that exploited the new technologies made possible by the microprocessor. Companies that pioneer new fields are inherently risky, but the potential reward equals that risk. Using this philosophy with extraordinary success, Milken was responsible for the launch of such companies as Cable News Network (CNN), which revolutionized the television news business, and McGraw Cellular, a company that offered cellular telephone service. Undreamed of before the 1980s outside of science fiction, today cell phones are nearly as common a sight on urban streets as wristwatches.

As the leveraged-buyout craze emerged in the mideighties, Milken and Drexel began using junk bonds to help finance these types of deals as well. Ron Perelman got control of Revlon in 1985 with the help of Milken and Drexel junk bonds. The following year, as the LBO craze reached its height and the stock market continued its climb into uncharted territory, Milken received a bonus from Drexel of $550 million, making him the highest-salaried employee in history. Had Michael Milken been dead flat broke on January 1, his 1986 bonus alone would have put him in the upper third of the *Forbes* Four Hundred list the following year.

But at the end of that year, as Ivan Boesky was trying to save his own skin by naming names, he pointed to Milken as a source of illegal inside information. The jury is still out, more than ten years later, on whether and to what extent Michael Milken was guilty of criminal behavior or the victim of jealousy, self-serving crooks like Boesky, and ambitious prosecutors who lusted after so high profile a case. But charged with no less than ninety-eight felonies that might have put him in jail for five hundred years, and threatened with having his brother indicted as well, he was allowed to plead guilty to only a handful of minor felonies. Although the judge said she could not find more than a few hundred thousand dollars in discrepancies (less than one-twentieth of 1 percent of his bonus in 1986 alone), she nonetheless sentenced him to ten years in jail—more than three times Boesky's sentence—and a fine of $600 million, certainly the largest criminal fine of an individual in the history of commerce.

Milken's biggest crime, certainly, was hubris. He was convinced that he was capable of carrying off any deal that he put his hand to, and he underestimated his enemies. Milken came to ruin as a financier because he lacked J. P. Morgan's sense of limits and of the strength of the forces arrayed against him. In this way, like hundreds of other Wall Streeters in the 1980s who were making money hand over fist and thought it would go on forever, he conceived of himself as a Master of the Universe.

Sherman McCoy made the same mistake and will perhaps prove the most enduring character of all to come out of the Wall Street of the 1980s, even though he is the entirely fictional protagonist of Tom Wolfe's novel *Bonfire of the Vanities,* published in 1989. It is, without a doubt, the greatest novel ever written about Wall Street. Like Grant's *Memoirs,* Wall Street's other great contribution to American literature, *Bonfire of the Vanities* became an instant classic. It captures its time and place—the New York of the 1980s—with nearly Dickensian precision and is a window into that world, just as *Bleak House* will forever be a window into the London of the 1840s.

Despite the crash of 1987, the 1980s saw the Dow Jones industrial average rise 228.3 percent, a rise previously exceeded only by the 239.5 percent of the 1950s, when Wall Street was still recovering from the psychology of the Great Depression. (The only losing decade of the twentieth century was the 1930s, when the average declined by 39.5 percent.)

Very good decades on Wall Street have always been followed by much less prosperous ones. Not so the 1980s. The 1990s are not quite over, and a lot can happen on Wall Street quickly. (The 1920s would have been up 255.5 percent if the decade had only ended on September 3, instead of December 31. By the latter date it was up only 131.7 percent.) But by the summer of 1999 the Dow Jones was up not far from 400 percent over its opening in 1990. Since 1980, the market is up a staggering 1,300 percent. Meanwhile volume has so risen that the average daily trading volume on the New York Stock Exchange in 1999 is well above the record volume of the 1987 crash, a record that had itself doubled the previous record. Average daily volume now exceeds the *yearly* volume of any year in the 1940s.

Can it continue? No one knows the answer to that, certainly not a historian. But one thing is inevitable: all bull markets end. Whether with a crash, as in 1929, or with a whimper, as in 1966, depends mostly on the interplay of forces beyond our control. But as 1987 showed, crashes don't have to be catastrophic if the regulatory forces are on watch and empowered to act with sufficient vigor.

That is precisely what makes Wall Street troubling at the dawn of a new millennium. Adequate regulation usually comes about only as a result of experience, often disastrous experience, just as the North Atlantic Ice Patrol was the result of the *Titanic* sinking. The brokers were able to curb the actions of the speculators in the 1860s only after the speculators had shown what they could do if left unregulated. The SEC finally was able to exert authority over the brokers only when Richard Whitney had shamed the entire profession.

But the SEC's effective regulation of the Street gave it sixty years of stability and—even with intermittent bear markets—great prosperity, while the country enjoyed the fruits of the largest and most efficient capital market on earth. Today, however, the situation is changing. A new medium of communication, the Internet, has united the world more rapidly than the telegraph did in the middle of the nineteenth century. And it is, of course, an almost infinitely more powerful medium. In the 1920s only floor traders—owners of seats on the New York Stock Exchange— could, as a practical matter, trade in and out of stocks dozens of times a day. But thanks to the Internet, anyone with a few thousand dollars, a computer, and a phone can do so. These are called day traders because they close out their positions at the end of the day. At the present time about 5 million people have accounts with on-line brokerages, and about a million of them, it is estimated, day trade, a number that is growing exponentially. They buy and sell on average twelve times more frequently than those with traditional brokerage accounts, sometimes as often as a thousand times a day. So quickly is on-line trading coming to dominate Wall Street that Merrill Lynch, the firm with the largest stake in the status quo (and fourteen thousand registered reps whose commission income is directly threatened), announced in mid-1999 that it will offer Internet trading to its customers. Wall Street will change profoundly in the next few years as a result.

Meanwhile, the Internet has proved fertile ground for a nearly endless number of get-rich-quick schemes and forums where traders can discuss stocks and egg each other on to trade in a certain way, just as tips used to pass from mouth to mouth in the 1920s. Already many of the excesses of the 1920s are appearing in the Wall Street of the late 1990s. The bubble in Internet stocks themselves, such as Amazon.com, an on-line bookseller that has yet to make a dime in profit, is the biggest bubble in decades. And many stocks are moving for reasons that clearly have little if anything to do with their intrinsic prospects. When Ticketmaster, a ticket-selling service with the stock symbol TMCS, went public and rose 300 percent in its first day of trading, a building-maintenance firm named Temco Services, with the stock symbol TMCO, also rose, otherwise inexplicably than for its symbol, 150 percent.

Quite simply, the Internet is the best system yet devised for propagating mob psychology. But who is regulating this emerging trading? The answer is essentially, no one. As François Mitterrand found out nearly twenty years ago, the markets are entirely globalized and operate as one. Wall Street now reaches to the ends of the earth, with power to match. But regulation still largely stops at each country's borders.

That will be difficult to change, as effective regulation of a worldwide market will necessarily involve a substantial surrender of sovereignty by the major nations. And nothing is more difficult for a national leader to do than relinquish his or her country's freedom to act independently. Human nature being what it is, probably only the financial equivalent of a *Titanic* disaster will bring about the needed result.

But even if Wall Street and the politicians fail to devise the regulatory framework needed to keep the Street on an even keel and—because the trouble with capitalism is always capital*ists*—Wall Street therefore has another disaster of 1929 proportions, that won't be the end of the story. Not by a long shot.

For just as men, despite untold maritime disasters, will always go down to the sea in ships, so will human beings go to the marketplace, to buy cheap and sell dear, to offer dreams of future prosperity in exchange for cash today, to play the great game. It is as much a part of what makes us human as our need to explore, to see what lies beyond the horizon. Indeed both activities arise from the same human impulse, for the market's horizon is the future.

And by doing so, by playing the great game, by pursuing our infinite self-interests within the rules of that game, we will continue to move the invisible hand that has made so much of the world so very rich.

NOTES

ONE: "A CLOACINA OF ALL THE DEPRAVITIES OF HUMAN NATURE"

1. White, xi.

TWO: "A LINE OF SEPARATION BETWEEN HONEST MEN & KNAVES"

1. Sobel, *Panic on Wall Street,* 19.
2. Sobel, *Big Board,* 21.
3. Sobel, *Panic on Wall Street,* 19.
4. Miller, 305.
5. Sobel, *Panic on Wall Street,* 27.
6. Ibid., 28.
7. Miller, 305.
8. Lomask, 227.
9. Miller, 511.

THREE: "THAT TONGUE THAT IS LICKING UP THE CREAM OF COMMERCE"

1. Smith, 770.
2. Ibid., 772.
3. Gordon, *Scarlet,* 30.
4. Smith, 774.
5. Gordon, *Scarlet,* 30.
6. Sobel, *Panic on Wall Street,* 42.
7. Chancellor, ix.
8. Fowler, 40.
9. Sobel, *Panic on Wall Street,* 40.
10. Sobel, *Big Board,* 44–45.

FOUR: "WHAT CAN BE THE END OF ALL THIS BUT ANOTHER GENERAL COLLAPSE?"

1. Sobel, *Big Board,* 50.
2. Norman, 54.
3. Hadley, 65.
4. Medbery, 9.
5. Stedman, 70.
6. Fowler, 125.
7. Ibid., 127.
8. Clews, 122.
9. Marks, 27.
10. Sobel, *Panic on Wall Street,* 92.
11. Train, 209.
12. Sobel, *Panic on Wall Street,* 96.
13. Stampp, 219.
14. Sobel, *Panic on Wall Street,* 99.
15. Ibid., 99.
16. Stampp, 222.

FIVE: "VANITY FAIR WAS NO LONGER A DREAM"

1. McPherson, 444.
2. Oberholtzer, vol. 2, p. 141.
3. Sobel, *Big Board,* 75.
4. Medbery, 247.
5. Ibid., 277.
6. Mott, 69.
7. Parton, 384.
8. Smith, 119.
9. *The Railroad Man's Magazine,* February 1910.
10. *Herald,* March 25, 1863.
11. Fowler, 204.
12. Ibid., 208.
13. Stedman, 175.
14. Fowler, 208.
15. Lane, 107.
16. Stedman, 178.
17. Fowler, 355.
18. Croffut, 79.
19. Clews, 115.

SIX: "WHO . . . COULD BLAME THEM
FOR DOING WHAT THEY PLEASED?"

1. *Fraser's Magazine,* May 1869.
2. Fowler, 439.
3. Ibid., 441.
4. Croffut, 281.
5. Fowler, 482.
6. Ibid.
7. Snow, 115.
8. *Herald,* February 5, 1868.
9. Clews, 125.
10. Adams, 6.
11. Ibid., 17.
12. Stedman, 200.
13. Nevins, vol. 2, 331.
14. Gustavus Meyers, "History of Public Franchises in New York City," *Municipal Affairs,* 4 (1900).
15. Tanner, iv.
16. Ibid., vi.
17. Nevins, vol. 2, 202.
18. *Fraser's Magazine,* May 1869.
19. *American Law Review,* October 1868.
20. *Herald,* January 26, 1868.
21. Fowler, 499.
22. Stedman, 202.
23. Fowler, 500.
24. Ibid., 499.
25. Croffut, 91.
26. Fowler, 501.
27. *Herald,* March 14, 1868.
28. Fowler, 502.
29. *Harper's Weekly,* May 1868.
30. Adams, 54.
31. *Fraser's Magazine,* May 1869.
32. *Herald,* April 15, 1868.
33. Adams, 53.
34. Ibid., 54.
35. Crouch, 29.
36. *Times,* November 13, 1868.
37. *Chronicle,* October 31, 1868.
38. Medbery, 344.

SEVEN: "THE BULLS, TRIUMPHANT, FACED THEIR FOES"

1. Adams, 114.
2. *House Report,* 113.
3. Gordon, *Scarlet,* 260.
4. *House Report,* 35.
5. Ibid.
6. Ibid., 444.
7. Ibid., 7.
8. *Herald,* September 25, 1869.
9. *House Report,* 15.
10. Harris, 48.
11. *House Report,* 90.
12. Sobel, *Panic on Wall Street,* 165.
13. Lane, 259.
14. *Herald,* January 7, 1872.
15. Mott, 491.
16. Sobel, *Panic on Wall Street,* 179.
17. Ibid., 184.
18. Ibid., 180.

EIGHT: "ALL YOU HAVE TO DO IS BUY CHEAP AND SELL DEAR"

1. Sobel, *Big Board,* 104.
2. Frederick Lewis Allen, 7.
3. Ibid., 13.
4. Ibid., 203.
5. Sparkes, 139.
6. Ibid., 160.
7. Sobel, *Panic on Wall Street,* 211.
8. Ibid., 215.
9. Ibid.
10. Ibid., 218.
11. Ibid., 227.

NINE: "HAVE YOU ANYTHING TO SUGGEST?"

1. Sobel, *Panic on Wall Street,* 245.
2. Ibid., 251.
3. Strouse, 341.
4. Ibid.

5. Ibid., 342.
6. Ibid., 343.
7. Ibid., 349.
8. Ibid., 350.
9. *Wall Street Journal,* May 28, 1996, R26, "Review and Outlook" column.
10. Previts, 81.
11. Ibid.
12. *Tribune,* January 21, 1870.
13. Sobel, *Panic on Wall Street,* 248.
14. Ibid., 249.
15. Garraty, *Encyclopedia,* 490.
16. *New York Times,* May 12, 1901.

TEN: "WHY DON'T YOU TELL THEM WHAT TO DO, MR. MORGAN?"

1. Frederick Lewis Allen, 77.
2. *Wall Street Journal,* February 27, 1901.
3. Holbrook, 152.
4. Frederick Lewis Allen, 220.
5. Sobel, *Panic on Wall Street,* 303.
6. Ibid., 313.
7. Satterlee, 583.
8. Ibid., 477.
9. Frederick Lewis Allen, 257.
10. See *Oxford Dictionary of Quotations,* 3rd ed.

ELEVEN: "DOES THIS HAPPEN OFTEN?"

1. Sobel, *Big Board,* 207.
2. Sobel, *Panic on Wall Street,* 328.
3. *Oxford Dictionary of Quotations,* 3rd ed., 236.
4. Sobel, *Panic on Wall Street,* 345.
5. Colby, 190.
6. Hessen, 216.
7. Chernow, *House of Morgan,* 186.
8. Ibid., 197.
9. Ibid., 198.
10. Brooks, 7.
11. Ibid., 18.

TWELVE: "THE STOCK EXCHANGE CAN DO ANYTHING"

1. Garraty, *Encyclopedia,* 954.
2. Brooks, 29.
3. Ibid., 30.
4. Ibid., 31.
5. Ibid., 33.
6. Ibid., 36.
7. Gustin, 213.
8. Paul, 125.
9. Greider, 296.
10. Sobel, *Panic on Wall Street,* 371.

THIRTEEN: "NOT DICK WHITNEY!"

1. Brooks, 111.
2. Sobel, *Panic on Wall Street,* 371.
3. Ibid., 368.
4. Ibid., 374.
5. *New York Times,* December 6, 1974.
6. Sobel, *Panic on Wall Street,* 379.
7. Garraty, *Depression,* 32.
8. Greider, 298.
9. Brooks, 198.
10. Koskoff, 26.
11. Ibid., 27.
12. Beschloss, 65.
13. Collier, 75.
14. Beschloss, 94.
15. Seligman, 157.
16. Ibid., 176.
17. Sobel, *NYSE,* 49.
18. Seligman, 168.
19. Brooks, 273.
20. Seligman, 169.
21. Ibid.
22. Louchiem, 132.
23. Ibid., 144.

NOTES

FOURTEEN: "WALL STREET IS . . . MAIN STREET"

1. Fowler, 20.
2. Sobel, *Big Board,* 335.
3. Lowe, 96.
4. Drucker, 277.
5. Sobel, *Big Board,* 347.
6. Ibid., 349.
7. Jeffrey, R42.

FIFTEEN: "IT'S TIME WE PUT IN A GOOD WORD FOR GREED"

1. Sobel, *NYSE,* 317.
2. Ibid., 324.
3. *New York,* October 7, 1974.
4. Taken from illustration in Buck, 19.
5. Sobel, *NYSE,* 211.
6. Ibid., 336.
7. Ibid., 337.

EPILOGUE

1. Chancellor, 269.
2. Greider, 298.

BIBLIOGRAPHY

Adams, Charles Francis, and Henry Adams. *Chapters of Erie, and Other Essays*. Boston, Massachusetts: James R. Osgood, 1871.

Allen, Frederick Lewis. *The Great Pierpont Morgan*. New York: Harper & Brothers, 1949.

Allen, Oliver E. *New York, New York: A History of the World's Most Exciting City*. New York: Atheneum, 1990.

Beschloss, Michael R. *Kennedy and Roosevelt: The Uneasy Alliance*. New York: Norton, 1980.

Brookhiser, Richard. *Alexander Hamilton, American*. New York: The Free Press, 1999.

Brooks, John. *Once in Golconda: A True Drama of Wall Street, 1920–1938*. New York: Harper & Row, 1969.

Buck, James E., ed. *The New York Stock Exchange: The First Two Hundred Years*. Essex, Conn.: Greenwich Publishing Group, Inc.

Burrows, Edwin G., and Mike Wallace. *Gotham: A History of New York City to 1898*. New York: Oxford University Press, 1999.

Chancellor, Edward. *Devil Take the Hindmost: A History of Financial Speculation*. New York: Farrar, Straus and Giroux, 1999.

Chernow, Ron. *The House of Morgan: An American Banking Dynasty and the Rise of Modern Finance*. New York: Atlantic Monthly Press, 1990.

———. *Titan: The Life of John D. Rockefeller, Sr.* New York: Random House, 1998.

Clews, Henry. *Fifty Years in Wall Street*. New York: Irving Publishing Company, 1908.

Colby, Gerard. *Du Pont Dynasty: Behind the Nylon Curtain*. Secaucus, N.J.: Lyle Stuart, 1984.

Collier, Peter, and David Horowitz. *The Kennedys: An American Drama*. New York: Summit Books, 1984.

Croffut, William A. *An American Procession*. Boston, Mass.: Little, Brown, 1931.

Crouch, George. *Erie Under Fisk and Gould*. New York: n.p., 1870.

Drucker, Peter. *Adventures of a Bystander*. New York: HarperCollins, 1991.

BIBLIOGRAPHY

Fowler, William Worthington. *Ten Years in Wall Street*. Hartford, Conn.: Worthington, Dustin, 1870.

Garraty, John. *The Great Depression*. Garden City, N.Y.: Anchor Books, 1987.

———, ed. *Encyclopedia of American Biography*. New York: Harper & Row, 1974.

Gordon, John Steele. *Hamilton's Blessing: The Extraordinary Life and Times of Our National Debt*. New York: Walker and Company, 1997.

———. *The Scarlet Woman of Wall Street: Jay Gould, Jim Fisk, Cornelius Vanderbilt, the Erie Railway, and the Birth of Wall Street*. New York: Weidenfeld & Nicholson, 1988.

Grant, James. *Bernard M. Baruch: The Adventures of a Wall Street Legend*. New York: John Wiley & Sons, 1997. (A reprint of the 1983 edition.)

———. *Money of the Mind: Borrowing and Lending in America from the Civil War to Michael Milken*. New York: Farrar, Straus and Giroux, 1992.

Greider, William. *The Secrets of the Temple: How the Federal Reserve Runs the Country*. New York: Simon and Schuster, 1987.

Gustin, Lawrence R. *Billy Durant: Creator of General Motors*. Grand Rapids, Mich.: William B. Eerdmans Publishing Company, 1973.

Hadley, Arthur T. *Railroad Transportation—Its History and Its Laws*. New York: G. P. Putnam's Sons, 1886.

Harris, Charles Townsend. *Memories of Manhattan in the Sixties and Seventies*. New York: Derrydale Press, 1928.

Hessen, Robert. *Steel Titan: The Life of Charles M. Schwab*. New York: Oxford University Press, 1975.

Holbrook, Stewart H. *The Age of the Moguls: The Story of the Robber Barons and the Great Tycoons*. Garden City, N.Y.: Doubleday, 1954.

House of Representatives. *House Report Number 31*. 41st Cong., 2nd sess. Washington, D.C.: U.S. Government Printing Office, 1870.

Jeffrey, Nancy Ann. "What's Wrong With This Picture?" *Wall Street Journal*, May 28, 1966, R42.

Kindleberger, Charles P. *Manias, Panics, and Crashes: A History of Financial Crises*. 3rd ed. New York: Wiley, 1996.

Koskoff, David E. *Joseph P. Kennedy: A Life and Times*. Englewood Cliffs, N.J.: Prentice-Hall, Inc., 1974.

Lamb, Martha J. *Wall Street in History*. Burlington, Vt.: Fraser Publishing Company, 1992. (A reprint of the 1883 edition.)

Lane, Wheaton. *Commodore Vanderbilt, an Epic of the Steam Age*. New York: Knopf, 1942.

Lefèvre, Edwin. *Reminiscences of a Stock Operator*. New York: Wiley, 1994. (A reprint of the 1923 edition.)

Lomask, Milton. *Aaron Burr: The Years from Princeton to Vice President, 1756–1805*. New York: Farrar, Straus and Giroux, 1979.

Louchiem, Katie, ed. *The Making of the New Deal*. Cambridge, Mass.: Harvard University Press, 1983.

BIBLIOGRAPHY

Lowe, Janet. *Benjamin Graham on Value Investing: Lessons from the Dean of Wall Street*. Dearborn, Mich.: Dearborn Financial Publishing, 1994.

Mackay, Charles. *Extraordinary Popular Delusions and the Madness of Crowds*. New York: John Wiley & Sons, 1996. (Republication of the 1841 edition.)

Marks, Paula Mitchell. *Precious Dust: The American Gold Rush Era: 1848–1900*. New York: William Morrow and Company, 1994.

McPherson, James M. *Battle Cry of Freedom: The Civil War Era*. New York: Oxford University Press, 1988.

Medbery, James K. *Men and Mysteries of Wall Street*. Boston, Mass.: Field, Osgood & Company, 1870.

Miller, John C. *Alexander Hamilton: Portrait in Paradox*. New York: Harper & Row, 1959.

Mott, Edward Harold. *Between the Oceans and the Lakes*. New York: John S. Collins, 1901.

Nevins, Allan, and Milton Thomas Halsey, eds. *The Diary of George Templeton Strong*. New York: Macmillan, 1952.

Norman, Bruce. *The Inventing of America*. New York: Taplinger Publishing Company, 1972.

Oberholtzer, Ellis Paxson. *Jay Cooke, Financier of the Civil War*. New York: Burt Franklin, 1970.

Parton, James. *Famous Americans of Recent Times*. Boston, Mass.: Ticknor and Fields, 1867.

Paul, Randolph E. *Taxation in the United States*. Boston, Mass.: Little, Brown, 1954.

Previts, Gary John, and Barbara Dubis Merino. *A History of Accounting in America*. New York: Wiley, 1979.

Satterlee, Herbert L. *J. Pierpont Morgan: An Intimate Portrait*. New York: Macmillan, 1939.

Schwed, Fred, Jr. *Where Are the Customers' Yachts: Or a Good Hard Look at Wall Street*. New York: Wiley, 1995. (A reprint of the 1940 edition.)

Seligman, Joel. *The Transformation of Wall Street: A History of the Securities and Exchange Commission and Modern Corporate Finance*. Boston, Mass.: Houghton Mifflin, 1982.

Smith, Page. *The Shaping of America*. New York: McGraw-Hill, 1980.

Snow, Alice Northrop (with Henry Nicholas Snow). *The Story of Helen Gould*. New York: Fleming H. Revell, 1943.

Sobel, Robert. *The Big Board: A History of the New York Stock Market*. New York: The Free Press, 1965.

———. *The Curbstone Brokers: The Origins of the American Stock Exchange*. New York: Macmillan, 1970.

———. *NYSE: A History of the New York Stock Exchange, 1935–1975*. New York: Weybright and Talley, 1975.

———. *Panic on Wall Street: A History of America's Financial Disasters*. New York: Macmillan, 1968.

BIBLIOGRAPHY

Sparkes, Boyden, and Samuel Taylor Moore. *The Witch of Wall Street, Hetty Green.* Garden City, N.Y.: Doubleday, Doran and Co., 1935.

Stampp, Kenneth M. *America in 1857: A Nation on the Brink.* New York: Oxford University Press, 1990.

Standage, Tom. *The Victorian Internet: The Remarkable Story of the Telegraph and the Nineteenth Century's On-Line Pioneers.* New York: Walker, 1998.

Stedman, Edmund Clarence. *The New York Stock Exchange.* New York: Stock Exchange Historical, 1905.

Strouse, Jean. *Morgan: American Financier.* New York: Random House, 1999.

Tanner, Hudson C. *"The Lobby," and Public Men from Thurlow Weed's Time.* Albany, N.Y.: George MacDonald, 1888.

Train, George Francis. *Young America in Wall-Street.* New York: Derby & Jackson, 1857.

White, Norval. *New York: A Physical History.* New York: Atheneum, 1987.

Ziegler, Philip. *The Sixth Great Power: A History of One of the Greatest Banking Families, the House of Barings, 1762–1929.* New York: Knopf, 1988.

INDEX

accounting practices, 171–74, 264
Adams, Alvin, 81
Adams, Charles Francis, 113, 114, 121–22
Adams, Henry, 113, 127
Adams, John, 30, 46
advertising, 226, 254
agriculture, 136, 149, 225
airline stocks, 58, 227
Alexander, William, 40
Allen, Frederick Lewis, 184
Amalgamated Copper Company, 188–90
Amazon.com, 295
American Express, 81, 130, 262, 263
American Revolution, 29, 30–31, 40, 53, 92
American Stock Exchange, 274, 279
Angell, Norman, 198
Anne, Queen of England, 72
annual reports, 173, 255, 264
anti-Semitism, 174–76
apex law, 188
arbitrage, 291
Articles of Confederation, 31, 41
Astor, John Jacob, 29
AT&T, 261
Atlantic cable, 123, 126, 151, 182
AutEx, 273
automobile industry, 221–22, 224, 225
Averell, William J., 176

Babson, Roger, 231, 240, 288–89
Babson Break, 231

Bache & Co., 254, 271
Baker, James, 288
Baltimore and Ohio Railroad, 74, 153
Bank of England, 26, 28, 31, 67, 85, 90, 127, 163, 208, 227
Bank of New York, 33, 36, 42, 46
Bank of the United States, 16, 32, 37, 41, 42, 50, 181
    second, 50, 63, 64, 66, 69, 181, 186
banks:
    depository vs. investment, 238
    discount rate for, 228, 229, 270
    establishment of, 37, 42, 46–49, 65–66, 87
    failures of, 67, 68, 69, 89, 90, 158–59, 163, 225
    FDR's closing of, 237
    in Federal Reserve System, 193–94, 228, 229
    French attempted nationalization of, 286
    interbank deposits among, 87
    panics on, 186–87, 190–93, 271
    rural, 225–26
    state, 37, 65–66
bank stocks, speculation in, 37, 41–45
Baring Brothers, 15, 57, 163
Barker, Jacob, 60
Barnard, George G., 114–15, 116, 117, 118, 120
Baruch, Bernard, 215, 257
bear markets, 60–61, 68
bear raids, 23

Beebe, Samuel, 51, 59
Bellomont, Richard Coote, Lord, 28
Belmont, August, Jr., 167, 168
Belmont, August (Schoenberg), Sr., 174
Benjamin, Judah P., 174–75
Bennett, James Gordon, 88
Bethlehem Steel, 199–200, 203, 204, 228
Biddle, Nicholas, 63
Big Board, 137, 280, 281
Bingham, William, 41
Black Friday, 135–36
blacks, NYSE membership of, 264
Black Thursday, 232–33, 238, 243
Bland-Allison Act, 165, 166
Bleak House (Dickens), 293
Bleecker, Leonard, 38–39
Bliss, Cornelius, 175
block trades, 268, 278
blue-chip stocks, 37
Boesky, Ivan, 290, 291, 292
bonds, 31, 32
    convertible, 78
    junk, 291–92
    for railroad construction, 143, 144–45
    Telerate system and, 285
    wars and, 50, 94–95, 208, 226
Bonfire of the Vanities (Wolfe), 293
Boutwell, George S., 131
brokerage business:
    commission houses in, 274
    expansion tactics of, 253–59
    on-line services of, 294
    protection against failures of, 262–64, 269, 270, 271, 272
    public stock offerings on, 269–70
brokers:
    curbstone, 71, 87, 96, 97, 201, 275
    earnings of, 96, 294
    exchange facilities developed by, 38–40, 50–51
    investors' interests vs., 19
    origin of, 36–37
    in over-the-counter market, 275–76

speculators stabilized by, 18, 123–26, 264, 294
    transfer clearinghouse for, 169
    women as, 139, 267
Brown, James, 135
Browne, Joseph, 47
Bryan, William Jennings, 32, 169, 171, 204, 205, 281
Buffett, Warren, 257
bull markets, 37, 62, 68, 203–4, 259–60, 264, 293–94
Burr, Aaron, 46–49
Butterfield, Daniel, 130, 133, 134, 135
Buttonwood Agreement, 39, 50–51, 274, 278
buyer's options, 105–6

Calahan, Edward A., 109
California gold mining, 84–86, 89, 90
call-money market, 228, 229
canal securities, 57–58, 73
capitalism, 16, 295–96
    Dutch invention of, 22–23
    government regulation of, 181–82, 185–86, 295
    minimal restrictions on, 17
    socialism vs., 286
Carnegie, Andrew, 116, 149, 184, 185, 187, 224
Carr, Fred, 267
cartels, 111
Carter, Jimmy, 280, 286–87
cash flow, 172
Cassel, Sir Ernest, 61
cattle sales, 82–83, 138
cellular telephones, 292
certificates of deposit, 273
certified public accountants, 173
Chapters of Erie (Adams and Adams), 113
Chase, Salmon P., 94
Chase Manhattan Bank, 49, 232
Churchill, Winston, 98
cities, population shift to, 149
Civil War, U.S., 18, 87, 90, 91–95, 127, 136, 148–49, 151, 174–75, 208, 280

Claflin, Tennessee, 139
Clark, Horace, 94
Clay, Henry, 99
Cleveland, Grover, 164, 167, 168, 169
Clews, Henry, 84, 90, 98, 108, 173
Clinton, De Witt, 16, 54–56, 76
Clinton, George, 16, 54
closed-end funds, 258, 259
coffeehouses, securities business conducted in, 38, 39–40
Cohen, Manuel, 277
Colfax, Schuyler, 137
commissions, fixed, 274, 276, 278
commodities markets, 183, 261–62, 281–83
communism, 208
computer technology, 19, 264, 268, 278, 279, 280, 286, 289, 294
Comstock Lode, 165
Congress, U.S.:
    early fiscal policy of, 31–32
    monetary decisions of, 127–28, 165–68
    on securities market, 278, 280
Continental Congress, 30–31, 40
continuous auction, 96, 126
Cooke, Jay, 94–95, 142–43, 144, 208
Cooper, Peter, 74, 75
copper trust, 188–90
Corbin, Abel Rathbone, 129–30, 131, 132
corners, 23, 62, 281
corporations:
    accountancy in, 172–73, 264
    consolidation of, 184–85
    institution of, 45–46
    leveraged-buyouts of, 290–91, 292
    limited liability of, 45, 49
    state laws on, 49–50
    trust form of, 170
Cortelyou, George B., 191, 192
cotton market, 87, 89, 112, 202–3
Crédit Mobilier scandal, 137, 155, 176
credit purchases, 226
Cruger, Nicholas, 30

curb brokers, 71, 87, 96, 97, 201, 275
currency, 26–27, 28–29, 31, 85, 127–28, 281
currency market, global, 285, 286
Curtis, William Edmund, 167
customers' men, 253
Customs House, 35, 72

Davis, Howland S., 245
Davison, Henry, 227, 228
day traders, 214, 279
De Angelis, Anthony (Tino), 261–62
Debs, Eugene V., 258
deflation, 165, 236
Democratic Party, 169, 195, 202–3, 277
Democratic-Republican Party, 46–47
Depew, Chauncey, 175
depressions:
    economic efficiency fostered by, 148
    of 1837, 68, 69, 84
    of 1857, 91
    of 1870s, 145, 148, 163
    of 1890s, 165, 166, 167, 187
    of 1930s, 234–36, 240, 242–43, 249, 287, 293
    recession vs., 242–43
Dewey, Thomas, 247
Diana, Princess of Wales, 98
Dickens, Charles, 293
discount rate, 228, 229, 270, 287
Dodd, David L., 257
double-entry bookkeeping, 171
Douglas, William O., 242, 248
Dow, Charles, 170–71, 260, 261
Dow Jones industrial average, 170–71, 226, 229, 236–37, 250, 260–61, 263, 264, 271, 272–73, 287, 293
Drake, Edwin, 97
Drew, Daniel, 61, 81–84, 90, 103, 106–7, 143, 218
    Erie stock and, 108, 110–23, 125
Drexel, Anthony, 143
Drexel, Burnham, Lambert, 291, 292
Drucker, Peter, 258

Duer, Catherine Alexander (Lady Kitty), 40
Duer, William, 40–44, 46, 60
Du Pont family, 203, 222, 223
Durant, William C., 221–23
Dutch West India Company, 21–22, 24–25

economies of scale, 75, 149, 184, 226
E. F. Hutton, 288
E. I. Du Pont, 203, 256
Eisenhower, Dwight D., 259, 260, 261
elections:
    of 1896, 169, 171
    of 1912, 195
    of 1928, 237
    of 1968, 270
    of 1972, 272–73
electric power, industrial use of, 226
electronic display boards, 268–69, 279–80
Elizabeth I, Queen of England, 79
Emergency Banking Relief Act, 237
Eno, John C., 159
Erie Canal, 16, 51, 53–58, 59, 73, 75, 76–77, 104
Erie Railway, 76–78, 89, 108–25, 128, 131, 138, 141, 142, 153, 158, 172
Evans, Oliver, 73, 74
Ewing, William, 210
express services, 81, 148

Fahnstock, H. C., 144
fails, 264–65
fast food, 97
Federal Deposit Insurance Corporation, 237–38, 271
Federal Hall, 35
Federalist Party, 46–47, 48
Federal Reserve System, 193–94, 195, 227–29, 235–36, 272, 283, 287, 289–90
Federal Securities Act, 237
financial reports, 172–73, 255, 264
Fischer, Edwin P., 211–12
Fish, James D., 157–58, 160

Fisher, Irving, 231, 232
Fisher, John Arbuthnot, Lord, 204
Fisk, James, Jr., 98, 112–13, 138, 139
    cornering of gold market attempted by, 127, 129, 130, 132, 133, 134–35
    in Erie War, 108, 111, 112–13, 117, 118, 119, 122, 123
    murder of, 140–42
floor traders, 214–15, 279, 294
Fowler, William Worthington, 62, 83, 103, 107, 110, 112, 113, 117, 254
France:
    global financial pressure on socialist reforms in, 286
    pre-Revolutionary trade within, 16–17
franchise company stocks, 58
Franklin, Benjamin, 30
Franz Ferdinand, Archduke, 195, 198–99
free market, 17–18, 19, 286
Frick, Henry Clay, 224
Fulton, Robert, 100
Funston, Keith, 263
fur trade, 24–25, 26

Gallatin, Albert, 50
Garfield, James A., 128, 132, 133, 136
Garzarelli, Elaine, 288–89
Gay, Charles, 246
General Electric, 171, 184, 261
General Motors (GM), 199, 204, 221–23, 256, 258, 259
Gesell, Gerhard, 247
Gibbons, Thomas, 99–100
Gibbons v. Ogden, 100
Girard, Stephen, 50
Glass-Steagall (Banking) Act, 237–38
global financial market, 285–86, 291, 295
gold:
    mining of, 84–86, 89, 90
    speculative market in, 92–94, 127–36, 282
    wartime liquidations and, 198, 199, 200, 202

Goldman, Henry, 206–8
Goldsmith, Sir James, 289
gold standard, 85, 127, 136, 165–69,
    187, 237, 281, 282, 286
golf, 185
Goodwin, James, 150
Gould, Jay, 98, 111–12, 138, 142,
    290
    cornering of gold market
        attempted by, 127–36
    in Erie War, 108, 111–13, 117,
        118, 119–23, 125
government officials, conflicts of
    interest of, 41, 46, 114–16,
    130
Graham, Benjamin, 251, 255–57
grain trade, 27, 75, 202, 203
Grand Illusion, The (Angell), 198
Grant, Ulysses S., 106, 110, 137,
    142, 144
    financial losses of, 157–60
    gold panic and, 129–32, 136
    memoirs of, 160–61, 293
Grant, Ulysses S., Jr. (Buck), 157,
    158, 159
Gratuity Fund, 244, 245
Great Depression, 234–36, 240, 243,
    249, 287, 293
Greater Fool Theory, 23
Greeley, Horace, 86, 115, 172
Green, Hetty, 154–57
greenbacks, 92, 93, 127–28, 136
Greene, Belle, 192
Greenspan, Alan, 290
Gresham's law, 92, 127–28, 166, 281
Grey, Sir Edward, 200–201
gross national product, 171
Guggenheim Exploration, 256

Haack, Robert, 271, 275–76
Hadley, Arthur T., 75
Hamilton, Alexander, 30–33, 35–36,
    37, 41, 43–46, 48, 63, 88, 290
Harding, Warren, 223
Harriman, E. H., 176–79, 184, 186
Hayden, Stone, 271, 272
hedging, 128–29
Heinze, F. Augustus, 188, 189–91

Henriques, George, 117
Hill, James J., 177–79, 186
Hitler, Adolf, 249
holding companies, 185–86
Holmes, Oliver Wendell, 57
Hone, Philip, 67, 68
Hoover, Herbert, 234–35, 236, 237,
    265, 273, 287, 289
Howey, Walter, 239–40
Hudson River Railroad, 102, 104–7,
    108
Hunt, Nelson Bunker, 281–83
Hunt, William Herbert, 281–83

IBM, 261, 272
immigration, 29, 30, 149
income tax, 92, 151, 195, 224
industrialization, 18, 148–49, 165,
    170, 181–82
inflation, 26, 165–66, 236, 251, 270,
    272, 273, 280, 282, 286–87
insider trading, 238–39, 291
institutional investors, 267–68, 274,
    276, 278
Intel, 279, 280
Intermarket Trading System (ITS),
    280, 285
international currency standards, 85,
    286
Internet, 185, 214, 294–95
investment, diversification of, 289
Ira Haupt and Company, 262, 263,
    269, 271

Jackson, Andrew, 32, 62–64, 66–67,
    68, 75, 181, 186
James II, King of England, 22
Jay, Bernard, 39
Jay, John, 48
Jefferson, Thomas, 24, 44, 54, 181,
    193, 225, 290
Jeffersonians, 31–32, 44–45, 46
Jerome, Addison, 98
Jerome, Leonard, 90, 98, 107–8, 110
Jews, in financial industry, 169,
    174–76, 206–7, 221
John J. Cisco and Son, 155
Johnson, Lyndon, 270

joint-stock companies, 24, 148
junk bonds, 291–92

Kahn, Otto, 221
Keenan, George, 195
Kennedy, John F., 55, 263, 271
Kennedy, Joseph P., 210, 234,
    239–42, 267, 290
Ketchum, E. B., 93
Kitchener, Horatio Herbert, Lord,
    205
Knickerbocker Trust Company, 189,
    191
Knox, Henry, 41
Kuhn, Loeb, 176, 178, 206, 207,
    221

Lamb, William, 51
Lamont, Thomas, 233, 245
Landis, James, 242
land sales, western, 65–66
Lansing, Robert, 204–5, 207
Lease, Mary E., 169
Lee, Henry, 41
Lefèvre, Edwin, 11
leftist politics, 181–82
Legal Tender Act, 128
Leisler, Jacob, 27
leveraged-buyout (LBO), 290–91,
    292
leveraging, 42–43
Levine, Dennis, 291
L. F. Rothschild, 288
Lincoln, Abraham, 92, 93, 142
Lindbergh, Charles A., 227
liquidity, 186
liquor stocks, 244–45
Litchfield, Edwin C., 89
Little, Jacob, 59–62, 78, 83, 89–90
Livermore, Jesse, 267, 290
Livingston, Robert R., 48, 100
Livingston, Walter, 43–44
London Stock Exchange, 31, 123,
    200, 278
Ludendorff, Erich von, 205
lunch counters, 97
Lusitania, sinking of, 205–6
Lynch, Edmund, 252, 253

McAdoo, William, 200
McCoy, Sherman, 293
McDonnell & Co., 270–71
McEvers & Barclay, 38–39
McKinley, William, 169, 171, 185
Macomb, Alexander, 41–42, 44
Madison, James, 16, 50
Mansfield, Josie, 140
Marshall, James, 84, 85, 86
Marshall, John, 100
Marxist theory, 17
mass-class marketing, 221–22
May, Lewis, 155–56
Medbery, James K., 81, 96, 125
Medina, Harold, 175
Mellon, Andrew, 223–24
Mellon, Thomas, 224
Merchants' Exchange, 59, 65, 72, 79
mergers, 226
Merrill, Charles E., 251–55, 257–58,
    261
Merrill Lynch, 252, 253–55, 263,
    270, 272, 277, 294
Mexican War, 72, 84, 85
microprocessors, 279
middle class, securities investment
    by, 19, 226
military-industrial complex, 205
Milken, Michael, 290, 291–93
mining securities, 87, 96–97, 125, 148
Mitterrand, François, 286, 295
money supply, regulation of, 26, 31,
    128, 165–66, 187
Monitor Money Rates, 285
Moody, John, 177
Morgan, J. Pierpont, 94, 98, 116,
    143, 164, 175, 188, 194–95,
    218, 255, 291, 293
    background of, 149–53, 154, 176
    bank panic ended by, 191–93, 200
    corporations formed by, 184–86,
        187
    on railroad management, 177–78
    U.S. monetary policy and, 167–69
Morgan, J. Pierpont, Jr. (Jack), 200,
    206, 210, 233, 238, 247
Morgan, Julius, 210
Morgan, Junius Spencer, 149–50

Morgan Bank, 195, 204, 205, 207, 208, 209, 223, 238
Morgan Guaranty, 272
Morris Canal and Banking Company, 58, 61–62, 68
Morrow, Dwight, 206
Morse, Charles W., 189–91
Morse, Samuel F. B., 79–80
Morton, Levi P., 94
Mount, J. R., 65
munitions production, 203, 205, 249
mutual funds, 258–59, 267, 268, 273, 275

Nader, Ralph, 32
Nast, Thomas, 137
National Association of Securities Dealers (NASD), 276
National Association of Securities Dealers Automated Quotation System (Nasdaq), 59, 278–79, 280, 285
national debt, 31, 50, 63–64, 91, 208, 224
Navigation Acts, 27
Nelson, Donald, 251
Netherlands, capitalism invented in, 22–23
Newton, Sir Isaac, 85
New York:
    in British colonial period, 25–29
    as capital city, 32, 35
    defensive wall built in, 21–22, 27
    early Dutch control of, 21–25
    1835 fire in, 64–65
    as global center of finance, 16, 125, 183
    immigrant groups in, 25, 29–30
    mayoralty of, 54, 87
    Philadelphia market eclipsed by, 68–69
    population of, 27, 29, 32, 51, 57
    port activities of, 27–28, 36, 98–99, 183
    in post-Revolutionary period, 32–33, 35–36
    water-supply system of, 47–49, 65
    wealthy society in, 40–41, 96

New York and Harlem Railroad, 101, 102–4, 105, 106, 107–8
New York Central Railroad, 104, 108, 110, 111, 121, 138, 152–53, 164, 175
New York Stock Exchange (NYSE):
    brokerage failures protected by, 262–64, 269, 270, 271, 272
    closings of, 144, 145, 200, 201–2, 268, 288
    corporate finance reports required by, 173
    federal regulation of, 238–39, 248, 294
    fractions used in prices of, 29
    Gratuity Fund of, 244, 245
    individual investors vs. institutional portfolios in, 267–68
    industrial stocks traded on, 148
    inner circle of, 213–14, 217–21
    investors' vs. members' interests in, 213, 215, 218, 241–42
    membership in, 51, 60, 64, 90, 147, 163, 201, 220, 232, 237, 264, 267, 268, 274, 276
    operating rules of, 96, 213–14, 217–18, 220, 248, 268, 275, 276
    origins of, 39–40, 50–51, 59–60, 95
    public stock offerings by members of, 269–70
    recordkeeping of, 264–65, 268, 269
    reorganization of, 277–78
    rivals of, 95–96, 97, 125, 274–76, 278–79, 280
    seat prices on, 147, 163, 201, 220, 232, 237, 268, 274, 290
    self-regulatory efforts of, 124–25, 238–39
    site of, 51, 59, 68, 183
    technological changes at, 279
    trading volume of, 59, 64, 87, 95, 96, 126, 137, 163, 199, 234, 237, 250, 260, 264–65, 268, 269, 270, 276, 288, 293
Nippon Telephone and Telegraph, 287–88

Nixon, Richard M., 270, 271, 272–73, 281–82
Norris, George, 224
Northern Pacific Railroad, 143, 177–79, 186
Northern Securities Corporation, 185–86
NYSE, *see* New York Stock Exchange

Ochs, Adolf, 178
oil prices, 273
oil securities, 97
on-line brokerages, 294
Open Board of Brokers, 96, 124–25, 126, 264
Osborne, Charles J., 128
overseas telephone service, 285–86
over-the-counter (OTC) stocks, 275–76, 277

Pacific Mail Steamship Company, 137–38
panics, 186–87
  federal efforts in limiting of, 44–45, 289–90
  of 1837, 84, 88, 90
  of 1857, 62, 89–90
  of 1873, 139, 142–45, 147
  of 1907, 190–93
  in silver market, 283
Peabody, George, 150
Pecora, Ferdinand, 238, 239, 241
Pennsylvania Railroad, 111, 114, 152–53, 164, 176
pension funds, 258
Perelman, Ron, 292
periaugers, 98–99
Perkins, George W., 193
Perry, Oliver Hazard, 174
Philadelphia Stock Exchange, 32, 51
Philipse, Frederick, 25
Pickard & Co., 269
Pierce, E. A., 241–42
Piggly Wiggly, 281
Pintard, John, 38–39
political office, conflicts of interest and, 41, 46, 115–16, 130

political patronage, 115, 240–41
Polk, James K., 86
Ponzi schemes, 59, 158
pools, 214–15, 238
Porter, Horace, 131
portfolio insurance, 289
power, economic vs. governmental, 15–17
price controls, 272, 273, 280
Progressive Party, 195
Prohibition, 244
Prosser, Seward, 210
protectionism, 235
Pulitzer, Joseph, 169
puts and calls, 37–38, 105

railroads:
  competition between, 138, 152–53
  construction of, 73–75, 76–77, 86, 136, 137, 143, 144
  in securities market, 58, 68, 75–78, 84, 87, 88, 89, 101–25, 141, 142, 143, 147–48, 152, 163–64, 169, 172, 176–79
  transport on, 73–75, 76–78, 80, 86, 138, 149, 165
Railroad Transportation (Hadley), 75
Reading, Rufus Daniel Isaacs, Lord, 207
Reagan, Ronald, 285, 287, 289
recession, 243, 287
Reminiscences of a Stock Operator (Lefèvre), 11
Republican Party, 175, 195
Revlon, 292
Richelieu, Armand Jean du Plessis, Duc de, 15
Robinson, Edward, 154
Rockefeller, John D., 116, 149, 185, 189, 191, 194, 234
Rockefeller, William, 189
Rogers, H. H., 188, 189–90
Roosevelt, Franklin D., 205, 237, 238, 239, 240–41, 242, 247, 249
Roosevelt, John, 43
Roosevelt, Nicholas, 43

Roosevelt, Theodore, 175, 185–86, 191, 193, 195, 251
Root, Elihu, 175
runners, 80, 169
rural economy, 53–54, 149, 225–26
Ryan, Allan A., 215–20
Ryan, Thomas Fortune, 215

Sage, Russell, 105
Schell, August, 90
Schell, Richard, 121, 122
Schiff, Jacob, 176, 177, 178, 184, 187, 206, 207, 221
Schiff, Therese Loeb, 176
Schuyler, Philip, 88
Schuyler, Robert, 88
Schwab, Charles, 184–85, 203, 204, 220
Scott, Thomas, 111
scripts, 38
Searles, Joseph L., III, 267
Second Bank of the United States, 50, 63, 64, 66, 69, 181, 186
Securities Acts Amendments, 278
securities analysis, 255–58
Securities and Exchange Commission (SEC), 239, 241–42, 263, 277
    investigations by, 246, 247, 271
    NYSE reforms and, 241–42, 248, 276, 294
Securities Investor Protection Corporation, 271
securities market:
    bank stocks in, 37, 41–45
    brokerage firm stocks in, 269–70
    canal stock in, 57–58, 73
    foreign presence in, 57–58, 67, 71, 86, 87, 90, 143, 147–48, 163, 198, 202, 208, 285, 287–88
    globalization of, 285–86, 291, 293
    government oversight of, 237, 238–39
    industrial, 148, 169–70, 171
    international, 151
    margin loans on, 226, 228
    in national linked system, 278, 280
    1929 crash of, 231–34, 240, 243, 288–89, 294, 295
    1987 crash of, 287–90, 293, 294
    on-line brokerages in, 294
    in OTC market, 275–76
    postwar expansions of, 253–59
    regulatory efforts in, 59, 97–98, 123–26, 237, 238–39, 294, 295
    short-term performance pressure in, 268
    twenty-four hour trading in, 97
    see also bonds; brokers; New York Stock Exchange
Seligman, Jesse, 175
Seligman, Joseph, 134
Seligman, Theodore, 174–75
seller's options, 105–6
Sherman Antitrust Act, 185–86
Sherman Silver Act, 166
short selling, 23, 37–38, 61–62, 105, 216–20, 239
Siebert, Muriel, 267
Siegel, Martin, 291
silver, 165–66, 167, 168, 281–83
Sinclair, Upton, 193
skyscrapers, 183
slavery, 24, 27
Sloan, Alfred P., 222
Smith, Adam, 11, 16, 17, 18, 100, 264
Smith, Al, 237
Smith, Winthrop, 253
Smoot-Hawley Tariff, 235
socialism, 19, 286
Soule, John B. L., 86
specialists, 214, 238–39, 274, 278
Special Trust Fund, 263–64, 269, 270, 271
speculation:
    brokers' stabilization of, 18, 19, 123–26, 264, 294
    detriments vs. contributions of, 60–61
    dynamics of, 23–24
    in pools, 214–15, 238

Speyers, Albert, 134–35
Stalin, Joseph, 249
Standard Oil, 170, 188, 190–91
steamboats, 100–101, 112, 148
Stebbins, Rowland, 231–32, 240
Stedman, E. C., 82, 106–7, 115, 117, 134
steel industry, 148, 149, 182, 183, 184–85, 199–200, 204
Steichen, Edward, 153
Stephenson, George, 74, 79
Stettinius, Edward, 205–6
Stillman, James, 188–89
stockholder interests, corporate management vs., 172
stock market, see National Association of Securities Dealers Automated Quotation System; New York Stock Exchange; securities market
stock market average, 170–71
    see also Dow Jones industrial average
stock tickers, 109, 126, 264, 268–69
Stockwell, Alden, 137–38
Stokes, Edwin, 140–41
Straus family, 226
Strong, Benjamin, 227–29, 235–36, 290
Strong, George Templeton, 115
Stutz Motor Car Company of America, 215–20
Stuyvesant, Peter, 21–22, 25, 26
subscription stock, 38
Sutton, John, 39
Sutton, Willie, 209
Sweeney, Peter, 120
Sweet, Edward, 210
syndicates, 23

Taft, William Howard, 195
takeovers, 291, 292
Talleyrand-Périgord, Charles Maurice de, 32
Tammany Hall, 115, 136
Tanner, Hudson C., 115
tariffs, 17, 148, 235
taxation:

federal institution of, 31
of income, 92, 151, 195, 224
wars financed by, 92, 151
telegraph, 78–81, 90, 109, 148, 182, 280, 294
telephone communication, 275, 285–86, 292
Telerate system, 285
Temco Services, 295
Theory of Moral Sentiments, The (Smith), 11
Third Market, 275, 278
Thorne, Oakleigh, 192
ticker-tape parades, 209, 269
Ticketmaster, 295
Tobias, Andrew, 273
Tobin, John, 98, 107, 110
Tontine Coffee House, 39–40
Train, George Francis, 88
transatlantic travel, 60
transportation, overland, 53–54, 56–57, 73–75, 86
Treasury, U.S.:
    financial panics bailed out by, 44–45
    gold supply of, 129, 130–31, 134, 135, 164, 166–69, 282
    silver policies of, 165, 166, 281, 282
    speculation forbidden to officials of, 41
Treasury bills (T-bills), 236
Trevithick, Richard, 73
Trinity Church, 21, 22, 27, 29, 35, 72, 211
Truman, Harry S., 254, 260
Trust Company of America, 191–92
trusts, 170, 185–86
Tsai, Gerald, 267
tulips, speculation on, 23
turning, 105
Twain, Mark, 160
Tweed, William M., 136–37
Tweed Ring, 136–37, 142

Underwood, Levi, 111
Union Club, 84, 174, 175
Union League Club, 174–75

Union Pacific Railroad, 74, 137, 176–77
union pension funds, 258
United States:
British financial alliance with, 182–83, 205
central bank of, 31, 50, 63, 186, 187, 193–94, 289–90; *see also* Bank of the United States
as common market, 16–17, 100
economic power of, 182, 202, 208–9
unfettered capitalism developed in, 17
western expansion of, 53–54, 65–66, 86
in World Wars, 204–9, 249–51
U.S. Steel, 178, 184–85, 203, 233, 243

Vail, Alfred, 79–80
Van Buren, Martin, 68
Vanderbilt, Cornelius, 90, 94, 98–108, 138–39, 144, 155, 176, 267, 290
in boat businesses, 98–101
Erie Railway and, 108, 110–11, 113, 114–22
Vanderbilt, William H., 152, 159, 160
Volcker, Paul, 287, 289

Wall Street:
architecture on, 71–72, 183
bombing of, 209–12
city wall as start of, 22
initial commercial development of, 35–36
leftist opposition to, 181
London finance vs., 123, 151, 163, 182–83
as metonym for national system, 69, 181, 274
novel on ethos of, 293
outdoor trading on, 59, 64

Senate hearings on, 238
stabilization of, 153
Wall Street Journal, 170
wampum, 25, 26–27, 28
Ward, Ferdinand, 157–59, 160
Ward, John Quincy Adams, 183
Ward, Thomas W., 57
War of 1812, 50, 63, 82, 99
War Production Board (WPB), 251
Washington, George, 30, 35, 46, 72
wash sales, 51, 215
watered stock, 82–83
Watt, James, 73
Wealth of Nations, The (Smith), 16, 18
Webster, Daniel, 46
Wellington, Arthur Wellesley, Duke of, 16
Western Union, 142, 144
Whalen, Grover, 209
Whitney, George, 243, 245
Whitney, Richard, 233, 234, 238–39, 241, 242–48, 253, 294
Whitney, William C., 215
Wiggin, Albert H., 232, 240
Wilhelm II, Kaiser of Germany, 197
Williston and Beane, 262, 263
Wilson, Charles E., 258
Wilson, Harold, 286
Wilson, Woodrow, 195, 203, 204, 207, 227
Winchell, Walter, 260
Wolfe, Tom, 293
Wood, Fernando, 87
Woodhull, Victoria, 139, 267
Work, Frank, 114, 117, 121, 122
World War I, 195, 197–201, 202–9, 215, 222, 250
World War II, 249–51
Worth, Frank, 98
WPB (War Production Board), 251

Yellow Cab Corporation, 239–40

Zeckendorf, William, 287